Fresh All The Year

Gail Duff lives in the Medway area with her husband, Mick Duff, the photographer. She is well known for her original and lively broadcasts on Radio Medway and for her contributions to *Kent Life* and other local magazines and papers, taking her topics from all her main interests — cookery, wine-making, country life and local customs. She also writes a monthly cooking feature with Robert Carrier in *Homes and Gardens* which concentrates on fresh, seasonal ingredients. This emphasis, and the strikingly original quality of her personality and approach, makes Gail Duff the most exciting new voice to emerge in the field of cooking and food writing.

D1614667

Other cookery books available in Pan

Mrs Beeton
All About Cookery

Ada Boni
The Talisman Italian Cook Book

Lousene Rousseau Brunner
New Casserole Treasury

Savitri Chowdhary
Indian Cooking

Jane Donald and Gail Firth
What's For Lunch, Mum?

Theodora FitzGibbon
A Taste of Ireland
A Taste of London
A Taste of Scotland
A Taste of Wales
A Taste of the West Country

Dorothy Hall
The Book of Herbs

Robin Howe
Soups

Rosemary Hume and Muriel Downes
The Cordon Bleu Book of Jams, Preserves and Pickles

Kenneth Lo
Quick and Easy Chinese Cooking

Claire Loewenfeld and Philippa Back
Herbs for Health and Cookery

edited by R. J. Minney
The George Bernard Shaw Vegetarian Cook Book

Marguerite Patten
Learning to Cook

Jennie Reekie
Traditional French Cooking

Constance Spry and Rosemary Hume
The Constance Spry Cookery Book

Katie Stewart
The Times Cookery Book

Marika Hanbury Tenison
Eat Well and Be Slim
Deep-Freeze Cookery
Deep-Freeze Sense

Gail Duff
Fresh All The Year

illustrated by Gillian Zeiner

Pan Books in association with
Macmillan London

First published 1976 by Macmillan London Ltd
This edition published 1977 by Pan Books Ltd,
Cavaye Place, London SW10 9PG,
in association with Macmillan London Ltd
© Gail Duff 1976
ISBN 0 330 25002 7
Printed and bound in Great Britain by
Richard Clay (The Chaucer Press) Ltd, Bungay, Suffolk

Contents

For Mick

Introduction

The recipes in this book are all based on vegetables and fruit. Not the frozen or tinned ones which go against our seasonal clocks, but the fresh ones which can be harvested in our gardens or bought in our greengrocers' shops each at their own time of the year. It is fascinating to see how their growing times are related to the weather and the way we feel during the different months – earthy root vegetables make warming winter stews, the rich, tender spring greens come in the warmer days of spring when we want to leave cold weather food behind, and the fresh-tasting peas and beans make perfect light summer meals.

Herbs also have their seasons, and they too seem to appear at just the right moment – mint in June for the new potatoes and peas, and basil in July and August when tomatoes are plentiful; and in April, when all the vegetables in the shops are either past their best or have been around for so long that we are longing for something new, the perennial herbs like rosemary and sage start to grow fresh tender leaves to liven up our meals.

I was brought up in a country district where everyone I knew seemed to have a large garden or an allotment; perhaps this is why I always relate foods to seasons and feel such pleasure when something new comes into the shops, just when I feel I can't wait any longer for it: the new carrots at the end of June after weeks of tough old woody ones, and that first punnet of English strawberries – always the most expensive but so sweet and good after several months of imported fruit.

Shopping itself can be more enjoyable as you learn to look for specific vegetables at different times of the year, and if you take a real interest in his produce, a good greengrocer will be only too pleased to tell you the best things to buy.

Some people might think it boring to rely on a limited number of fresh foods all through the winter, but it is even more boring to live on the same frozen or tinned ones all year round. What I have tried to do in this book is to find as many different ways with fresh vegetables and fruit as possible so that they remain a pleasure throughout their season.

Vegetables have for a long time been pushed to one side of the dinner plate and the cook is judged more often by the quality and originality of her meat dishes, rather than by the number of ways in which she can cook a swede, or a turnip or a runner bean.

What many people do not realise is that vegetables have been a staple part of the English diet at least since the twelfth century. We hear so often of 'roast beef of olde England' and the great Medieval banquets consisting of twelve different meat courses and no vegetables at all, but these were usually for the rich. The ordinary people had to supplement what little meat they had with any vegetables that they could grow themselves, often cooking them together so that the flavours blended and the dish seemed larger and more substantial. I have tried to adapt some of these methods to be used practically in vegetable cookery today.

As I possess no garden or allotment myself at present I have used only foods that have been widely available in my local shops, trying to buy as much British and locally-grown produce as possible. I have not included anything too expensive, such as asparagus or mange-tout peas, because although they are delicious they will not make a cheap meal for the average family, and they are also rarely found in shops outside the main centres.

I have tried to keep most of the recipes fairly simple. The housewife I have had in mind wants to produce practical and tasty meals for her family and the occasional elaborate dinner or supper dish. Preparing fresh vegetables does, I admit, take more time than opening a packet or a tin, but the final result is worth it. I have myself cooked many of the recipes after coming in from work – having sometimes thought them up in a traffic jam on the way home.

I have also tried not to pile on the calories too much. I am weight-conscious myself and know how frustrating it can be to prepare a beautifully mouth-watering dish for other people and then sit down to a plate of plain cottage cheese reminiscent of soggy polystyrene! I'm not pretending for a minute that this book will help you lose weight, but on the other hand it shouldn't make you put too much on.

Some people find it more satisfying to add their own ideas to a recipe instead of following it to the letter. For this reason I have given hints for alternative herbs, for instance, and sometimes only suggested the cooking method, leaving some recipes open to variation. In recipes that use both meat and vegetables, for example, you could easily alter the proportions of one to the other to suit your family's needs.

The vegetables that I have recommended for each month are generally those that are in peak condition at that particular time, but in most cases they are not the only ones available and I don't envisage you living all through the month on those alone. So I have also given brief lists of whatever else is available, usually leaving out onions and potatoes and anything we can buy all the year round.

I hope that in producing this book I have helped to revive even a little interest in the craft of using the available foods in imaginative ways; and I hope too that I have managed to share some of the pleasure that I find in producing meals to go with our moods and the natural progression of the seasons.

All recipes are for four people

Basic ingredients

Herbs

Although we don't grow our own vegetables, we do possess a
herb garden and I have made wide use of fresh herbs throughout
the book. They are very easy to grow and take up very little
room – they can even be grown in a window-box or in pots –
and I would encourage anyone who is seriously interested in
cookery to have a go. If, however, you are unable to grow, beg
or buy any particular herb, use dried herbs instead, remembering
to halve the quantities as their flavour is far more concentrated.
If you know someone with a large bay tree in their garden ask
them to let you have a few branches when they trim it, and hang
them up in a dry place.

Herbs used in the recipes

basil	marjoram
bay	mint
chervil	parsley
chives	rosemary
dandelions (not really a herb	sage
but always springing up	savory
somewhere in the garden)	sorrel
dill	tarragon
fennel	thyme
lovage	

Flavourings

As well as herbs I have used a variety of pickles, mustards and
spices, all of which stand in readiness in the store cupboard.

Starting from scratch, this large array of bottles and jars may seem expensive, but they don't all get used at the same rate and will never have to be bought all at the same time again.

Spices used in the recipes

allspice – whole berries
caraway seeds
cayenne pepper – ground
cinnamon – both ground and in sticks
cloves – whole
coriander – whole berries
curry powder

dill seeds
ginger – ground
juniper – whole berries
mace – both ground and whole blades
nutmeg – whole
paprika – ground
turmeric

Spices always maintain their flavour better if they are left whole. Keep a small stone pestle and mortar for the allspice, juniper and coriander and a special nutmeg grater or small cheese grater for the nutmeg.

Pickles and preserves

capers
pickled dill cucumbers
large pickled Hungarian gherkins
preserved grated horseradish
black and green olives

Mustards

English mustard powder – essential
Dijon mustard – essential
German mustard
Moutarde de Meaux (whole grain mustard)
Tarragon mustard

Other flavourings

olive oil
tabasco sauce
tomato purée
wine vinegar
Worcestershire sauce

Salt and pepper
I always use sea salt and black pepper freshly ground from the mill. I have only specified quantities of seasoning where they are particularly important to the recipe. Otherwise I feel it is very much a matter of personal taste, best left to the individual.

Wines
It is not a great extravagance to keep a couple of bottles of cheap wine, one red and one white (both dry), in the store-cupboard. I use cider a lot and prefer a dry still type.

Stock
One of the essentials in any kitchen is the stock-pot. I make up about six pints at a time and keep it in the refrigerator. I use bones, giblets, a chicken carcase from which I have removed the legs, wings and breast, or sometimes a chicken quarter. This latter isn't quite as extravagant as it sounds as the meat remains intact and is really quite tasty when it has been boiled up with all the root vegetables and herbs. It usually turns up the next day in an omelette or soufflé for lunch, or chopped up in a salad.

To make stock, put whatever meat or bones you have into a large saucepan with a couple of carrots sliced down the middle, a large onion cut in quarters with the skin still on, two sticks and a few leaves of celery, a small potato cut in half but not peeled and any other root vegetables that are handy. Put the saucepan on a very low heat with no fat until the contents begin to brown, and turn them about so they will cook evenly. Pour in cold water to about an inch (2·5 cm) from the top and put in a large bouquet garni, two bayleaves and a few peppercorns. Bring to the boil on a high heat, skim, and simmer for 1½ hours.

Flour
Unless a recipe specifies self-raising flour, use plain flour. I always use either a plain wholemeal or the 81 % or 85 % wholemeal flours for both flavour and goodness, but you can also, and just as easily, use white.

Brown sauce
This is not the brown sauce that comes in bottles but a variation on the French demi-glace sauce, which I make myself and keep

in a screw-topped jar in the refrigerator. These quantities will
make between half and three-quarters of a pint.

2 tablespoons olive oil (or other cooking oil)
1 small onion, finely chopped
1 small carrot, finely chopped
½ stick celery, finely chopped

1 tablespoon wholemeal flour
1 teaspoon tomato purée
1 pint (6 dl) stock
bouquet garni
1 mushroom, or 2 stalks, chopped

Heat the oil in a small saucepan on a fairly low heat. Stir in the
vegetables and cook them until they are just beginning to brown.
Take the pan off the heat and stir in the purée and then ¾ pint
(4·5 dl) of the stock. Add the bouquet garni and the mushrooms.
Put back on the heat. Bring to the boil, stirring, and skim.
Simmer, covered, for half an hour. Pour in the rest of the stock
and bring to the boil again. Skim, and simmer for a further ten
minutes. Strain the sauce through a sieve or conical strainer,
pressing down well to extract all the juices. Return it to the pan
and simmer for a further five minutes.

Horseradish sauce
This is also better home-made. Here are the proportions that I
always use, but they can be varied to suit your own taste.

3 oz (75 gr) jar grated horseradish
1 heaped teaspoon English mustard powder
1 heaped teaspoon soft brown sugar

1 dessertspoon wine vinegar
5 fluid oz (1·5 dl) sour cream

Basic French dressing
4 tablespoons olive oil, or other good quality oil
2 tablespoons wine vinegar
black pepper
1 clove of garlic crushed with ¼ teaspoon fine sea salt

To this you can add any mixture of chopped herbs, or paprika,
Tabasco sauce, mustard or a little sugar to suit your salad or
your fancy.

Sour cream dressing
4 tablespoons sour cream
juice of ½ lemon, or more
1 clove garlic, very finely chopped

1 teaspoon soft brown sugar
black pepper

Mayonnaise

2 egg yolks
1 teaspoon English mustard
  powder
black pepper
pinch salt

8 fluid oz (2·2 dl) plus 2 tablespoons olive oil
up to 2 tablespoons wine vinegar

Work the egg yolks, mustard, pepper and salt in a bowl and
gradually add the tablespoons of oil, drop by drop, creaming
after each addition. When this oil is all mixed in, beat in a
dessertspoon of the vinegar. After this you can switch to an
electric mixer or carry on by hand. Both ways are just as good.
By hand, gradually beat in the rest of the oil, about a teaspoon
at a time at first and increasing the amount as you go. With a
beater, add it in a thin trickle. When all the oil is used up, beat
in the vinegar teaspoon by teaspoon with a wooden spoon,
tasting as you go to make sure you don't make it too sharp. I
usually end up with about a dessertspoon left over, but here
again it is a question of personal taste.

Bread and breadcrumbs

I use granary bread which I bake myself, for everything. You
can buy it, however, or if you can't find granary, use another
variety of wholemeal instead.

Here is my basic recipe for granary bread, using 1 lb (450 gr)
flour. If you need to make more at a time, simply double or
treble the quantities.

Granary bread

1 lb (450 gr) granary bread meal
1½ oz (38 gr) fresh yeast or ¾ oz
  (22 gr) dried yeast
scant tablespoon soft brown sugar

½ pint (3 dl) warm water
1 heaped teaspoon fine sea salt
1 tablespoon oil

Put the flour in a mixing bowl and let it stand in a warm place.
Put 4 fluid oz (1·1 dl) of the water in a bowl with a teaspoon of
the sugar. Crumble the fresh yeast into it, or sprinkle on the
dried yeast and let it stand in a warm place until it bubbles up
the sides of the bowl. Dissolve the rest of the sugar and the salt
in the remaining 6 fluid oz (1·8 dl) of water.

When the yeast is ready, make a well in the centre of the flour.

Pour in the sugar and salt solution, the yeast mixture and the oil. Mix them into the flour with a rounded knife. Turn the dough onto a floured board (I usually use some ordinary wholemeal flour for this) and knead it until it is smooth, flouring your hands all the time if they get tacky. Put the dough into a greased bowl, make a deep cross-cut in it with a knife, and cover it with a tea-towel. Put it in a warm place to rise for an hour.

Preheat the oven to Reg 5/375°F, 190°C. Knead the dough again and divide it into two. Knead each half once or twice. Shape the two halves into round or long shapes and put them on a greased baking sheet. Cover them with the cloth again and let them stand on top of the heating oven for 30 minutes. Then bake them in the centre of the oven for 45 minutes, or until they sound hollow when you tap the bottom, and have stopped 'singing'. Cool them on a wire tray.

To make browned crumbs, crumble some bread (preferably several days old) either in the blender or by hand. Put the crumbs into an ovenproof dish in the bottom of the oven while you are cooking something else on a moderate or low heat until they are dried out completely and slightly brown, turning them about from time to time so they dry evenly.

Rendered fat from meat or poultry

In some meat recipes I have suggested using fat instead of butter. To obtain this fat, cut off some of the excess from the chops or joint and put it in the pan or casserole you are going to use, on a low heat on top of the stove, to render down. You can do this with lamb or pork, or with poultry, using the two lumps of fat that are usually just inside the body of the bird.

Kneaded butter (*Beurre manié*)

This is made by mashing butter and flour together with a fork. Many people use twice as much butter as flour, but I usually use half and half. Only a very little is required to thicken most sauces – never more than a tablespoon and usually less.

Making soufflés

As there are several soufflé recipes in the book I shall describe here how to prepare the dish to get a good high soufflé.

Butter a six-inch (15-cm) soufflé dish and tip in some browned crumbs. Tip the dish backwards and forwards so the crumbs stick to the butter, and then tip out all the loose ones. Cut some greaseproof paper just longer than the circumference of the dish and fold it so it is about twice as high. Butter and crumb the paper in the same way as you did the dish and tie it round with string (beware of nylon string – it disintegrates in the oven – so does Sellotape).

This will support the soufflé as it rises in the oven and the paper can be removed just before you run to the table with the dish.

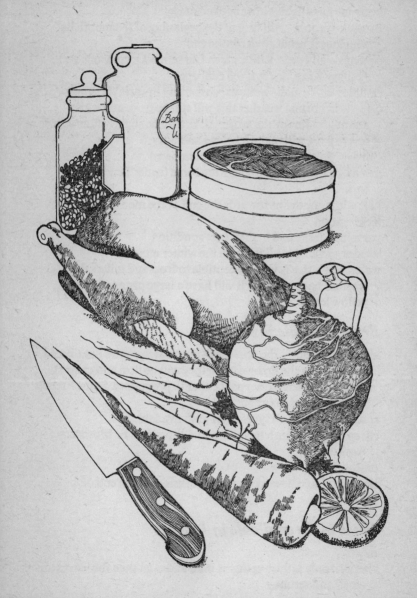

Vegetables available in January

beetroot – available either cooked or raw

Brussels sprouts – still firm at the beginning of the month but
    with looser heads towards the end

cabbage – all types: white, green Christmas Drumheads and
    January King, Savoys, red cabbage

cauliflower – usually quite expensive and in variable supply

celery – in normal weather this will still be fresh and white
    although some of the larger sticks may be slightly floury; too
    severe frost will make it brown and tatty

chicory (Belgian endive) – mostly imported

greens – a bit tough, but there are some tender Brussels
    tops

kale – in some shops towards the end of the month

leeks – good

parsnips – large and in their best condition

swedes – available all through the winter months

watercress – this is very susceptible to frost and unless the
    weather has been mild it will have a large proportion of
    yellow leaves

Fruit available in January

apples and pears – the post-Christmas batch comes out of cold
    store during the first week, so they will be firm and crisp at
    first but become softer as the month progresses. Some French
    Golden Delicious about too

cooking apples – all types of English available

citrus fruit – Spanish including Seville oranges or Moroccan;
    fresh and juicy

pineapples

rhubarb (forced) – arrives from Yorkshire at the end of
    December

Fresh herbs available in January

bay

chervil – only if the weather is mild and even then the leaves are
    small and scrubby

marjoram – woody stems but tiny tender leaves
parsley – not quite so good as the rest this month – I always have
   to buy extra to supplement my own home-grown supply
rosemary – tough stems but plenty of tender leaves
sage – tough, almost dry leaves
savory – woody stems and slightly tough leaves
thyme and lemon thyme – very tough stems but tender leaves

ॐ   ॐ   ॐ

When the year begins, most of us are still in the middle of Christmas celebrations, eating richer, more extravagant foods than usual, and by the end of the final party of Twelfth Night we are ready to welcome long comfortable winter nights at home by the fire and hearty, warming food.

And what better to provide this than root vegetables, which are all in excellent condition in January? Carrots are fairly large but crisp, and are good raw in salads as well as cooked in stews or on their own, and there are some even-sized firm white turnips to be found.

One vegetable which has not enjoyed a very good reputation for some years is the swede. Our loathing of it probably stems from the over-cooked, badly-mashed, watery mush that seemed to appear so often on the school lunch table. In fact it has greater possibilities than one is led to believe. Even mashed, it can be a tasty vegetable, but it must have plenty of butter, lashings of black pepper and a little cream, and most important of all, no lumps or stringy pieces. You can use nutmeg instead of pepper and add a few chopped fresh herbs as well.

Here are two recipes for mashed or puréed swede which should make it more interesting:

Swede and bacon mash

1 large swede
3 rashers bacon
1 oz (25 gr) butter

Grill the bacon until it is crumbly, and cut it into small pieces. Boil a large swede (cut into chunks) in salted water until it is tender (about 45 minutes), drain it and mash it well, removing any stringy lumps. Add the butter and some freshly ground pepper, stir in the bacon and serve.

Swede with onion and green pepper

1 large swede
1 large green pepper, chopped
1 medium onion, sliced
1 oz (25 gr) butter

Cut the swede into chunks, boil it in salted water until tender and mash it. Meanwhile, melt the butter in a frying pan on a low heat and cook the onion until it is soft. Add the chopped pepper, cover, and simmer for five minutes. Stir this mixture, butter and all, into the mashed swede.

Swede can be baked in small cubes in very much the same way as potatoes, either in plenty of butter for an hour in a hot oven, or more slowly round a roasting joint so it absorbs the flavour of the dripping. If you want to surprise people with a more elaborate form of baked swede, try the two following recipes.

Swede Anna

2 medium swedes (or more if required)
2 oz (50 gr) butter
nutmeg

Preheat the oven to Reg 4/350°F, 180°C and thickly butter a seven-inch cake tin or small skillet.
Clean and peel the swedes and slice them into paper-thin rounds with a mandolin or sharp knife. Arrange two layers of swede in the bottom of the tin in overlapping circles. Sprinkle with salt, pepper and nutmeg and dot with butter. Repeat those two layers until the tin is full, remembering that the swede shrinks slightly during cooking.

Cover it with buttered foil and either a lid that fits the tin or an ovenproof plate. Set it on a moderate heat on top of the stove for ten minutes to colour the bottom lightly, then put it into the oven for one hour. To serve, turn it out of the tin and present it as a round flat cake.

Cut roasted swede

1 lb (450 gr) small swedes
2 oz (50 gr) butter for every four swedes
browned breadcrumbs

Preheat the oven to Reg 6/400°F, 200°C.
Wash and peel the swedes and cut each one in half. In each half, make deep incisions with a knife, ⅛ inch (3 mm) apart and almost all the way through. Thickly butter an ovenproof dish and stand the swedes, flat side down, in it. Melt the rest of the butter and dribble it over the swedes. Season. Bake for 45 minutes, basting occasionally. Scatter the crumbs over the swedes, baste again, and put back for a further 15 minutes.

Next, to warm you up on a chilly night, a soup using swedes.

Swede and bacon soup

8 oz (225 gr) swede, finely sliced
1 oz (25 gr) butter
1 large onion, finely sliced
4 oz (100 gr) lean bacon, diced
1½ pints (9 dl) stock

Melt the butter in a heavy saucepan on a low heat. Stir in the swede, onion and bacon and cook gently until the swede and onion are beginning to soften. Pour in the stock and simmer for ten minutes. Put through the blender, season and reheat.

For those who like egg dishes for lunch or supper, swede makes a light soufflé; its bulk is sufficient for the usual bechamel sauce to be omitted.

Swede soufflé

12 oz (325 gr) swede, weighed
  before cooking
1 oz (25 gr) butter
2 oz (50 gr) lean bacon
2 oz (50 gr) chopped raw onion
2 tablespoons chopped mixed
  herbs
4 eggs, separated
browned crumbs for the dish and
  top

Preheat the oven to Reg 6/400°F, 200°C. Prepare a six-inch (15-cm) diameter soufflé dish (page 15).

Boil the swede in salted water until tender and mash it to a purée. Dice the bacon and cook it in the butter on a moderate heat until it is beginning to brown. Mix it into the swede together with the onion, herbs, salt and freshly ground black pepper. Beat in the egg yolks. Stiffly whip the whites and fold them into the swede mixture. Pile this quickly into the prepared soufflé dish and scatter a tablespoon of browned crumbs on top. Bake in the centre of the oven for 30 minutes.

Swede goes very well with beef, and here are two warming winter dishes, one with a very British flavour, the other hot and spicy and reminiscent of the East.

Beef stew with swede crust

2 lb (900 gr) shin of beef, or other stewing cut
3 medium onions, thinly sliced
3 tablespoons beef dripping
¾ pint (4·5 dl) light ale (or ½ pint (3 dl) ale and ¼ pint (1·5 dl) stock)
4 tablespoons chopped parsley

2 bayleaves
4 tablespoons Worcestershire sauce
1-1½ lb (450-675 gr) swede, cut into chunks
1 oz (25 gr) butter
1 tablespoon grated horseradish

Preheat the oven to Reg 4/350°F, 180°C.

Cut the beef into one-inch cubes. Melt the dripping in a heavy flameproof casserole on a high heat and brown the pieces of meat all over. Remove and set aside. Lower the heat and cook two of the onions very gently in the dripping until they are soft. Pour in the ale (and stock if used), add the parsley and bay-leaves, season and bring to the boil. Replace the meat and add the Worcestershire sauce. Cover, and cook in the oven for 1½ hours.

Meanwhile, boil the swedes in salted water until they are tender (about 45 minutes). Drain and set aside. Melt the butter on a low heat in a saucepan and cook the remaining onion in this until it is golden. Put in the cooked swede, turn off the heat, and mash it with the onion and butter.

Take the lid off the casserole and remove the bayleaves.
Scatter the horseradish over the top of the stew, and then spread
the swede mixture on the top like potatoes on a shepherd's pie.
Scatter over the crumbs and put the dish back into the oven for
a further 20 minutes, by which time it should be brown and crisp.

Hot spiced beef and swede loaf

1 lb (450 gr) minced beef
1 oz (25 gr) butter
1 medium onion, finely chopped
½ teaspoon cayenne pepper
1 teaspoon paprika
1 teaspoon ground cumin
1 teaspoon ground coriander

4 tablespoons stock
1 tablespoon chopped mixed
 herbs
1 tablespoon tomato purée
1 medium swede, peeled and cut
 into ⅛-inch slices

Preheat the oven to Reg 6/400°F, 200°C. Butter a cake tin eight
inches in diameter and two inches deep with a fixed base.
Melt the butter in a frying pan on a low heat. Add the onion and
simmer gently for five minutes. Stir in the cayenne, paprika,
cumin and coriander and continue cooking for a further five
minutes. Add this mixture to the minced meat in a large mixing
bowl and beat it in well. Pour the stock into the frying pan and
swirl it about, off the heat, to absorb the remaining spice. Then
beat it into the meat along with the herbs and tomato purée.
   Put half the chopped swede in the bottom of the buttered tin
in overlapping rings. Cover this with half the meat mixture. Add
all the rest of the swede slices in another layer, and finish with
the rest of the meat. Set on the top of the stove on a moderate
heat for ten minutes to brown, then cook in the oven for 1½
hours. Turn out after running a knife round the edges, and serve
with steamed or boiled rice.

೫   ೫   ೫

Another root vegetable in its prime in January is the parsnip.
At this time of the year there are few or no soft brown patches
on them. What is more, they are large – an essential quality, as
the proportion of edible vegetable in comparison to the waste
once they have been peeled or scraped and the woody core
removed is really quite small.

Parsnips, like swedes, are good roasted round a joint, or puréed with nutmeg and herbs. Being almost equal in bulk and calorific value to potatoes, they can either replace them in a meal or be served in combination with them in a number of ways.

Potato and parsnip dice

1 lb (450 gr) parsnips, peeled, cored and cut into ¾-inch (2 cm) dice
1 lb (450 gr) potatoes, peeled and cut into ¾-inch (2 cm) dice
1½ oz (38 gr) butter
2 tablespoons chopped mixed herbs (or parsley alone)

Preheat the oven to Reg 7/425°F, 210°C.
Put the butter in an ovenproof dish into the oven to melt. Stir the cubes of vegetables around in the melted butter, making sure they are separated as much as possible. Cook in the oven for 45 minutes (or until golden brown) turning them around occasionally. Transfer them to a warmed serving dish, season and toss in the herbs.

Parsnip chips

1 lb (450 gr) parsnips
12 oz (325 gr) potatoes
oil or fat for deep frying
mixed herbs or parsley, chopped

Cut the potatoes and cored parsnips into very small thin chips, and dry them. Season and deep fry as for ordinary potato chips in hot oil or fat. Serve them plain or tossed with herbs.

Provided they are thin enough these can also be served cold with drinks, with a little salt, like potato crisps.

Potato and parsnip patties

1 lb (450 gr) parsnips, cored
12 oz (325 gr) potatoes
4 tablespoons grated cheddar cheese
1 beaten egg or 1 egg white for glaze

Preheat the oven to Reg 6/400°F, 200°C. Butter a baking sheet.

Scrub the potatoes and cut them into convenient sizes for boiling, but leave the skins on for a better flavour. Boil them with the parsnips until tender (about 20 minutes). Drain and skin the potatoes. Mash the parsnips and potatoes together with the cheese and seasoning.

Form the mixture into balls about 1½ inches (3·75 cm) in diameter, put them onto the baking sheet and press them down into flat patties. Brush them with the beaten egg or egg white, and cook in the oven for 30 minutes until golden.

Parsnips, like potatoes, make good croquettes, and a plateful of the two sorts formed into different shapes can look very attractive.

Parsnip croquettes I

2 large parsnips, cored   seasoned flour
½ oz (13 gr) butter   breadcrumbs
1 egg, separated   oil or fat for deep frying
1 dessertspoon chopped mixed
  herbs

Boil the parsnips until tender. Mash them with butter, and blend in the egg yolk and herbs. Form them into about twelve balls the size of a walnut. Coat them first with flour, then with the egg white and then the crumbs and deep fry them in fat until golden.

To make the potato croquettes to serve with them, first boil the potatoes in their skins, peel them and mash them with butter, egg yolk and a dessertspoon of chopped sage. Form them into tiny sausage shapes and coat and fry them like the parsnips.

Here is a simpler recipe for croquettes, using only parsnips, with onions for flavour.

Parsnip croquettes II

2 large parsnips, cored
1 medium onion, thinly sliced
dry breadcrumbs (preferably granary)
1½ oz (38 gr) butter for frying

Boil the parsnips and sliced onion in salted water until the parsnips are tender. Drain and mash them together. Leave them to cool, so they will be firmer to handle. Form them into ten to twelve sausage shapes. Roll them in breadcrumbs and fry them in the butter on a moderate heat.

When the core is removed from a parsnip, particularly a big one, it seems a shame to disregard the hollow that is left, so why not fill it with some sort of stuffing? Here is a recipe for a filling of onions and mushrooms, but you could equally well use bread-crumbs and herbs.

Baked stuffed parsnips

2-3 lb (1-1·350 kg) large parsnips
½ oz (13 gr) butter
grated nutmeg
2 medium onions, finely chopped

½ lb (225 gr) mushrooms, finely chopped
a little double cream

Preheat the oven to Reg 6/400°F, 200°C.
Peel the parsnips, cut them in half lengthways, and remove the cores. If they are exceptionally large, cut them in half crossways as well. Smear a little butter in the hollows of the parsnips, as though lightly greasing a dish. Put the parsnips in a buttered ovenproof dish and grate a little nutmeg over them. Fill the hollows with a mixture of the onions and mushrooms, season, and dribble the cream over them. Cover with foil and bake for one hour.

Here are two more warming soups using parsnips.

Parsnip and carrot soup

2 large parsnips, finely sliced
2 large carrots, finely sliced
1 large onion, finely sliced
½ oz (13 gr) butter
1½ pints (9 dl) stock

1 clove garlic
1 heaped teaspoon brown sugar
nutmeg
¼ pint (1·5 dl) milk

Melt the butter on a low heat. Put in the vegetables, cover them and let them sweat for seven minutes. Pour in the stock, bring slowly to the boil and simmer, covered, for fifteen minutes. Cool. Add the chopped garlic, sugar, salt, pepper and a little grated nutmeg and put through the blender. Return the soup to the saucepan, stir in the milk, and reheat.

Cream of parsnip soup

3 medium parsnips, cored and chopped
1½ oz (38 gr) butter
1 pint (6 dl) stock
½ oz (13 gr) flour
grated nutmeg
¼ pint (1·5 dl) milk

Melt 1 oz (25 gr) butter on a low heat, stir in the parsnips and cook them, covered, on a low heat for five minutes. Pour in the stock, bring to the boil and simmer for fifteen minutes. Cool and put through the blender. Melt the remaining ½ oz (13 gr) butter. Stir in the flour and keep stirring until it bubbles. Off the heat blend in the milk and then the parsnip stock. Bring to the boil and simmer, stirring, until creamy. Season if necessary, and serve with a little nutmeg grated over the top.

The floury texture of mashed parsnips and the pungent sweetness of the flavour makes them an ideal basis for a stuffing, particularly for chicken.

Chicken stuffed with parsnips

a 3½ lb (1·5 kg) roasting chicken
for the stuffing:
8 oz (225 gr) parsnips, weighed without their cores
½ oz (13 gr) chicken fat or butter
4 oz (100 gr) bacon
1 small onion
1 dessertspoon chopped sage
½ oz (13 gr) fat or butter
1 small parsnip, diced
1 small onion, chopped
½ pint (3 dl) stock
bouquet garni
1 tablespoon chopped parsley
1 oz (25 gr) kneaded butter

Preheat the oven to Reg 4/350°F, 180°C.
To make the stuffing, peel the parsnips and boil them in salted

water until tender. Mash them to a purée. Melt the fat in a small frying pan and cook the onion and bacon in this until the onion is soft. Remove from the heat and mix in the mashed parsnips, sage and seasoning. Stuff the chicken with this mixture and truss it.

Melt the fat in a large flameproof casserole on a moderate heat and brown the chicken all over in this. Remove it and set aside. Lower the heat, stir in the diced parsnip and onion, cover them and sweat for five minutes. Set the chicken on the top. Season, pour over the stock and tuck in the bouquet garni. Cover and cook in the oven for 1½ hours.

Remove the chicken, carve it, arrange it on a warm serving dish with the stuffing, and put it to keep warm. Strain the juices from the casserole and skim them if necessary. Return them to the casserole on a moderate heat on top of the stove. Whisk in the kneaded butter and parsley and simmer gently for two minutes. Serve the sauce and the chicken separately.

ജ   ജ   ജ

Mixtures of root vegetables make ideal flavourings for beef, whether the sauce is strained or whether the vegetables themselves are a part of the final dish. Here is one of each kind of recipe, both using beer to bring out the rooty taste.

Beef marinated in barley wine

4 slices beef sirloin
1 medium onion
1 stick celery
1 small carrot
1 small parsnip
bouquet garni of parsley, thyme
    and bayleaf

6 fluid oz (1·8 dl) barley wine
1½ tablespoons beef dripping
approx ½ pint (3 dl) stock
1 clove garlic, finely chopped
2 tablespoons chopped parsley
horseradish sauce for serving

Finely dice the vegetables and put them into a saucepan with the bouquet garni and barley wine. Bring to the boil and simmer for five minutes. Cool. Pour this marinade over the slices of beef and let them stand for a least four hours at room temperature, turning the beef once. Remove the beef and pat it dry. Strain the marinade and reserve both the liquid and the vegetables and bouquet garni.

Melt the dripping in a sauté pan or heavy frying pan on a high heat and brown the slices of beef on both sides. Remove and set aside. Lower the heat right down, add the reserved vegetables, cover them and let them sweat for five minutes. Measure the marinade and make it up to ¾ pint (4·5 dl) with the stock. Pour it into the pan and bring it to the boil. Replace the meat and add the bouquet garni, garlic and seasoning. Cover and simmer for 45 minutes, turning the beef once.

Remove the beef and put it on a heated serving dish to keep warm. Strain the sauce, pressing down hard on the vegetables to extract all the juice. Return it to the pan and boil it to reduce it a little. Stir in the parsley, and pour the sauce over the meat. Serve horseradish sauce separately.

Beef with winter vegetables

1½ lb (675 gr) skirt of beef, cut into ¾-inch (2-cm) dice
1 small onion, finely diced
6 oz (150 gr) carrots, finely diced
6 oz (150 gr) white turnips, finely diced
3 oz (75 gr) parsnip (weighed without the core), finely diced
2 tablespoons beef dripping

½ pint (3 dl) strong beer (Gold Top, John Courage, Newcastle Amber)
2 bayleaves
1 clove garlic crushed with a pinch of salt
1 tablespoon tomato purée
1 tablespoon grated horseradish

Melt the dripping in a large sauté pan or wide-bottomed flame-proof casserole on a high heat and brown the meat all over. Remove and set aside. Lower the heat, stir in the vegetables, cover them and let them sweat for five minutes. Pour in the beer, raise the heat slightly, and add the bayleaves, garlic and seasoning. Bring to the boil, replace the beef, and simmer gently on top of the stove for an hour, using the lowest heat possible. By this time most of the liquid will have been absorbed by the vegetables. Just before serving, stir in the tomato purée and horseradish and keep warm for five minutes to let the flavours blend.

୫   ୫   ୫

Any meal, whether it is an everyday family one or a formal dinner, always needs a contrast in taste and texture, and all these hearty stews and soups need something light and refreshing to go with them.

White cabbage is still available in January, and is really good for crunchy salads. Shredded raw it can be served on its own with a plain French dressing, or with celery and apples and a few chopped walnuts. Mixed with shredded carrot it is good with a sour cream dressing; and with carrot, onion and a little thyme (but no garlic) and mayonnaise it becomes cole slaw.

One of my favourite salads is a fruity one, made from a base of shredded white cabbage mixed with sliced orange, halved and seeded grapes, a crisp eating apple and a few peanuts and raisins. The dressing for this should be simple, with no garlic but a lot of black pepper, and two parts olive oil to one of lemon juice.

If the day is cold and you would rather have a hot dish but still want something crunchy and light, how about trying a hot salad?

Hot cabbage salad with raisins

1 small white cabbage (or a Christmas Drumhead which is green and firm), shredded
1 clove garlic, finely chopped
4 tablespoons olive oil

2 tablespoons raisins
2 tablespoons wine vinegar
1 dessertspoon English mustard powder

Heat the oil on a very low heat in a large frying pan or paëlla pan. Put in the cabbage, garlic and raisins and cook gently for about five minutes, stirring from time to time, until the cabbage is just beginning to soften. Blend the mustard powder with the vinegar, and when the cabbage is ready raise the heat to moderate and stir the dressing in. Bring just to boiling point and serve immediately.

Hot cabbage salad with Dijon mustard and caper dressing

1 small white cabbage, shredded
1 small onion, thinly sliced
4 tablespoons olive oil

2 tablespoons wine vinegar
1 teaspoon Dijon mustard
2 teaspoons chopped capers

Heat the oil in a large frying pan or paëlla pan on a low heat. Put in the cabbage and onion and cook gently for about five minutes, stirring around, until the cabbage is just beginning to soften. Blend the vinegar, mustard and chopped capers together. When the cabbage is ready, raise the heat to moderate and quickly stir in the dressing. Bring to the boil and serve immediately.

෯ ෯ ෯

Chicory (sometimes known as endive) is also a good salad vegetable. It has not been grown very much in Britain so far, but during December, January and February we import it from Belgium.

Chicory braised with orange

3 medium heads chicory, cut into
  ½-inch (1·25 cm) slices
1 oz butter

grated rind and juice of 1 medium
  orange

Melt the butter on a low heat in a heavy frying pan. Put in the chicory and orange rind and pour in the juice. Cover and simmer for fifteen minutes, when the chicory should be soft and just on the point of colouring.

Hot chicory and carrot salad

2 heads chicory, cut into ½-inch
  (1·25 cm) slices
2 medium carrots, sliced paper
  thin

3 tablespoons olive oil
1 clove garlic, finely chopped
2 tablespoons wine vinegar
1 teaspoon brown sugar

Heat the oil on a high heat in a large frying pan. Put the chicory, carrot and garlic in the pan and stir them about for three minutes. Blend the sugar with the wine vinegar and mix them into the salad, keeping the pan on the heat for a further two minutes. Serve immediately.

ଛ୍ଥ   ଛ୍ଥ   ଛ୍ଥ

If you want to refresh your palate with an unusual flavour, Seville oranges come into the shops, usually in the second week in January. Britain buys over ninety per cent of all the Spanish crop, mostly for the jam and marmalade industry. But the bitter juice can be used in cooking in much the same way as lemon. Duck with orange is probably our first thought and in Spain one of the few ways the fruit is used is rubbed over the inside and outside of a wild duck before it is cooked. Here are six recipes using Sevilles in various other ways, but when one thinks how much we use lemons, there must be many more waiting to be devised.

Seville chicken

3-3½ lb (1·3-1·5 kg) roasting
  chicken, jointed
seasoned flour
2 small Seville oranges

2 tablespoons olive oil
½ pint (3 dl) chicken stock
1 oz (25 gr) butter

Coat the chicken joints in seasoned flour. Cut one orange into paper-thin slices and squeeze the juice from the other. Heat the olive oil in a sauté pan on a moderate heat and brown the joints in this, skin side down first. Pour off all but a thin film of fat from the pan, set it on a high heat and pour in ¼ pint (1·5 dl) of the stock. Bring to the boil, scraping in any brown pieces in the pan. Put in the chicken joints with two orange slices on each. Cover and simmer for thirty minutes.

When the chicken is tender and the juices run clear, remove the joints from the pan and arrange them on a warm serving dish. Add the remaining stock to the pan and boil it to reduce a little. Swirl in the butter and when it has melted stir in the orange juice to taste (not less than one tablespoonful and more if liked). Pour the sauce over the chicken before serving.

Seville orange soup

pared rind and juice of 1 small
Seville orange
1 small onion
1½ oz (38 gr) butter

1½ tablespoons flour
1½ pints (9 dl) stock
2 egg yolks

Melt the butter in a saucepan on a low heat and cook the onion in this until it is soft. Stir in the flour and blend in the stock. Bring to the boil, stirring, and simmer for five minutes. Add the orange juice and pared rind to the soup and simmer for fifteen minutes. Strain through a sieve. Work the egg yolks together in a bowl and gradually beat the hot soup into them a very little at a time, until about a quarter is mixed with the yolks. Return the rest of the soup to the saucepan and stir in the egg yolk mixture. Season and reheat slowly, but do not boil.

Stuffed lamb chops with Seville oranges

4 loin lamb chops, with the long
bone removed
8 oz (225 gr) good sausage meat
2 tablespoons chopped marjoram
2 tablespoons chopped parsley

2 tablespoons finely chopped
onion
grated rind and juice of 1 Seville
orange
½ pint (3 dl) brown sauce

Mix the sausage meat with the marjoram, parsley, onion, and orange rind. Divide the mixture into four equal portions and wrap the tail end of each chop round the stuffing. Shape each chop and its stuffing into an oval and tie round with string. Let them stand for about 30 minutes to set so they don't come apart during cooking. Sprinkle with pepper.

Preheat the grill to high, and grill the chops, turning them once (with care, so that the stuffing does not come out). When they are done, set them aside and keep them warm. Remove the rack from the grill pan and pour off any excess fat. Set the pan on a moderate heat on top of the stove and deglaze it with the orange juice. Stir in the brown sauce, bringing in any residue from the pan. Check the seasoning and serve the sauce either separately or poured over the chops.

Pork and carrots with Seville oranges

1½ lb (675 gr) lean boneless pork, cut into ½-¾-inch (1·25-2 cm) cubes
1 clove garlic, finely chopped
12 oz (325 gr) carrots, cut into thin julienne strips
1 medium onion, thinly sliced
½ pint (3 dl) stock
grated rind and juice of 1 small Seville orange
2 teaspoons chopped rosemary

Heat a heavy sauté pan or large frying pan on a high heat with no fat and when it is hot put in the pork pieces and garlic. Cook them, stirring them about all the time, until the pork is brown. Lower the heat slightly and stir in the vegetables. When they are coated with fat, pour in the stock and bring it to the boil. Stir in the grated orange rind and juice and the chopped rosemary. Cover and set on a very low heat for 30 minutes. Check the seasoning and serve with buttered noodles.

Grilled mackerel with Seville orange sauce

4 small mackerel
for the sauce:
1 egg yolk
2 teaspoons grated onion
grated rind and juice of 1 small Seville orange
2 oz (50 gr) unsalted butter cut into small pieces
1 dessertspoon tomato purée
salt, pepper

Fillet the mackerel. Preheat the grill to high and lay the mackerel on the hot grill pan, skin side down, and grill them close to the heat until they are golden (about five minutes). They need not be brushed with oil or fat as they have enough of their own to prevent them from sticking.

To make the sauce, blend the egg yolk in a bowl with the onion, salt, pepper, orange rind and juice, adding the latter by degrees. Set the bowl in a pan of warm water on low heat and stir with a wooden spoon until the mixture begins to thicken. Beat in the butter piece by piece and when it is all used up and the sauce is really thick, stir in the tomato purée. Do not let the water boil under the bowl. The sauce should be just about ready as boiling point is reached. Do not let it cook or it will curdle. Serve the sauce hot, either in a warm dish separately, or spooned over the mackerel.

Seville salad (for a first course)

1 small lettuce
½ bunch watercress (if available, if not, use a carton of mustard and cress)
2 Spanish navel oranges
4 oz (100 gr) blue cheese (Stilton, or Danish or Norwegian)

for the dressing:
4 tablespoons olive oil
juice of 1 medium Seville orange
pepper

Chop the lettuce and cress. Divide the navel oranges into segments and cut them into small pieces. Mix them with the lettuce and cress. Blend the oil, Seville orange juice and pepper and dress the salad. Put it into individual bowls, and crumble 1 oz (25 gr) blue cheese over each bowl.

Vegetables available in February

artichokes – the Jerusalem variety
beetroot – available cooked or raw
Brussels sprouts – overblown and rather large by now
cabbage – all the winter varieties
carrots – still good and crisp
cauliflower – expensive and sometimes slightly brown from
    frost damage
celery – English celery will have brown rotten parts on it at this
    time of the year if there have been severe frosts
greens – a bit tough, and brussels tops have finished as well
kale – a good alternative to greens
leeks – still in very good condition
mushrooms – a very useful standby
parsnips – large and for the most part very sound still
purple sprouting broccoli – towards the end of the month
swedes – still very good
turnips – also very good
watercress – only if the weather is mild

Fruit available in February

apples and pears – the last batches of English eating apples and
    pears come crisp and fresh out of the cold store at the
    beginning of the month. There are plenty of cooking apples
    too.
citrus fruit – as well as Jaffa grapefruit there are Israeli oranges
    and lemons which are sweeter than the Spanish. There are
    still some Spanish and Moroccan oranges. Seville oranges are
    usually available all through February
rhubarb – forced at first, but later in the month some shops will
    have supplies from local farms of rhubarb grown in the open,
    and by the end of the month this should be widely available

Fresh herbs available in February

bay
chervil – this occasionally lasts until February but it will be very

scrappy, and only usable if the weather is very mild

marjoram – the leaves are very tiny at first but get larger as the month progresses

parsley – this should begin to grow up quite well again towards the end of the month

rosemary – good tender leaves

sage – very tough leaves

savory – small leaves at first, gradually becoming larger

thyme and lemon thyme – plenty of leaves but very tough stems

❧   ❧   ❧

In February we feel that winter is never going to end. The weather is dark and dreary and the same vegetables seem to have been in the shops for ages. Our palates need livening up, so if you happen to see anything different or unusual in your green-grocer's the motto should be 'Buy it and try it'.

Some shops will be selling Jerusalem artichokes, those strange, colourless, knobbly objects which have a very distinct flavour and can be served either as a first course or as an accompanying vegetable. To cook them, first peel them like a potato and cut them into walnut-sized pieces, and then put them into gently boiling salted water with the juice of half a lemon, simmer for seven minutes and drain them.

Cream of artichoke soup

1 lb (450 gr) Jerusalem artichokes, peeled and thinly sliced
1 large onion, thinly sliced
2 oz (50 gr) butter

1½ pints (9 dl) stock
1 tablespoon flour
½ pint (3 dl) milk
1 tablespoon tomato purée

Melt 1 oz (25 gr) of the butter on a low heat. Stir in the artichokes and onion, cover and set on a very low heat for five minutes. Pour in the stock and simmer for ten minutes. Cool slightly, and work in the blender until smooth. Melt the remaining 1 oz (25 gr) of butter, stir in the flour and mix in the milk. Stir until it is thick and bubbly, then quickly stir in the tomato purée and the artichoke mixture. Check seasoning, reheat and serve.

Artichoke salad

1 lb (450 gr) Jerusalem artichokes
4 tablespoons olive oil
juice of 1 lemon
2 tablespoons parsley

Prepare and cook the artichokes as described above. Allow them to cool and chop them coarsely. Blend the oil and lemon juice and cover them with this dressing. Season and sprinkle with the parsley.

Artichokes with lemon and onions

1 lb (450 gr) Jerusalem artichokes
2 tablespoons spring onions,
  chopped, or a small onion,
  thinly sliced

1 oz (25 gr) butter
lemon juice

Prepare and cook the artichokes as above. Gently sauté the onion in the butter, and when it is golden stir in the artichokes and the lemon juice to taste. Season, heat through again, and serve immediately. They should accompany rather a plain meat dish.

Artichokes with savoury sausage

1 lb (450 gr) Jerusalem artichokes
1 oz (25 gr) butter
1 medium onion, finely sliced
2 tablespoons chopped parsley

4 oz (100 gr) spicy
  sausage, such as Spanish
  Chorizo, Italian or Polish
  Cabanos or an English Saveloy

Prepare and cook the artichokes as above. Fry them in the butter with the onion and the sausage, chopped into pieces. Toss in the parsley and serve hot as a first course.

※   ※   ※

Curly kale makes a welcome change from spring greens, which are rather tough in February anyway. Kale is the basis of the Irish dish, Colcannon, mixed with mashed potatoes, cream and sometimes leeks as well. Here is another recipe for kale and potatoes, which I have called Kale lyonnaise, after the French method of sautéing together potatoes and onions.

Kale lyonnaise

½ lb (225 gr) kale
1 lb (450 gr) potatoes
1 oz (25 gr) butter

2 tablespoons olive oil
1 small onion, finely sliced

Remove the stalks from the kale and break it into small pieces. Put it into boiling salted water for two minutes. Drain. Boil the potatoes in their skins until they are just tender. Drain them and peel them while still hot, and then dice them. In a large frying pan, heat the oil and butter on a moderate heat. Put in the onion and cook until it is just beginning to soften. Raise the heat a little, add the potatoes, kale and seasoning to the pan and fry, moving them around thoroughly until the potatoes and onions are a golden brown.

This is best served as a potato dish, accompanied perhaps by another vegetable, but in the next recipe the kale is served as a green vegetable.

Curly kale and bacon

1 lb (450 gr) curly kale
2 oz (50 gr) lean bacon, diced
½ oz (13 gr) butter
grated parmesan cheese (optional)

Wash the kale, remove the thicker stems and tear the rest into small pieces. Plunge it into boiling salted water and boil for no more than three minutes. Drain it well. Meanwhile, cook the diced bacon in the butter in a large frying pan on a moderate heat until the bacon is just beginning to brown. Put the drained kale in the pan, season, and cook, stirring about from time to time, for ten minutes.

Just before serving, sprinkle over the cheese, if you like it.

When vegetables and meat are cooked together one flavour complements and merges happily with the other. Here is a recipe that combines kale and lamb in this way.

Curly kale and lamb chops with tomatoes

4 good-sized lamb chops
1 clove garlic
1 dessertspoon chopped rosemary
½ lb (225 gr) kale
2 tablespoons melted lamb fat or
  ½ oz (13 gr) butter

½ glass dry white wine
2 tablespoons double cream
1 teaspoon tomato purée
2 firm tomatoes, skinned, seeded
  and sliced

Crush the garlic and rosemary with salt and pepper and rub them into the chops. Remove the stalks from the kale and break it into small pieces. Put it into boiling water for two minutes. Drain. Heat the fat or butter on a high heat in a large frying pan and brown the chops on both sides. Lower the heat a little and continue to fry the chops until they are done to your liking. Remove them from the pan and keep them warm.

Over a moderate heat put the kale into the pan, and cook it, moving it around a little, until it is just tender. Raise the heat, pour in the wine and boil to reduce it by half. Stir in the cream, tomato purée and tomatoes. Check the seasoning, let it bubble for about a minute, then pile it onto a warmed serving dish and set the chops on the top.

ಐ   ಐ   ಐ

Among the more usual vegetables, all types of winter cabbage are in the shops in February, still firm and tightly packed. Like swede, for a long time cabbage has not enjoyed a very good reputation in Britain, being often associated with back-street seaside boarding houses, shoddy cafés serving 'meat and two veg' and, above all, with schools and institutions. Cooked for ages in far too much water it becomes sloppy and tasteless, but there is no need for this. It can, in fact, be one of the most delicious of vegetables, if it is served still slightly crisp and fresh, straight from the stove.

On its own cabbage is best cooked with a knob of butter and about an inch (2·5 cm) of salted water or stock. Put these into a covered saucepan on a low to moderate heat for about twenty minutes, stirring occasionally. As long as the lid is tightly on no more water should need to be added, and by the time the cabbage is done there will be just sufficient liquid to keep it moist. This way of cooking it will preserve the freshness of the leaves. If you like, you can add some chopped fresh herbs or a chopped clove of garlic to the pan before cooking.

Using this as a basic method, cabbage can take on a surprising number of guises.

Lemon cabbage

1 small Christmas Drumhead or January King cabbage, shredded and with the outer leaves discarded

grated rind and juice of ½ lemon
a knob of butter
scant ¼ pint (1·5 dl) stock

Put all the ingredients into a thick-bottomed saucepan with the butter at the bottom. Cover tightly and set on a moderate heat for 25 minutes, shaking occasionally to make sure it does not stick.

Here is recipe using caraway seeds, this time cooked in an open pan to make it into a hot salad.

Caraway salad

1 medium January King cabbage, shredded and with the outer leaves discarded
3 tablespoons olive oil

1 medium onion, thinly sliced
1 tablespoon caraway seeds
2 tablespoons sour cream

Heat the oil in a large frying pan or paëlla pan on a low heat. Cook the onion and caraway seeds in this until the onion is just turning golden. Add the cabbage and cook on a slightly higher heat, stirring about, for five minutes, when the cabbage should be wilted but still slightly crunchy. Remove the pan from the heat, season and stir in the sour cream. Serve immediately.

Caraway cabbage

1 small Christmas Drumhead or January King cabbage, shredded and with the outer leaves discarded	1 small onion, sliced 1 tablespoon chopped savory 1 dessertspoon caraway seeds 2 tablespoons olive oil

Put the cabbage and onion into a saucepan with the savory, caraway seeds, seasoning and oil, and not more than an inch (2·5 cm) of water. Cover tightly and cook on a moderate heat for 25 minutes, stirring occasionally.

The salty flavour of anchovies also makes a good basis for a hot salad dressing for a cabbage.

Hot cabbage salad with tomato and anchovy dressing

1 medium January King or Christmas Drumhead cabbage, shredded and with the outer leaves discarded 2 tablespoons wine vinegar	1 dessertspoon tomato purée 1 dessertspoon anchovy essence 4 tablespoons olive oil 1 large clove garlic, finely chopped black pepper

Combine the vinegar, tomato purée, anchovy essence and some black pepper. Heat the olive oil in a large frying pan or paëlla pan on a moderate heat. Stir in the shredded cabbage and the garlic and cook, stirring, for ten minutes. Quickly stir in the vinegar mixture. Bring it to the boil and remove it from the heat immediately.

This dish of cabbage cooked in the oven in a casserole is very rich.

Anchovy cabbage

1 small green cabbage, finely shredded 2 flat anchovy fillets 1 medium onion, sliced	1 oz (25 gr) butter pinch ground mace pinch ground allspice 1 bayleaf

Preheat the oven to Reg 4/350°F, 180°C.
Pound the anchovies to a paste. Melt the butter on a low heat in a heavy flameproof casserole and cook the onion slowly, until it is soft. Stir in the anchovies and then the spices and cabbage. Tuck in the bayleaf, cover and put in the oven for 45 minutes.

Herrings make an ideal winter meal, so much more satisfying and substantial than many white fish. This herring and cabbage recipe uses apples to provide sharpness.

Herrings with cabbage and apple

4 herrings	1 large onion, thinly sliced
2 tablespoons made English mustard	1 large cooking apple, peeled, cored and sliced
1 tablespoon chopped thyme or (preferably) lemon thyme	1 small green cabbage, shredded
1 oz (25 gr) butter	¼ pint (1·5 dl) dry cider

Preheat the oven to Reg 4/350°F, 180°C.
Remove the heads, fins and backbones from the herrings, keeping them joined down the back. Spread each one fairly thickly with mustard and sprinkle over the lemon thyme. Fold the herrings back into shape again. Melt the butter in a heavy flameproof casserole on a low heat and soften the onion and the apple slices in this. Add the cabbage to the casserole, stirring round to mix all the ingredients and to coat the cabbage well with butter. Pour in the cider, check the seasoning and bring to the boil. Bury the prepared herrings in this mixture and put the casserole in the oven for 45 minutes.

Marinated pork chops with cabbage

4 pork chops
for the marinade:

½ pint (3 dl) stock	1 medium green cabbage, finely shredded
1 tablespoon wine vinegar	
1 large clove garlic, crushed with salt	½ teaspoon freshly ground allspice
	1 bayleaf, torn up and crumbled
½ teaspoon freshly ground black pepper	1 oz (25 gr) butter

Mix together the stock, vinegar, garlic, spices and bayleaf. Pour this over the chops and leave them for at least four hours and preferably longer, turning occasionally. Remove the chops from the marinade, pat them dry and brush off any pieces of bayleaf.

Melt the butter in a large flameproof casserole or heavy enamelled saucepan on a high heat. Brown the chops in this on both sides. Pile the cabbage on top and strain in the marinade. Cook, covered, on a moderate heat for thirty minutes, keeping the chops at the bottom and stirring the cabbage about on the top from time to time. Serve the chops on a bed of cabbage.

The flavours of pork and cabbage go very well together, particularly if the dish has an added sharpness.

☻   ☻   ☻

To provide a contrast in your February meals, the first Jaffa grapefruit find their way into the shops now, and can make unusual fresh salads with which to start a meal. Peel them, cut each segment into about four pieces, depending on their size, and mix them with grated carrot and sour cream dressing; or mix them with an equal amount of chopped tomato and some watercress or cress and serve them with a peppery French dressing or coat them with plain yoghurt into which you have mixed some crushed garlic and a little cayenne pepper or paprika; or use mayonnaise instead of yoghurt and leave out the garlic.

All types of cheese go well with grapefruit.

Grapefruit and Stilton cheese

2 Jaffa grapefruit
approx 6 oz (150 gr) Stilton cheese

Cut and prepare the grapefruit as if they were to be served cold, removing all the pithy core from the centre. Put each half into a small heatproof dish. Fill up the centre hole with crumbled Stilton and put them under a high grill until the grapefruit are warmed through and all the cheese has melted. Cover the surface of the grapefruit with more cheese and put them back under the grill until it melts. Serve hot straight away and provide a fork as well as a spoon to eat it.

Grapefruit and Derby Sage

2 Jaffa grapefruit
6 oz (150 gr) Derby Sage cheese
French dressing using
 3 tablespoons olive oil and
 1½ tablespoons wine vinegar,
 garlic, salt and pepper

1 tablespoon chopped parsley

Cut the grapefruit in half and scoop out the segments, reserving the shells. Cut each segment in half again. Dice the cheese and mix it with the chopped grapefruit. Mix in the French dressing. Pile the whole mixture back into the shells and scatter over some chopped parsley if you like.

Grapefruit and tomatoes with curd cheese

2 Jaffa grapefruit
4 oz (100 gr) curd cheese
1 clove garlic, very finely chopped
2 tablespoons chopped mixed
 herbs

4 small firm tomatoes
2 tablespoons French dressing
 (without garlic)
8 lettuce leaves

Blend the cheese with the garlic and herbs. Peel the grapefruit and chop the segments. Chop the tomatoes, mix them with the grapefruit and coat them with the dressing. Arrange them either on one large serving dish on top of the lettuce leaves or on four small plates with spoonfuls of the cheese mixture on top.

Grapefruit also combines well with chicken or fish.

Grapefruit and chicken mayonnaise

2 Jaffa grapefruit
4 oz (100 gr) cooked chicken
4 tablespoons mayonnaise

a few drops Tabasco sauce (or a
   pinch of cayenne pepper)
1 teaspoon chopped thyme or
   lemon thyme

Cut the grapefruit in half and separate the segments. Chop the chicken very finely, as though you were chopping herbs. Combine the chicken with the mayonnaise and Tabasco and put a spoonful on each cut grapefruit. Sprinkle the chopped thyme or lemon thyme over the top.

Grapefruit and prawn salad

2 Jaffa grapefruit
1 pint (6 dl) prawns (or 8 oz
   (225 gr) shelled prawns)
3 tablespoons olive oil

juice of $\frac{1}{2}$ lemon
1 teaspoon paprika
pinch cayenne pepper
1 tablespoon chopped parsley

Cut the grapefruit in half. Scoop all the flesh from the shells, and cut each segment into half again. Combine the grapefruit and prawns. Mix together the oil, lemon juice, paprika and cayenne and coat the grapefruit and prawns with this. Pile back into the reserved shells. Sprinkle with the chopped parsley.

ध   ध   ध

Mushrooms were once only available in the autumn and were quite a luxury addition to the breakfast table as it took so much trouble to find and pick them. Nowadays cultivated mushrooms are available all the year round and have become commonplace. Even if the flavour bears no comparison to that of field mushrooms they have many possibilities in the kitchen; served either on their own or in combination with other ingredients they can help greatly in livening up meals in the dull February days.

The tiny button mushrooms have a more delicate flavour than the flat open ones and they go very well with lemon.

Button mushrooms and lemon

½ lb (225 gr) button mushrooms
1 oz (25 gr) butter
juice of ½ lemon, or more to taste

Slice the mushrooms thinly, leaving the stalks on. Put them in a saucepan with the melted butter and the lemon juice. Cover, and simmer gently for ten minutes.

Lamb is often improved by the sharpness of lemon which counteracts its fattiness, and adding mushrooms as well will make a rounded and flavourful dish.

Braised lamb provençal

1 shoulder of lamb, boned,
  keeping the bones
6 flat anchovy fillets
8 green olives
2 tablespoons olive oil
for the sauce:
4 large mushrooms, finely
  chopped
1 tablespoon flour

1 medium onion, diced
1 medium carrot, diced
1 stick celery, diced
1 mushroom stalk, diced
1 wineglass white wine

1 dessertspoon tomato purée
½ pint (3 dl) stock

Preheat the oven to Reg 6/400°F, 200°C.
Pound the anchovies and olives together and spread them over the cut surface of the lamb. Roll up the joint and tie it with strong thread or fine cotton string. Melt the oil in a heavy flameproof casserole on a high heat and brown the lamb on all sides. If there is room for the bones add them to the casserole for extra flavour. Remove the meat and bones and set aside.

Stir the vegetables into the casserole, cover them and sweat them on a very low heat for seven minutes. Replace the lamb and the bones. Season and pour over the white wine. Cover and put into the oven for one hour. Take out the lamb, carve it, and keep it warm on a serving dish. Discard the bones.

Strain the remaining contents of the casserole through a sieve. Skim the liquid and put the skimmed fat into a small saucepan on a moderate heat. (If there isn't sufficient fat, use ¾ oz (19 gr) butter). Put the chopped mushrooms into the pan and cook them for three minutes. Stir in the flour and tomato purée and blend in the stock. Bring to the boil, stirring, and stir in the juices reserved from the casserole. Simmer for two minutes and pour over the lamb before serving. Baked potatoes in their jackets go very well with this dish.

Lamb and mushrooms in lemon sauce

1 shoulder of lamb, boned out
8 flat anchovy fillets
8 black olives, stoned
1 tablespoon chopped marjoram
grated rind and juice of 1 lemon
½ oz (13 gr) butter (or 2 tablespoons melted lamb fat)
½ pint (3 dl) stock
½ lb (225 gr) button mushrooms
2 egg yolks

Preheat the oven to Reg 4/350°F, 180°C.
Pound the anchovies and olives together in a pestle and mortar and work in the marjoram and the grated lemon rind. Spread this mixture over the cut surface of the lamb. Roll up the joint and tie it with strong thread or fine cotton string. Heat the fat or butter in a heavy flameproof casserole on a moderate heat and brown the joint all over. Remove the lamb and pour off all the fat from the casserole. Stir in the stock and bring it to the boil. Replace the meat and add the whole button mushrooms. Cover, and put in the oven for 1¼ hours. Remove the meat, carve it, and keep it warm.

Stir the lemon juice into the juices in the casserole. Work the egg yolks together in a bowl and gradually blend four table-spoons of the hot sauce into them. Pour the egg mixture into the casserole. Check the seasoning, and reheat without boiling. Pour the sauce over the sliced lamb, arranging the mushrooms around the slices of meat.

In this next recipe for shoulder of lamb and mushrooms the meat is not only boned, but diced as well.

Shoulder of lamb with caraway

2 lb (900 gr) lean shoulder of
  lamb, diced
4 tablespoons olive oil
1 large onion, finely chopped
1 clove garlic, finely chopped
2 tablespoons paprika

juice of 1 lemon
2 tablespoons caraway seeds
½ lb (225 gr) mushrooms, sliced
½ pint (3 dl) stock
4 tablespoons chopped parsley

Heat the oil on a high heat in a large heavy frying pan or casserole and when it is smoking, put in the cubes of lamb to brown all over. Remove the lamb and set it aside. Reduce the heat, put in the onion and garlic and cook them gently until they are soft. Stir in the paprika and cook for two minutes. Stir in the lemon juice, stock, caraway seeds and mushrooms. Bring slowly to the boil and stir in the browned lamb. Season, cover, and set on the lowest possible heat on top of the stove for an hour, adding the parsley for the last 30 minutes.

Mushrooms are really compatible with any meat. Here are some beef recipes.

Beef duxelles

1½ lb (675 gr) silverside or topside, cut into four fairly thin slices
for the stuffing:
1 oz (25 gr) butter
3 oz (75 gr) onion, finely chopped
2 oz (50 gr) flat mushrooms,
  finely chopped
2 oz (50 gr) granary breadcrumbs
2 tablespoons chopped parsley
1 dessertspoon Worcestershire
  sauce

1 tablespoon olive oil
½ oz (13 gr) butter
1 wineglass sherry
½ pint (3 dl) stock
4 oz flat mushrooms

To make the stuffing, melt the butter over a low heat in a frying pan and gently cook the onion in this until it is soft. Raise the heat, add the chopped mushrooms and cook briskly for three minutes. Remove the pan from the heat and work in the bread-crumbs, parsley and Worcestershire sauce. Season. Spread this mixture evenly over the slices of meat, roll up each slice and tie it with strong thread.

Heat the oil on a high heat in a heavy sauté pan, add the butter, and when the foam subsides put in the rolls of beef to brown. Remove and set aside. Pour the sherry and stock into the pan and rapidly bring them to the boil, scraping in any brown pieces from the bottom of the pan. Replace the meat rolls, cover and simmer for 30 minutes, turning them occasion-ally. Add the whole mushrooms to the pan and simmer for 15 minutes more.

This stuffing mixture can also be put into a boned piece of brisket before it is rolled up for roasting. When it is cooked, make a sauce with the basic brown sauce to which you have added the pan juices and a further tablespoon of Worcestershire sauce.

Steak with mushrooms and sour cream

1½-2 lb (675-900 gr) steak, of any cut suitable for frying
garlic
1 oz (25 gr) butter
½ lb (225 gr) mushrooms
5 fluid oz (1·5 dl) sour cream

Fry the steak in the butter with plenty of garlic. Set it aside to keep warm, and quickly cook the sliced mushrooms in the pan juices. Stir in the sour cream, season and pour the mixture over the steak.

Beef and mushroom loaf

1 lb (450 gr) good minced beef (coarsely minced if possible)
1 large clove garlic, finely chopped
3 tablespoons chopped parsley
¼ lb (100 gr) flat mushrooms, finely chopped
1 oz (25 gr) butter

Preheat the oven to Reg 4/350°F, 180°C. Lightly butter a loaf tin.

Put the meat into a large mixing bowl with the garlic, parsley and seasoning. Melt the butter on a moderate heat and cook the mushrooms in this for three minutes. Add them to the meat in the bowl and beat all the ingredients together well.

Press the meat mixture into the tin and bake in the oven for an hour. Allow the loaf to cool in the tin before turning it out. Serve cold with horseradish sauce.

Mushrooms and chicken both have a mild, delicate flavour, but here they form the basis of a hot, spicy dish.

Spiced grilled chicken and mushrooms

3-3½ lb (1·3-1·5 kg) roasting
  chicken, jointed
4 oz (100 gr) butter
1 dessertspoon ground cumin
1 dessertspoon ground coriander

1 teaspoon cayenne pepper
1 dessertspoon ground turmeric
2 cloves garlic, crushed with salt
8 oz (225 gr) small flat
  mushrooms, sliced

Soften the butter and blend in the spices and garlic. Spread this mixture over the chicken joints and leave them in the refrigerator for two hours for the butter to set. Preheat the grill to high. Lay on the chicken joints, skin side down first and grill them as close to the heat as possible, turning them several times, until the juices run clear when they are pierced. Lay the joints in the bottom of the grill pan, without the rack. Put in the mushrooms, and continue to cook under a high heat for a further ten minutes, when the chicken should be tender and the mushrooms cooked through. Serve with rice.

Vegetables available in March

beetroot – available cooked or raw

broccoli, purple sprouting

Brussels sprouts – too old and yellow to be worth using

cabbage – savoys are finished, but there should still be plenty of
January King and Drumhead varieties

carrots – quite large now and sometimes too bitter and woody
for eating raw, but still good for cooking

cauliflowers – expensive at first but by the end of the month they
are more plentiful and cheaper

celery – very little English about and what there is is only
suitable for cooking, not for salads

leeks

parsnips – these now have more soft brown patches and should
only be bought with care

spring onions – thin at first but gradually filling out

spring greens

swedes – still good

turnips – now too soft to be used as a vegetable, but still usable
in stocks and soups

watercress

Fruit available in March

apples – most English varieties are finished by the end of the
month and their place is taken by French Red and Golden
Delicious and South African Granny Smiths

pears – Conference are finished now but there are still some
Comice about. Others are mostly Spanish

citrus fruit – Spanish and Moroccan fruits finish and are
replaced by the sweeter Israeli fruits.

rhubarb – all home-grown, in the open, and crisp and fresh

Fresh herbs available in March

bay

chives – the first young, tender crop appears in the middle of
March

marjoram – the stems become longer and more tender and the
   leaves more tender as the month progresses
parsley – should still be growing fairly steadily
rosemary – the leaves become softer and more aromatic
sage – new, more tender leaves begin to grow
savory – the stems begin to soften and become greener
thyme – new soft stems and bright green new leaves grow

⁓   ⁓   ⁓

March is the month of 'many weathers', sometimes really rough
and cold, sometimes just dull and grey, and occasionally warm
and sunny enough to kid you into thinking that spring is really
here. As the weather gets brighter and milder, we no longer
need the earthy comforting root vegetables, which by now are
past their best, but something fresher and greener.

To fill this need, as soon as the hard frosts are over, watercress begins to grow again. There won't have been enough sun
yet to make the leaves the shiny bronze colour that they become
later in the year, but they will be hot and crisp. On the warmer
days in March watercress can be included in all kinds of green
salads, either chopped up very fine and mixed into the dressing,
or used as one of the main ingredients of a green salad. Oranges
and tomatoes both go well with watercress.

Watercress, tomato and Gorgonzola salad

1 bunch watercress
8 firm tomatoes
2 oz (50 gr) Gorgonzola cheese
4 tablespoons olive oil
2 tablespoons wine vinegar

Chop the watercress and tomatoes and mix them together.
Cream the cheese and gradually blend in the oil and vinegar.
Season. Combine this dressing with the tomatoes and water-
cress, and serve it as a first course.

On warmer days, watercress and eggs combine well for a light
first course.

Watercress eggs

4 hard-boiled eggs	1 tablespoon mayonnaise
4 tablespoons grated Cheddar	4 tablespoons chopped watercress
cheese	1 teaspoon made English mustard

for serving:
1 bunch watercress
for coating:
4 tablespoons mayonnaise
2 tablespoons chopped watercress

Cut the eggs in half lengthways. Rub the yolks through a sieve and work them with the cheese, mayonnaise, watercress and mustard. Fill the cavities in the egg whites with this mixture and sandwich the halves together with any that is left over. Lay them on a 'nest' of watercress.

Mix the remaining chopped watercress and mayonnaise together and spoon it over the eggs.

Green eggs

4 eggs
1½ bunches watercress, chopped
3 oz (75 gr) butter
2 tablespoons wine vinegar
1 dessertspoon chopped capers
1 dessertspoon chopped parsley

Use either one large serving plate or four small ones and arrange the watercress as a base for the eggs. Soft-poach the eggs in about two inches (5 cm) of simmering water to which has been added a spot of wine vinegar. Drain thoroughly and cool. Put each on to the bed of watercress. Melt the butter in a frying pan on a fairly high heat and let it brown. Quickly stir in the vinegar, capers and parsley, and let it boil for a few seconds. Remove from the heat and shake the pan while the mixture continues to bubble. When it has reduced by half and is thick, pour it over the eggs. Let it cool before serving.

And for the colder days, here is a sustaining soup.

Watercress and potato soup

1 bunch watercress, finely
  chopped
1 large potato, peeled and thinly
  sliced

1 medium onion, thinly sliced
1½ pints (9 dl) stock
bouquet garni
2 fluid oz (60 ml) double cream

Put the sliced potato and onion into a saucepan with the stock,
bouquet garni and seasoning, bring to the boil, and simmer
gently for 20 minutes. Remove the saucepan from the heat, take
out the bouquet garni and put in the watercress. Allow the
liquid to cool slightly, then work it in the blender until it is
smooth. Return it to the saucepan, stir in the cream and reheat.
Serve garnished with a little more chopped watercress if liked.

Watercress makes a good alternative to herbs as a flavouring.

White fish with green anchovy sauce

2 lb (900 gr) white fish (cod, coley,
  or haddock), skinned
juice of 1 lemon
2 bayleaves
a few black peppercorns
½ pint (3 dl) fish stock (made by
  simmering the skin of the fish
  with 1 pint (6 dl) of water, a
  carrot, a small onion, a stick of
  celery, and a bouquet garni)

6 flat anchovy fillets
1 oz (25 gr) butter
1 tablespoon flour
2 teaspoons anchovy essence
2 teaspoons chopped capers
4 tablespoons chopped watercress

Cut the fish into even-sized pieces, lay them in a buttered ovenproof dish and pour over the lemon juice. Put a small piece of
bayleaf on each piece of fish, scatter over the peppercorns, and
leave the fish to stand for an hour. Preheat the oven to Reg
4/350°F, 180°C, cover the fish with foil and bake for 20 minutes.

Meanwhile, pound the anchovy fillets to a paste with a large
pestle and mortar or in a bowl with a wooden spoon. Beat in
the butter, flour and anchovy essence.

When the fish is done, take it from the oven, remove the pieces
of bayleaf, and put the fish on a warm dish. Strain any juices

from its cooking into a saucepan and add the stock. Heat the liquid and when it is on the point of boiling, whisk in the anchovy and butter mixture. Simmer for five minutes and stir in the capers and watercress. Pour over the fish and serve.

Lamb with mushrooms and watercress

1½ lb (675 gr) lean boneless lamb (shoulder or leg), cut into small dice
2 tablespoons olive oil
1 large onion, finely chopped
1 dessertspoon ground ginger
½ pint (3 dl) stock
6 oz (150 gr) mushrooms, sliced
2 bunches watercress, chopped

Heat the oil in a heavy sauté pan on a high heat and brown the lamb in this. Remove the meat and set aside. Lower the heat and stir in the onion and ginger. Cook until the onion is soft. Stir in the stock and bring to the boil. Stir in the lamb and mushrooms. Cover and simmer on a low heat for 40 minutes.

Stir the watercress into the pan. Check the seasoning, cover again, and cook for a further five minutes.

Watercress rice

10 oz (275 gr) uncooked long-grain rice
4 oz (100 gr) grated Cheddar cheese
1 bunch watercress, finely chopped

Boil the rice in salted water until it is just tender. Drain it and refresh it with hot water. Put the rice back into the saucepan on a very low heat and quickly fork in the cheese and the chopped watercress. Serve it as soon as the cheese has started to melt.

Beef sautéed with watercress

1½ lb (675 gr) top rump or blade bone of beef, cut into four fairly thin slices
¾ oz (19 gr) butter
1 large onion, finely chopped
1 tablespoon flour
½ pint (3 dl) stock
1 tablespoon Worcestershire sauce
1 bunch watercress, chopped

Melt the butter on a high heat in a sauté pan and brown the slices of beef very well on both sides. Remove them and set aside. Lower the heat and take the pan off the stove to cool a little. Put in the onion, return the pan to a low heat, and cook the onion gently until it is soft. Stir in the flour and cook, stirring until it is russet brown. Blend in the stock and bring it to the boil, still stirring. Stir in the Worcestershire sauce and watercress and replace the meat. Check the seasoning, cover and simmer on a low heat for one hour.

Creamed potatoes and watercress

4 medium potatoes, peeled
1 small onion, thinly sliced
2 oz (50 gr) butter

½ bunch watercress, finely
  chopped
4 tablespoons milk

Boil the potatoes and onion together in salted water until the potatoes are tender. Drain them. Melt the butter in the saucepan on a very low heat. Put the watercress and then the potatoes and onion into the butter and mash them all together. Beat in the milk and continue beating them all until they are smooth.

ಐ   ಐ   ಐ

Spring greens are usually a good buy in March. Although they are available throughout the winter it is at about this time that they become really tender and more tasty. Greens, like cabbage, can be ruined by overcooking, and 'eat up your greens, they're good for you' is a command that many children learn to dread from an early age. As with cabbage, less water and a few herbs can work wonders.

To cook 1 lb (450 gr) of spring greens, remove the stalks, wash the leaves and chop them into fairly small pieces. Put them into a saucepan with 1 oz (25 gr) butter and an inch (2.5 cm) of water. Cover them and set them on a moderate heat for 25 minutes, stirring them from time to time. If they become rather dry, add more water by the tablespoon.

Various combinations of fresh herbs can be added to the greens while they are cooking, according to the meat they are to accompany: a little chopped rosemary for lamb, for instance, or parsley and thyme with fish. A medium onion, thinly sliced, or some chopped spring onions can be added as well as, or instead of the herbs.

During the last two weeks of Lent it used to be a custom in the north of England to make what was known as Bistort or Ledger Pudding, using eggs and all the different sorts of wild leaves that spring up at this time of the year, such as bistort, dock and dandelion. Here is an adaptation of this pudding using spring greens, eggs and bacon.

Green pudding

1 lb (450 gr) spring greens, finely chopped
1 oz (25 gr) butter
2 oz (50 gr) lean bacon, finely diced

4 large or 6 small spring onions, chopped (or 1 small onion, sliced)
4 eggs
1 tablespoon chopped parsley

Put the washed greens into a saucepan with about an inch (2·5 cm) of salted water. Cover, and cook on a moderate heat for 20 minutes. If there is still any water in the pan when they have finished cooking, drain them in a sieve – they should not be sloppy for this recipe.

Meanwhile, melt the butter in a fairly large saucepan on a low heat. Add the bacon and onion to the butter and cook gently for ten minutes. Beat the eggs with the parsley and some pepper. Stir the cooked spring greens into the saucepan and mix them well with the bacon and onion. Pour in the beaten eggs and mix again. Continue to stir until the eggs are set (as for scrambled eggs).

Have ready a warm pudding basin and a heated flat plate to cover the top. Put the mixture into the basin and press it down with the back of a metal spoon. Cover it with the plate and let it stand for two minutes in a warm place to take shape. Turn it out.

This will serve two people for lunch or supper, or it can be used for more people to supplement a plain meat dish.

The mixture of eggs and greens is used again in the following recipe.

Green roulade with cheese

8 oz (225 gr) spring greens, finely chopped and with the stalks discarded
6 spring onions (or 1 small onion), chopped

2 tablespoons chopped parsley
4 eggs, separated
4 oz (100 gr) curd cheese
1 dessertspoon grated Parmesan cheese

Preheat the oven to Reg 6/400°F, 200°C. Line a Swiss roll tin with buttered greaseproof paper.

Put the washed greens into a saucepan with the onions and parsley and half an inch (1.25 cm) of salted water and set them, covered, on a moderate heat for 20 minutes. Beat the eggs yolks together. When the greens are cooked, allow them to cool a little and then mix them into the egg yolks. Stiffly beat the whites and fold them into the mixture, using a metal spoon. Season. Spread the mixture evenly over the paper in the tin and put it in the centre of the oven for 20 minutes, by which time it should be firm. Take it out of the oven and quickly spread the curd cheese over the surface. Roll it up and sprinkle the Parmesan cheese over the top. Put it back into the oven for three minutes to warm through.

This will serve two people as a main meal, but cut into slices, as a first course or to accompany another dish, it should serve four.

Spring greens and rosemary go excellently with lamb.

Lamb chops and spring greens in red wine

4 good-sized lamb chops (boneless if possible)
1 oz (25 gr) butter
1 large onion, sliced
1 clove garlic, finely chopped
2 sprigs rosemary, finely chopped

1 wineglass red wine
2 flat anchovy fillets, finely chopped
1 lb (450 gr) spring greens, washed and very finely chopped

Melt the butter in a casserole or heavy enamel saucepan on a high heat and brown the chops in this on both sides. Lower the heat a little and continue to cook until the chops are half done, turning them from time to time. Remove the chops and set aside. Lower the heat right down and put in the onion, garlic and rosemary and cook until the onion is soft. Pour in the wine and add the chopped anchovy fillets. Bring to the boil. Replace the chops and pile the spring greens on the top. Turn the heat up to moderate, cover and cook for 20 minutes, stirring the greens three or four times to ensure even cooking without disturbing the chops. The onions will gradually mix in with the greens.

To serve, check the seasoning, arrange the greens on a dish, put the chops on the top and spoon over any sauce that is left in the casserole. Buttered noodles are a good accompaniment.

Green lamb

1 best end of neck of lamb, boned
2 sprigs rosemary, finely chopped
2 sprigs thyme, finely chopped
up to 1 lb (450 gr) spring greens, washed and with the stalks removed
10 spring onions
for the sauce:
½ tablespoon flour
¼ pint (1·5 dl) stock
2 tablespoons chopped parsley

2 tablespoons lamb fat or ½ oz (13 gr) butter or dripping
1 small onion, sliced
1 small carrot, diced
1 small stick celery, diced
½ pint (3 dl) stock
bouquet garni

Preheat the oven to Reg 4/350°F, 180°C.
Scatter the chopped rosemary and thyme over the underside. Lay as many whole leaves of the greens as you can lengthways on the boned-out lamb, folding under any that are too long. Lay the onions between the greens, cutting any that are too long to the length of the joint. Roll the lamb round the greens and onions and tie as tightly as possible. Heat the fat on a high heat in a heavy flameproof casserole. Put in the lamb with its bones to brown. If the greens are showing through be careful not to put this part into the fat or the leaves will burn.

Take out the lamb and the bones, lower the heat and stir in the other vegetables. Cover them with a buttered paper and a lid and sweat them for five minutes. Return the lamb and the bones to the pan, pour in the stock and tuck in the bouquet garni. Bring to the boil, cover and put into the oven for an hour.

When the lamb is done, remove it from the casserole on to a warm plate and let it rest for a few minutes. Strain the juices from the casserole, pressing down hard on the vegetables to extract all the liquid. Skim, and put the fat back into the casserole. Set it on a moderate heat on top of the stove, stir in the flour and blend in the cooking juices and the stock. Stir until boiling, add the chopped parsley and simmer it for two minutes. Check the seasoning. Carve the lamb in fairly thick slices and serve with the sauce poured over it.

ஐ   ஐ   ஐ

Purple sprouting broccoli in many ways resembles spring greens, but it is also akin to cauliflower, and can stand being boiled. Like cauliflower it is delicious with cheese.

Purple sprouting broccoli with cheese sauce

1½ lb (675 gr) purple sprouting broccoli, trimmed
for the cheese sauce:
1 oz (25 gr) flour   1 teaspoon English, or
1 oz (25 gr) butter   1 dessertspoon Dijon mustard
½ pint (3 dl) milk   2 oz (50 gr) Cheddar cheese
2 oz (50 gr) grated Cheddar cheese

Cook the broccoli in boiling salted water until tender (about 10 minutes). Meanwhile make the cheese sauce, and add the mustard to it. Transfer the broccoli to a shallow ovenproof dish, pour the sauce over it, sprinkle liberally with the grated cheese, and brown it under the grill.

Purple sprouting broccoli with Parmesan cheese

1½ lb (675 gr) purple sprouting broccoli, trimmed
2 oz (50 gr) butter
1 tablespoon grated Parmesan cheese

Cook the broccoli in boiling salted water until it is just tender (about 10 minutes). Drain it well and put it into a warmed serving dish. Melt the butter in a saucepan on a moderate heat, stir in the Parmesan and cook it until it is golden. Pour the butter and cheese over the broccoli and serve.

Purple sprouting broccoli can also be cooked like spring greens with butter and only a little water.

Purple sprouting broccoli with onion, tomatoes and garlic

1 lb (450 gr) purple sprouting
  broccoli
1 oz (25 gr) butter
1 medium onion, thinly sliced
1 clove garlic, finely chopped

4 tomatoes, skinned, seeded and
  roughly chopped
1 tablespoon grated Parmesan
  cheese

Put the broccoli, onion and garlic into a saucepan with the butter and half an inch (1.25 cm) of salted water. Cover, and cook on a moderate heat until tender (20 minutes), when all the liquid should have evaporated. Toss in the tomatoes, season, and heat through. Serve with the Parmesan cheese sprinkled over the top.

This can make a very attractive dish if it is arranged round some cooked cauliflower, with the cheese sprinkled over the lot.

Using much the same method, cauliflower can be cooked in the saucepan with the broccoli.

Purple sprouting broccoli with cauliflower

1 lb (450 gr) purple sprouting broccoli
1 small cauliflower, broken into florets
1 medium onion, thinly sliced
1 oz (25 gr) butter

Put the vegetables and butter into a saucepan with half an inch (1.25 cm) of salted water and cook, covered, for 20 minutes on a moderate heat.

ॐ   ॐ   ॐ

There is an old saying:

Eat leckes in lide [leeks in March] and ramsins [wild garlic] in May
And all the year after physitians may play.

True or not, leeks are one of the few winter vegetables that remain as good in March as they were at the beginning of the season. Personally I prefer long thin leeks with plenty of white in proportion to green, and because of this, leeks are the only vegetable that I buy regularly in a supermarket instead of at the greengrocer, where often they are short and squat and sometimes well over an inch (2.5 cm) thick, with a lot of waste. For making soups, fat or thin are really equally suitable, but for the other recipes, if you have to use thick ones, cut them into thinner slices and vary the amount you use to fit your pot.

The best basic way of cooking leeks is in stock with a little butter and parsley.

Basic recipe for leeks

6 long white leeks, cut into one-inch (2·5 cm) lengths
¼ pint (1·5 dl) stock
1 oz (25 gr) butter   2 tablespoons chopped parsley

Put all the ingredients into a saucepan, season, cover, bring to the boil, and simmer for ten minutes.

There are several possible variations to this basic method. You can add a teaspoon of Dijon, German or tarragon mustard, *or* add some chopped spring onions, *or* cook some diced bacon in the butter first and when it has just begun to brown, add the leeks, parsley, stock and seasoning and continue as before, *or* when the leeks are cooked, put them into an ovenproof dish, scatter over four tablespoons each of browned crumbs and grated cheese, and brown them under a hot grill.

Grilled leeks

1½ lb (675 gr) leeks, cut into 1½-inch (4 cm) lengths
1 oz (25 gr) butter, softened
1 tablespoon Parmesan cheese   1 dessertspoon Dijon mustard

Cook the leeks in boiling salted water for ten minutes. Drain them and transfer them to a shallow ovenproof dish. Cream the butter, cheese and mustard together and spread the mixture over the leeks. Grill them under a high heat until golden.

Cold leek salad

6 thin white leeks, chopped into
  1½-inch (4 cm) lengths
¼ lb (100 gr) button mushrooms, sliced
3 tablespoons olive oil
1 teaspoon German mustard
1½ tablespoons wine vinegar

Cook the leeks in boiling salted water for ten minutes. Drain, refresh and drain again. Combine the leeks and mushrooms. Work the oil into the mustard and blend in the vinegar. Add a little pepper if liked. Mix this dressing into the leeks and mushrooms and let the whole stand for an hour before serving.

Leeks make all manner of tasty soups. In this recipe ham is added to the familiar smooth and creamy combination of leeks and potatoes known as 'Vichyssoise'.

Leek, potato and ham soup

4 small leeks, the white part only,   1½ oz (38 gr) butter
  finely sliced   1½ pints (9 dl) stock
8 oz (225 gr) raw potato, finely   4 oz (100 gr) lean ham, finely
  sliced   diced
for the garnish:
1 tablespoon chopped parsley
the green part of one leek cut into thin one-inch (2·5 cm) strips and
  blanched

Melt the butter on a low heat in a saucepan. Stir in the leek and potato. Cover them with a butter paper and a lid and let them sweat for five minutes without browning. Stir in the stock and add the ham. Simmer for 15 minutes. Cool slightly and work in the blender until smooth. Return to the pan and reheat.

Check the seasoning and serve in individual bowls with the parsley and green leek sprinkled on the top.

If they are finely chopped, leeks also make good clear soups. The following soup is an adaptation of a medieval recipe.

Leek and mushroom soup

3 thin leeks, finely chopped	1½ pints (9 dl) stock
¼ lb (100 gr) mushrooms, finely chopped	1 tablespoon chopped thyme and parsley
1 oz (25 gr) butter	1 bayleaf
1 tablespoon flour	1 wineglass red wine

Melt the butter in a saucepan on a low heat. Stir in the leeks and mushrooms, cover and cook them gently for ten minutes. Stir in the flour and blend in the stock. Bring to the boil, stirring. Add the chopped herbs and the bayleaf and simmer gently for ten minutes, uncovered. Stir in the red wine. Remove the bayleaf, check the seasoning, and reheat.

This next soup is also made without a blender.

Leek and tomato soup

4 small leeks, cut in half lengthways and finely sliced	4 tablespoons chopped mixed herbs
1 oz (25 gr) butter	1 pint (6 dl) stock
1 lb (450 gr) ripe tomatoes (they need not be best quality), skinned and chopped	

Melt the butter in a saucepan on a low heat. Stir the leeks into it, cover and cook slowly for 15 minutes, stirring occasionally, until they are just turning brown. When the leeks are done, add the tomatoes and herbs to the pan. Cover again and cook until the tomatoes are mushy. Pour in the stock, bring slowly to the boil and simmer for ten minutes. Check the seasoning before serving.

Leeks go very well with eggs and the combination makes good supper or lunch dishes.

Leek roulade

2 long white leeks, sliced
4 eggs, separated
2 tablespoons grated Parmesan
  cheese
2 tablespoons chopped chervil or
  parsley

3 oz (75 gr) lean bacon, chopped
½ oz (13 gr) butter or dripping
3 oz (75 gr) mushrooms, chopped
1 dessertspoon chopped thyme
1 teaspoon made English mustard

Preheat the oven to Reg 6/400°F, 200°C, and line a Swiss roll tin with buttered greaseproof paper.

Boil the leeks in salted water for four minutes. Drain and refresh them. Mix the egg yolks with half a tablespoon of the cheese and stir in the leeks and chopped chervil or parsley. Stiffly beat the egg whites and fold them into the leek and yolk mixture. Season. Spread the mixture evenly over the paper in the tin and cook in the oven for 20 minutes, or until firm.

Meanwhile, cook the bacon slowly in the dripping or butter until it is just starting to brown; raise the heat and add the mushrooms. Cook quickly for two minutes. Take the pan off the heat and stir in the thyme and mustard.

When the roulade is cooked, spread the bacon and mushroom mixture over the top and sprinkle over half a tablespoon of the Parmesan. Roll up the roulade, scatter over the rest of the cheese, and brown it quickly under a hot grill.

Pork is a particularly good accompaniment to leeks as both go perfectly with cider and spicy mustards.

Braised shoulder of pork with sage

a piece of shoulder of pork
  weighing about 2 lb (900 gr)
1 oz (25 gr) butter
1 small onion, chopped
1 small carrot, chopped
1 stick celery, chopped
1 wineglass dry cider

1 wineglass stock
6 sage leaves tied together, or a
  sprig of sage
6 thin white leeks cut into
  two-inch (5 cm) lengths
1 oz (25 gr) butter, kneaded
1 teaspoon tomato purée

Preheat the oven to Reg 4/350°F, 180°C.

Melt the butter in a heavy flameproof casserole on a high heat. Brown the joint on all sides and remove it. Lower the heat right down, stir in the onion, carrot and celery, cover and let them sweat for seven minutes. Set the meat on top of the vegetables, pour in the cider and stock, and tuck in the sage leaves. Season. Bring the liquid to the boil and put in the leeks. Cover, and cook in the centre of the oven for one and a half hours.

Remove the leeks and the meat from the casserole. Carve the meat, arrange it with the leeks on a warmed serving dish and put them to keep warm. Strain the juices from the casserole, pressing down hard on the vegetables to extract all the liquid. Skim the liquid if necessary and return it to the casserole. Set it on a moderate heat and bring it to the boil. Stir in the tomato purée and whisk in the kneaded butter. Pour the sauce over the meat and leeks and serve.

Pork chops and leeks in Dijon sauce

4 pork chops
2 small cloves garlic, chopped
2 teaspoons chopped rosemary
12 black peppercorns
8 small thin leeks, cut into
  one-inch (2·5 cm) lengths

1 oz (25 gr) butter, or
  4 tablespoons melted pork fat
½ pint (3 dl) dry cider
4 tablespoons double cream
1 dessertspoon Dijon mustard
1 tablespoon grated Parmesan
  cheese

Crush the garlic, rosemary, peppercorns and a pinch of sea-salt together and rub these into both sides of the chops. Melt the butter on a high heat in a wide-bottomed casserole and brown the chops in this on both sides. Remove them and set aside. Keeping the heat high, pour in the cider and bring to the boil. Replace the chops and put in the leeks. Cover and simmer for 30 minutes.

Remove the chops and leeks and arrange them on a warmed serving dish. Stir the cream, mustard and cheese into the juices in the pan. Bring them to the boil, pour them over the chops and serve.

ജ   ജ   ജ

Towards the end of March the herb garden begins to wake up, and I always get a surprise when the first crop of chives suddenly appears above the surface, almost overnight. I nearly weeded them out one year as I thought it was much too early for them and they must be grass! However, having saved them I found they were a good ingredient for fish pâtés as well as the more usual egg salads and cottage cheese.

Bloater and mustard pâté

2 bloaters
1 oz (25 gr) butter
juice of ½ lemon
1 tablespoon chopped chives and parsley
1 teaspoon made English mustard
1 hard-boiled egg, finely chopped
1 teaspoon Meaux or other whole grain mustard

Fillet and skin the bloaters and chop them very small. In a heavy frying pan melt the butter on a moderate heat. Put in the chopped fish and cook briskly, stirring, for about three minutes. Remove the pan from the heat. Put the fish into a bowl and pound with a wooden spoon until it is smooth, removing any remaining small bones. Beat in the lemon juice, chopped herbs, English mustard and seasoning.

In a separate bowl, work the Meaux mustard into the egg. Press half the fish mixture into a small terrine. Cover it with the whole of the egg mixture in an even layer, and then with the rest of the fish. Chill until firm and turn out before serving.

Mackerel pâté

¾-1 lb (325-450 gr) filleted mackerel
1 egg yolk
1 dessertspoon anchovy essence
1 tablespoon chopped parsley
1 tablespoon chopped chives
1 teaspoon flour

Preheat the oven to Reg 3/325°F, 170°C. Butter a 1 lb (450 gr) terrine.

Remove the skin from the mackerel fillets and mince them finely. Mix all the ingredients together. Press them into the terrine. Bake in a bain-marie for 1½ hours in the oven. Cool completely before turning out.

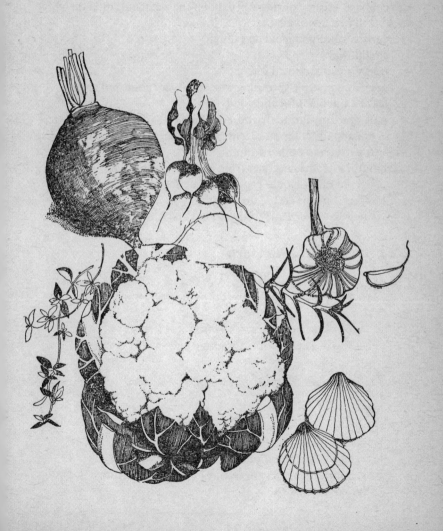

Vegetables available in April

asparagus – the season for this is from mid-April until
    midsummer day. Its availability depends very much on where
    you live
beetroot – raw as well as cooked
cabbage – scarce during April, but if the weather is mild there
    will be a few available
carrots – becoming old and tough
cauliflower
celery – scarce and all foreign
greens and purple sprouting broccoli – very good and tender
leeks – still plentiful and good
parsnips – my farmer friend says that you should never eat
    parsnips after Good Friday, and he's right – they really are
    too rotten to bother with
potatoes – some new ones from abroad creep into the shops as
    the old English ones become rather floury
radishes – by the end of the month
watercress – excellent: fresh and hot and sun-bronzed

Fruit available in April

apples – all eating apples are from France or South Africa now
pears – no English ones now, they are mostly Spanish or South
    African
rhubarb – the cheapest and best fruit
citrus fruit – Israeli Jaffas are sound and sweet

Fresh herbs available in April

bay
chives – growing rapidly
fennel – begins to get feathery leaves
lovage – the first red shoots appear above the surface
marjoram – the stalks are getting longer and more tender, and
    the leaves bigger

parsley – still growing steadily
rosemary – the leaves increasingly tender and aromatic
sage – lots of new growth and tender leaves
savory – the leaves and stems become larger and more tender
    as the month progresses
sorrel – starts to grow a few new leaves
tarragon – tiny shoots appear at the beginning of the month and
    by the end of April they should be about an inch long
thyme – lots of new tender stems and leaves

❧   ❧   ❧

With the arrival of Easter winter has gone for another year. As well as spring-cleaning and turning out the house it is time to forget about the old foods and welcome the new. The trouble is that there are very few fresh new vegetables about in April.

We can, however, turn to the herb garden where the perennial herbs – thyme, rosemary, sage, savory and marjoram – are producing plenty of soft, fresh green growth. Both the leaves and stems should be soft enough to be chopped into salad dressings, mixed with mayonnaise or cream cheese or sprinkled over thick soups.

Hot-house lettuce begins to be tastier and more robust at this time of the year, and makes an excellent simple salad.

Mixed spring salad with herb dressing

1 lettuce
1 bunch watercress
1 handful dandelion leaves
for the dressing:

3 tablespoons mixed fresh herbs   1 large clove of garlic, crushed
    of as many varieties as possible   with salt
4 tablespoons olive oil   black pepper
2 tablespoons wine vinegar

Chop the herbs very finely and mix them with the other ingredients for the dressing. Season with plenty of black pepper and let it stand for two hours. Chop the lettuce with the watercress and dandelion leaves. Pour the dressing over the salad and serve.

In the following recipes different combinations of fresh herbs are used.

Lemon lamb chops

8 small lamb chops
16 small sprigs thyme and
  marjoram, broken into twigs
2 sprigs rosemary, broken into
  twigs

grated rind and juice of 1½ lemons
6 tablespoons olive oil

Put half the herbs in the bottom of a baking dish, with half the lemon rind. Lay the chops on top and sprinkle over them the rest of the herbs and lemon rind. Blend the oil, lemon juice, salt and pepper together and pour this over the top. Let it stand for at least two hours. Preheat the oven to Reg 4/350°F, 180°C. Bake the chops in the centre of the oven for 45 minutes. Remove the chops from the dish and brush off any herbs that are clinging to them before serving.

Stuffed shoulder of lamb with red wine sauce

1 shoulder of lamb, boned
1 dessertspoon Dijon mustard
4 oz (100 gr) sausage meat
2 oz (50 gr) mushrooms, finely
  chopped
1 medium onion, finely chopped

2 sprigs rosemary, finely chopped
1 dessertspoon flour
1 wineglass stock
1 wineglass red wine
2 pickled dill cucumbers, finely
  chopped

Preheat the oven to Reg 4/350°F, 180°C.
Spread the cut surface of the lamb with mustard. Mix the sausage meat with the mushrooms, onion, rosemary and seasoning. Spread the mixture over the mustard. Roll up the joint and tie it with strong thread or fine cotton string. Roast the lamb in the centre of the oven for 1½ hours. When the meat is cooked, remove it from the roasting pan, carve it in fairly thick slices, and keep it warm.

Pour off any excess fat from the roasting tin and set it on a moderate heat. Sprinkle in the flour and blend it in well. Blend

in the wine and stock and bring them to the boil, still stirring.
Add the chopped cucumbers and simmer gently for two minutes.
Serve the sauce and the lamb separately.

Lamb's liver with thyme

1½ lb (675 gr) lamb's liver	6 oz (150 gr) mushrooms, sliced
4 tablespoons seasoned flour	1½ tablespoons tomato purée
2 tablespoons chopped thyme	12 fluid oz (4 dl) stock
2 oz (50 gr) butter	

Cut the liver into thin strips. Mix half the thyme into the seasoned flour and coat the liver with this, reserving any that you
do not use. In a heavy frying pan, melt 1½ oz (38 gr) of the butter
on a high heat. When the foam subsides, add the liver and brown
it, turning once. Lower the heat and cook for three minutes
more, turning whenever necessary. Remove the liver and set it
aside. Add the remaining ½ oz (12 gr) butter to the pan (if
necessary) and cook the sliced mushrooms on a moderate heat
for two minutes. Stir in a tablespoon of the reserved flour and
blend well. Take the pan off the heat and stir in the tomato
purée, stock and the rest of the thyme. Bring to the boil and
replace the liver. Cover and simmer for five minutes.

Chicken with rosemary and bay

a 3-3½ lb (1·3-1·5 kg) roasting chicken, jointed	1 oz (25 gr) butter
	1 wineglass sherry
4 tablespoons seasoned flour	¾ pint (4·5 dl) stock
4 short sprigs rosemary, finely chopped	1 tablespoon tomato purée
	3 bayleaves
1 clove garlic, finely chopped	

Mix the chopped rosemary and garlic with the seasoned flour.
Coat the chicken joints with this and leave them to stand for at
least 30 minutes. Melt the butter in a heavy sauté pan on a
moderate heat and brown the chicken joints on both sides, skin
side down first. Raise the heat, pour over the sherry and ignite.
When the flames have died down, pour in the stock. Stir in the

tomato purée and tuck in the bayleaves. Bring to the boil, cover and simmer for 40 minutes. Remove the bayleaves and skim if necessary. Serve with buttered noodles.

Pork in a packet

4 pork chops
2 cloves garlic crushed with salt and black pepper
6 oz (150 gr) flat mushrooms, finely chopped

1 tablespoon chopped parsley
1 tablespoon chopped thyme
1 tablespoon chopped sage
4 tablespoons double cream

Preheat the oven to Reg 4/350°F, 180°C.
Rub the crushed garlic into the surface of both sides of the chops. Cut four round pieces of foil big enough to encase each chop and lay the chops on them. Mix the mushrooms with the herbs and cream, and spread some of the mixture over each chop. Fold over the foil and seal the edges. Put the packets into the oven for one hour. Serve immediately from the packet.

Cod and cockles in red wine

1½ lb (675 gr) cod fillet, skinned and cut into 1½-inch (3·75 cm) cubes
8 oz (225 gr) shelled cockles
2 tablespoons flour seasoned with pepper, but no salt
1½ oz (38 gr) bacon fat or butter
4 rashers lean bacon, finely chopped

1 large onion, finely sliced
6 oz (150 gr) button mushrooms, quartered
2 wineglasses red wine
2 tablespoons chopped thyme
2 tablespoons chopped parsley

Coat the fish in the seasoned flour. Melt half the fat in a large frying pan on a low heat and cook the bacon and onion until they are golden (10–15 minutes). Remove and keep them warm. Raise the heat very slightly and brown the cubes of fish on all sides so they are almost cooked but still firm (about three minutes). Remove the fish from the pan and set it aside with the bacon and onion. Add the rest of the fat to the pan, raise the heat a little more and brown the cockles and mushrooms. Pour in the red wine and stir until it boils. Lower the heat right down and stir in the herbs.

Carefully replace the fish and the onion and bacon. Turn the fish over in the sauce, being careful not to break the pieces. Simmer gently for three minutes. To serve, lay the fish on a warmed serving dish, spoon the thick sauce mixture over the top and sprinkle with a little more chopped parsley.

Braised beef in cider

2 lb (900 gr) topside of beef (in a piece)
1 oz (25 gr) beef dripping
1 small onion, finely chopped
1 small carrot, finely chopped

½ pint (3 dl) dry cider
1 tablespoon tomato purée
4 bayleaves
½ oz (13 gr) kneaded butter

Preheat the oven to Reg 4/350°F, 180°C.
Melt the dripping in a heavy flameproof casserole on a high heat. Brown the beef all over and remove it. Lower the heat and stir in the onion and carrot. Cover them and let them sweat for seven minutes. Replace the meat. Pour over the cider, stir in the tomato purée and tuck in the bayleaves. Season. Cover and put in the centre of the oven for 1½ hours.

Take out the beef, carve it and keep it warm. Strain the sauce through a sieve, pressing down hard on the vegetables to extract all the juice. Return the sauce to the casserole and bring it to the boil. Whisk in as much kneaded butter as is necessary and pour it over the beef.

In recent years Easter has become another excuse for a good feed and now the shops are almost as crowded on Easter Saturday as they are on Christmas Eve, and Easter presents and even decorations are becoming more and more popular.

Chicken has for a long time been a popular meal on Easter Sunday, but now many people have a small turkey. Whichever you choose, here is a good, light way of roasting it, again making use of the herb garden.

Roast chicken or turkey with herbs

1 chicken or turkey
½ teaspoon paprika
1 oz (25 gr) butter, softened
a large bunch of herbs – parsley,
  marjoram, thyme and lemon
  thyme

1 pint (6 dl) stock, made from the
  giblets
1 tablespoon flour
2 tablespoons chopped parsley

Preheat the oven to Reg 4/350°F, 180°C.

Rub the paprika into the skin of the bird and spread it all over with the softened butter. Season the inside with salt and black pepper and put a piece of each herb inside. Lay all the other pieces of herb over the breast and legs and tuck them into the wings. Set the bird on a roasting tray and pour round half the stock. Cover the bird with foil and roast it in the centre of the oven for an hour for a chicken, longer for a turkey. Remove the foil and raise the heat for a further 45 minutes, keeping the herbs in place.

When the time is up and the bird is golden brown, take it from the oven, remove the herbs, and serve it either whole or carved. Pour off any excess fat from the pan and deglaze it with a little stock. Stir in the flour and blend in the remaining stock and the chopped parsley. Serve the sauce separately.

✢   ✢   ✢

One of the few vegetables both in good supply and excellent condition in April is cauliflower, which now should be large and white and tightly packed. Cauliflower is best cooked in boiling salted water with a bayleaf or a bouquet garni for about ten minutes, or until it is just tender. Once cooked it can be dressed up in a number of different ways.

Cauliflower with sorrel

1 cauliflower, cooked with a
  bayleaf (see above)
1 clove garlic

1 handful sorrel leaves, finely
  chopped
1 oz (25 gr) butter
juice of ½ lemon

Melt the butter over a high heat, add the chopped garlic and cook until it is just turning brown. Stir in the sorrel, season and cook for one to two minutes. Stir in the lemon juice and remove the pan from the heat immediately. Toss in the cauliflower.

Cauliflower and mushrooms

1 cauliflower, cooked with a
  bayleaf (see above)
½ oz (13 gr) butter
¼ lb (100 gr) flat mushrooms,
  quartered

1 small onion, finely chopped
1 dessertspoon Dijon or
  1 teaspoon Meaux or other
  whole grain mustard
1 tablespoon chopped parsley

Melt the butter in a saucepan on a low heat. Add the mushrooms and the onion. Cover and simmer for five minutes. Stir in the mustard and parsley. Gently add the cauliflower to the pan, turning it over carefully so it mingles with the other ingredients but doesn't break up. Heat through, check the seasoning and serve.

Cauliflower with white wine

1 cauliflower, cooked with a
  bouquet garni (see above)
½ oz (13 gr) butter
1 small onion, finely chopped
  (optional)

1 tablespoon chopped mixed
  herbs
1 wineglass white wine

Gently cook the onion in the butter until it is soft. (If you are not using the onion, melt the butter on a low heat.) Stir in the herbs. Pour in the wine and boil until it is reduced by half. Gently turn the cauliflower in the sauce, check the seasoning, and heat it through.

Cauliflower sautéed with garlic

Cook the cauliflower with a bayleaf. Gently sauté it with a clove of chopped garlic in butter until the cauliflower and the garlic begin to brown.

Cooked cauliflower is often served with a cheese sauce, but if you like your vegetables raw, try this salad instead.

Cauliflower cheese salad

1 cauliflower
¼ pint (1·5 dl) mayonnaise
3 oz (75 gr) grated Cheddar cheese

Pull the cauliflower into florets. Combine the cheese, mayonnaise and some pepper. Mix the dressing with the cauliflower and leave it standing for about four hours before serving.

Cauliflower with capers and herbs

1 cauliflower, cooked with a
  bouquet garni (see above)
1 oz (25 gr) butter
juice of ½ lemon

1 dessertspoon chopped capers
1 dessertspoon chopped parsley
1 dessertspoon chopped thyme or
  lemon thyme

Melt the butter on a high heat and cook it until it browns. Stir in the lemon juice, capers, herbs and seasoning. Gently mix in the cauliflower off the heat.

Cauliflower cheese soup

1½ pints (9 dl) chicken stock
1 small cauliflower, chopped into
  small pieces
1 small onion, sliced
1 bayleaf
1 oz (25 gr) butter

1 tablespoon flour
½ pint (3 dl) milk
2 oz (50 gr) grated Cheddar cheese
  (or more if you like a stronger
  flavour)
seasoning

Put the cauliflower and onion into a pan with the stock and bayleaf and a little salt and pepper and simmer for 30 minutes. Cool slightly and either rub them through a sieve or work them in the blender until they are smooth. Melt the butter on a moderate heat and blend in the flour and milk. Bring just to the boil and beat in the cheese. Blend in the cauliflower mixture and reheat but do not boil again.

Cauliflower can be cooked without the initial boiling, as in the following recipe, when it is casseroled with lamb.

Braised shoulder of lamb with cauliflower and tomatoes

1 shoulder of lamb	1 large cauliflower
½ oz (13 gr) butter or	¾ lb (325 gr) tomatoes, skinned,
2 tablespoons melted lamb fat	seeded and sliced
1 wineglass dry white wine	1 tablespoon chopped mixed
1 clove garlic, crushed with salt	herbs

Preheat the oven to Reg 4/350°F, 180°C.

Melt the butter (or heat the lamb fat) on a high heat in a heavy flameproof casserole. Brown the lamb in this on all sides. Pour off all but a thin film of fat. Pour in the white wine, add the crushed garlic and bring to the boil. Cover and put into the oven for 30 minutes. Remove the casserole from the oven and add the cauliflower, broken into florets, the tomatoes, herbs and seasoning. Cover, and put back in the oven for a further hour.

Remove the lamb from the casserole and carve it, while keeping the cauliflower and juices warm in the casserole. Arrange the sliced lamb and the cauliflower on a heated serving dish and pour over the juices.

The delicate flavour of cauliflower makes it a good accompaniment to fish.

White fish with cauliflower

1½ lb (675 gr) white fish (cod,	4 tablespoons olive oil
coley, haddock)	1 clove garlic, finely chopped
juice of 1 lemon	¾ lb (325 gr) ripe tomatoes,
black pepper	skinned, seeded and roughly
2 tablespoons flour	chopped
1 dessertspoon paprika	1 tablespoon capers, chopped
2 small cauliflowers	8 flat anchovy fillets, finely
1 bayleaf	chopped

Skin the fish and cut it into small serving pieces. Lay it in a flat dish and pour over the lemon juice. Grind some pepper over the top and leave it to stand for 30 minutes.

Mix the flour and paprika together. Shake the fish dry and coat it in this mixture. Cook the cauliflowers (broken into florets) in boiling salted water with a bayleaf for ten minutes. Drain and set aside.

Heat two tablespoons of the oil in a large frying pan on a moderate heat. Fry the fish, cut side down first and turning it once, until it is just cooked but still firm (about 3 minutes). Remove it and keep it warm. Add the cooked cauliflower to the pan, together with the garlic and any more oil if necessary. Fry, turning about, until it is just beginning to get brown. Add the tomatoes, capers and anchovies and mix them in well.

Replace the fish, being careful not to break up the pieces. Cook gently until the tomato is hot but not mushy. Serve immediately.

If cauliflower is cooked for a little longer, it can be rubbed through a sieve and used as a base for a sauce or a soup.

Eggs in cauliflower sauce

1 small cauliflower	6 oz (150 gr) lean bacon, diced
1½ lb (675 gr) potatoes	6 fluid oz (2 dl) double cream
2 oz (50 gr) butter	4 eggs
a little milk	2 tablespoons grated Cheddar
1 bayleaf	cheese

Boil the potatoes in their skins, peel them and mash them with half the butter and the milk.

Boil the cauliflower in salted water with the bayleaf for twenty minutes. Remove the cauliflower, reserving the water and the bayleaf in the saucepan. Cook the bacon in the remaining butter in a saucepan very slowly until it is beginning to brown. Rub the cauliflower through a sieve and mix it into the bacon and butter. Beat in the cream.

Put the mashed potato into an ovenproof dish and make four wells in it. Poach the eggs in the water that the cauliflower was boiled in. Drain them and put one in each well in the potatoes.

Season. Pour the cauliflower sauce over the eggs, sprinkle some grated cheese over the top and brown under a high grill. Serve with a green salad.

                    ⬧   ⬧   ⬧

Beetroot is available pretty well all the year round, but during the winter months some greengrocers only sell it cooked, and the cooking time is dependent on them. In April, however, you can buy raw beetroot again everywhere. At this time of the year, the longer and thinner type is in the shops. My farmer friend tells me it all used to be this shape, but as the smaller, rounder ones were found to be more popular these strains were encouraged. But once it is cooked the flavour is the same, so if you don't like the shape, now is the time to chop it and grate it and make it into soup.

Hot spiced beetroot

1 lb (450 gr) beetroot
4 tablespoons sour cream
2 tablespoons wine vinegar
1 dessertspoon chopped capers

Cook the beetroot in boiling salted water until tender. Drain, and as soon as you can handle them, peel and dice them. Return the beetroot to the saucepan and stir in the cream, vinegar, capers and seasoning. Reheat until they are on the point of boiling and serve immediately. This is good with cold roast beef.

Clear beetroot soup

12 oz (325 gr) raw beetroot, peeled and diced
1½ pints (9 dl) ham stock (no other kind is suitable)
1 clove garlic, crushed with salt
2 oz (50 gr) flat mushrooms, finely chopped
2 oz (50 gr) vermicelli
4 tablespoons sour cream
chopped parsley

Put the beetroot into a saucepan with the stock and crushed garlic and simmer gently for 30 minutes. Strain, and either reserve the beetroot for a salad or discard it. Put the clear liquid back into the saucepan with the chopped mushrooms. Break up the vermicelli. Bring the liquid to the boil, add the vermicelli, and simmer for ten minutes. Serve in individual soup bowls, garnished with the sour cream and chopped parsley.

Beetroot in cheese sauce

4-5 medium beetroot	½ pint (3 dl) milk
1 oz (25 gr) butter	4 oz (100 gr) strong Cheddar
1 bunch spring onions, chopped	cheese, grated
1½ tablespoons flour	

Cook the beetroot in boiling salted water until tender (this can take up to an hour). Drain, and as soon as they are cool enough to handle, peel and dice them. Melt the butter in a saucepan on a low heat and cook the chopped spring onions in this until they are soft. Stir in the flour and blend in the milk. Cook, stirring, until the sauce is thick and bubbly. Off the heat beat in half the cheese. Stir the beetroot into the sauce. Transfer it to a heat-proof dish, check the seasoning, scatter over the rest of the cheese, and brown under a hot grill.

Spiced burgers with beetroot sauce

for the burgers:

1½ lb (675 gr) good quality beef, coarsely minced	10 allspice berries
1 large onion, finely chopped	10 juniper berries
1 oz (25 gr) butter	10 peppercorns
	6 sage leaves, chopped

for the sauce:
1 medium beetroot
1 oz (25 gr) butter
1 egg yolk
2 tablespoons wine vinegar

First make the burgers. Melt the butter on a low heat and sauté the onion in this until it is soft. Put the meat in a mixing bowl and stir in the onion and butter. Crush the spices and seasoning together and work these and the sage into the meat. Divide the meat into flat burgers about half an inch (1·25 cm) thick. Refrigerate for 30 minutes. Preheat the grill to high and grill the burgers until they are crisp and dark brown on each side.

Beat the butter until it is soft and fluffy in a small bowl and then beat in the egg yolk. Set the bowl in a saucepan of water on a low heat and keep beating until the mixture starts to thicken. Grate in the beetroot, beating as you go, and then very gradually beat in the vinegar. Add salt and pepper to taste. Raise the heat slightly under the saucepan and continue to beat until the sauce is hot, taking it off the heat as soon as the water boils. Serve the burgers with the sauce on top.

Hot beetroot with onion and garlic

4 medium beetroot
2 tablespoons olive oil
1 medium onion, finely chopped

1 clove garlic, finely chopped
2 tablespoons wine vinegar

Cook the beetroot in boiling salted water until they are tender. Drain, allow them to cool, and then peel and dice them. Heat the olive oil in a saucepan on a gentle heat. Add the onion and garlic. Cover, and cook gently until they are soft. Stir in the diced beetroot and heat it through. Season. Raise the heat, stir in the vinegar, bring quickly to the boil and serve. This goes well with grilled or fried mackerel.

Sweet and sour beetroot salad

4 medium beetroot
1 tablespoon wine vinegar
1 teaspoon black molasses (or black treacle)

1 tablespoon prepared horseradish sauce
1 teaspoon dry English mustard
2½ fluid oz (70 ml) plain yoghurt

Cook the beetroot in boiling salted water until tender. Drain, and allow to cool. Peel them and slice them into rounds. Gently warm the vinegar and molasses together until they are blended. Off the heat, stir in the horseradish, mustard and seasoning. Cool a little and beat in the yoghurt. Mix the beetroot into the dressing. Put it into an earthenware or glass dish and chill.

Mackerel with beetroot and orange

4 small or 2 large mackerel
2 tablespoons seasoned flour
4 tablespoons olive oil
1 lb (450 gr) beetroot, cooked
  until tender and grated

grated rind and juice of 2 medium
  oranges
2 tablespoons grated horseradish

Fillet the mackerel and coat the fillets in seasoned flour. In a heavy frying pan, heat the oil on a high heat. Put in the mackerel, cut side down first, and fry them until they are golden brown on both sides, turning once. Remove and keep them warm.

Lower the heat to moderate. Stir in the grated beetroot, the orange rind and the horseradish and heat them through. Raise the heat again, quickly stir in the orange juice and bring it to the boil. Pour the beetroot mixture over the mackerel and serve.

ß   ß   ß

Cauliflower and beetroot, although they are good buys in April, have been available – if in variable condition – all through the winter, so aren't really a change. But coming into the shops for the first time towards the end of the month are bunches of crisp, crimson radishes, just right for mixing into salads with herbs. Here are three suggestions, all of them best served as a first course.

Grapefruit and radish salad

1 large grapefruit
1 bunch radishes, sliced
French dressing made with
  2 tablespoons olive oil

1 tablespoon chopped lemon
  thyme or thyme
2 oz (50 gr) curd cheese
watercress for garnish

Peel the grapefruit and remove all the pith. Divide it into two equal parts and then cut each half crossways into two. Slice each quarter into three. Put the grapefruit and radish slices in a flat dish and pour over the dressing. Let them stand for about thirty minutes.

Blend the lemon thyme and curd cheese together. Take the

slices of grapefruit from the dressing and arrange them on four individual plates with the radishes, leaving any dressing behind in the dish. Decorate with a blob of the curd cheese and sprigs of watercress.

Cheese, radish and cucumber salad

3 oz (75 gr) Cheddar or Danish
  Blue cheese, grated
4 tablespoons mayonnaise
¼ cucumber, diced but not peeled

1 bunch radishes, chopped
spring onions, chopped, for
  garnish
lettuce leaves

Mix the grated cheese with the mayonnaise. Add the cucumber and the radishes. Serve piled on to lettuce leaves with the chopped spring onions scattered over the top.

Bacon and radish salad

4 rashers lean bacon
4 sticks celery
24 large radishes
2 tablespoons olive oil

1 tablespoon wine vinegar
1 teaspoon made English mustard
1 dessertspoon chopped sage
  leaves

Grill the bacon until it is crisp and chop it into small pieces. Chop the celery and slice the radishes. Blend the oil, vinegar, mustard and seasoning together and mix in the chopped sage. Mix the dressing with the bacon, celery and radishes, and serve.

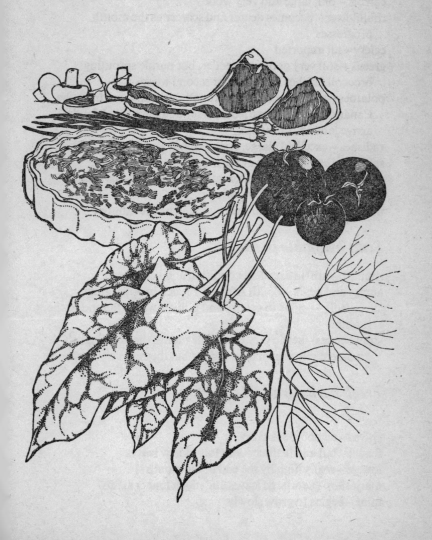

Vegetables available in May

asparagus
beetroot – raw, round varieties available
cabbage – very few
carrots – old, large and very woody
cauliflower – becomes dearer and scarcer as the month
  progresses
celery – all imported
greens – still very good and tender, but purple sprouting
  broccoli finishes in the first or second week
potatoes – still some old ones around. New ones are from the
  Canary Islands. Those from Jersey and the Scilly Islands
  arrive later in the month
radishes – excellent: large, crisp and hot
spinach – by the middle of the month
spring onions – a useful alternative to onions at this time
tomatoes – still mostly imported
watercress – excellent, at the beginning of the month

Fruit available in May

rhubarb – still in excellent condition and very cheap
apples and pears – South African, French or Australian
citrus fruit – begins to get dry and pithy towards the end of the
  month.
strawberries – at the very end of the month the first English
  commercially grown ones appear but they are very expensive

Fresh herbs available in May

bay
chives – a good thick crop
fennel – tall and feathery with lots of new leaves
lovage – really high by the end of the month
marjoram – new large leaves and much longer stems
mint – begins to grow slowly

parsley – there should be a good crop now as long as it hasn't
   been over-picked
rosemary – good, tender aromatic leaves
sage – the leaves become very soft and large all through May
savory – masses of new soft growth
sorrel
tarragon – growing steadily, but still not ready for picking
thyme – new bright soft leaves growing all the time

🐙　🐙　🐙

The traditionally merry month of May is something of a para-
dox for the cook. The weather tantalises us: occasional really
warm days bring the promise of summer and there is bright
fresh growth on the trees and flowers, but in the fields and
vegetable gardens the variety of fresh leaves and roots for eating
is very small. For the first part of the month at least, we have to
make the best of the old while eagerly awaiting the new.

In the nick of time, around the middle of the month, the first
crop of spinach is ready to be picked, its bright soft leaves pro-
viding a fresh, new, subtle flavour, delicate but slightly bitter.

The mountain of leaves that is needed to provide enough
cooked vegetable to go round often puts people off cooking
spinach. If it is cooked without gallons of boiling water it main-
tains its substance far better, but it does need a lot of water to
wash it, as it is very often grown in sandy soil and any grit which
escapes can ruin the best of dishes.

The best way to treat spinach is to nick off the stalks where
they join the leaf and then put the leaves into a saucepan with
only the water that remains clinging to them after they have been
washed. Cover it tightly and set it on a moderate heat for 15
minutes, stirring it occasionally. There will probably still be too
much moisture in the pan when the spinach is tender; if so,
either raise the heat for a few minutes with the pan uncovered,
to evaporate the moisture, or to prevent it becoming too soft,
simply drain the spinach. A knob of butter can be added to the
spinach while it is cooking. To vary the flavour, add a thinly
sliced onion, or some chopped spring onions, any combination
of chopped fresh herbs or some grated nutmeg.

Creamed spinach

1½ lb (675 gr) spinach
6 fluid oz (2 dl) double cream
grated nutmeg

Cook the spinach according to the basic recipe without the butter. Drain it well and press down on it to get rid of as much moisture as possible. Chop finely and return it to the saucepan. Stir in the cream and grated nutmeg and let it bubble a little before serving.

Spinach au gratin

1½ lb (675 gr) spinach, prepared and cooked as above
6 tablespoons double cream
grated nutmeg

4 tablespoons grated Gruyère (or Cheddar) cheese
4 tablespoons browned breadcrumbs

Chop the cooked spinach and put it into a flat heatproof dish. Spoon over the cream and grate over the nutmeg. Mix together the cheese and crumbs, sprinkle them on top of the cream and nutmeg, and brown the dish under a high grill. This makes a good first course or an accompanying vegetable.

Spinach soup

1 lb (450 gr) spinach
1½ pints (9 dl) stock
bouquet garni
1 oz (25 gr) butter
1 bunch spring onions, chopped

1 tablespoon flour
4 tablespoons grated Cheddar cheese
a little grated nutmeg

Wash the spinach and remove the stalks. Chop it finely and put it into a pan with the stock and bouquet garni. Bring it to the boil and simmer for 15 minutes. Allow it to cool slightly and work it in the blender. Melt the butter in a saucepan on a low heat and cook the chopped onions in this until they are just soft. Blend in the flour. Take the pan from the heat and blend in about a quarter of the spinach and stock mixture. Put back on the heat and stir until it boils. Beat in the cheese and stir in the rest of the mixture. Check the seasoning.

Reheat, but do not allow it to boil. Serve it in individual dishes, garnished with the nutmeg.

Spinach beurre noir

1½ lb (675 gr) spinach cooked
   and drained well
1 oz (25 gr) butter

juice of ½ lemon
2 tablespoons chopped parsley
a little grated nutmeg

Melt the butter in a frying pan on a moderate heat and cook it until it browns. Swirl in the lemon juice and stir in the chopped spinach and parsley. Grate over the nutmeg and add salt and pepper to taste. Stir round until the whole lot is bubbling and serve at once.

In the next two recipes spinach and eggs are combined. Both can be served as a light lunch or supper dish, or as a first course for a main meal.

Spinach omelette

½ lb (225 gr) cooked spinach
4 eggs
2 tablespoons chopped parsley
1 oz (25 gr) butter
6 spring onions, chopped

1 oz (25 gr) grated Cheddar or
   Gruyère cheese, if it is to be
   served hot
1 oz (25 gr) grated Parmesan
   cheese, if it is to be served cold

Drain the cooked spinach well and chop it finely. Beat the eggs with the parsley and seasoning and mix in the spinach. Melt the butter on a low heat in an omelette pan and cook the spring onions in this until they are soft. Raise the heat to moderate, pour in the spinach mixture and stir it round a little to mix in the onions.

Preheat the grill to high, while you cook the omelette until the underside is beginning to brown, lifting up the edges and tipping the pan occasionally to get as much egg as possible to the bottom. If you are going to eat the omelette hot, put it under the grill until it is firm but not brown. Remove it from the grill, scatter the grated cheese over the top and put it back under the grill until the cheese is bubbly. If you plan to serve it cold, strew the top with grated Parmesan cheese and put the omelette, still in the pan, under the grill to brown.

As a main dish these quantities will serve two, and as a first course, four to six. For larger helpings or to feed more people, you can use six eggs if your pan is big enough. It is very good cold and cut into wedges for a picnic.

Spinach and eggs niçoise

1 lb (450 gr) cooked spinach
2 tablespoons olive oil
1 large onion, thinly sliced
1 large clove garlic, chopped
½ lb (225 gr) firm tomatoes, skinned and roughly chopped

8 black olives, chopped
6 flat anchovy fillets, chopped
6 oz (150 gr) lean ham, diced
4 eggs
2 tablespoons grated cheese

Preheat the oven to Reg 4/350°F, 180°C.
Drain the spinach well and chop it finely. Melt the oil on a low heat in a frying pan and cook the onion and garlic in this until the onion is golden. Off the heat, mix the tomatoes, anchovies, olives and spinach into the onion. Put this mixture into a flat, ovenproof dish and make four indentations in the surface. Break an egg into each hollow. Season, scatter over the cheese, and bake in the centre of the oven for 30 minutes, or until the eggs are set.

Spinach and ham quiche

1 nine-inch (22 cm) diameter pastry shell
1 medium onion, thinly sliced
1 oz (25 gr) butter
2 eggs
¼ pint (1·5 dl) creamy milk

½ lb (225 gr) spinach, cooked, drained and chopped
6 oz (150 gr) lean ham, diced
1 tablespoon chopped mixed herbs
1 tablespoon chopped parsley

Preheat the oven to Reg 6/400°F, 200°C.
Cook the onion slowly in the butter until it is golden. Beat the

egg and milk together. Mix in the spinach, onion, ham, herbs and seasoning. Pour the mixture into the pastry shell and cook it in the centre of the oven for 30 minutes.

For the warmer days in May, spinach can make a salad, either cooked or raw.

Spinach and cod salad

1 lb (450 gr) spinach
1 oz (25 gr) butter
2 sprigs chopped rosemary
1 dessertspoon chopped parsley
1 dessertspoon chopped chives
1 lb (450 gr) cod
5 fluid oz (1·5 dl) plain yoghurt

for the court bouillon:
1 quart (1·2 litres) water
2 tablespoons wine vinegar
2 bayleaves
1 blade mace
1 slice onion
6 peppercorns
lettuce leaves and tomato slices
   for serving

Cook the spinach with the butter, herbs and seasoning. Chop it and cool it.

Put all the ingredients for the court bouillon into a saucepan, bring them to the boil and simmer them for 20 minutes. Remove the pan from the heat and put in the cod. Return it to the heat and cook the cod with the water just trembling for a further 10 minutes. Lift out the cod, drain it well, and when it is cool, flake it. Mix the spinach, cod and yoghurt together. Pile the mixture on to a bed of lettuce leaves and garnish with slices of tomato.

Raw spinach salad

½ lb (225 gr) raw spinach
½ cucumber
5 fluid oz (1·5 dl) plain yoghurt

4 tablespoons olive oil
juice of 1 lemon
1 dessertspoon Dijon mustard

Wash the spinach and remove all the stalks. Shake off as much water as possible and chop it finely. Wipe the cucumber and dice it finely without peeling it. Mix the spinach and cucumber together. In a bowl, gradually blend the olive oil into the yoghurt. Beat in the lemon juice, mustard and seasoning. Mix it well into

the spinach and cucumber. Leave it to stand for at least an hour
before serving slightly chilled.

Spinach pâté

½ lb (225 gr) spinach
1 good bunch sorrel leaves,
  chopped
6 spring onions, chopped

1 oz (25 gr) butter
4 oz (100 gr) curd cheese
juice of ½ lemon (or more to taste)

Remove all the stalks from the spinach, cook it without
butter, drain it well and chop it finely. Cook the spring onions
and sorrel on a fairly high heat in the butter for three minutes.
Keeping the pan on the heat, mix in the spinach and then allow
the mixture to cool a little. Put it into the blender with the
cheese, lemon juice and seasoning and blend it until it is smooth.
Taste it to see if there is sufficient lemon, add a few more drops
if necessary and blend again. Press the mixture into individual
soufflé dishes or ramekins and chill it until it is firm. Serve with
brown toast.

83　　83　　83

Sorrel is a close relation to spinach. It looks almost exactly the
same and is at its best at the same times of the year. Its flavour
is also similar but stronger and slightly lemony, making it far
more suited to being used as a herb than as a vegetable. I have
two sorrel plants growing in my herb garden and during May
they produce as many leaves as I can possibly use, even though
the flavour seems to go well with everything.

Sorrel soup

24 large sorrel leaves, chopped
1 oz (25 gr) butter
for the bechamel sauce:
1 oz (25 gr) butter
1 oz (25 gr) flour
1½ pints (9 dl) stock
½ pint (3 dl) milk, infused with a bayleaf, a blade of mace,
  peppercorns and a slice of onion

Divide the sorrel leaves into two piles. Make the bechamel sauce. Melt the butter on a high heat in a small frying pan. Put in half the sorrel and cook it until it bubbles. Add the cooked sorrel to the bechamel sauce and bring it to the boil. Blend in the stock and finally add the uncooked sorrel. Simmer for five minutes, and allow to cool a little. Work in a blender until smooth. Check the seasoning and serve it either hot or chilled.

Lamb chops with sorrel

4 good sized lamb chops, trimmed of excess fat
½ oz (13 gr) butter or 2 tablespoons melted lamb fat
1 medium onion, finely chopped

1 large or 2 small cloves garlic, finely chopped
1 good handful sorrel leaves, finely chopped
1 wineglass red wine
1 dessertspoon tomato purée

Melt the butter or heat the fat on a high heat. Brown the chops quickly on both sides and then lower the heat and continue to cook the chops until they are done. Remove them, set them on a serving dish, and keep them warm. Cook the onion and garlic gently in the pan until they are just turning brown. Raise the heat, add the sorrel, and cook it briskly, stirring it about, for two minutes until the sorrel is soft, dark and tender. Pour in the wine, stir in the tomato purée and boil the liquid until it is reduced by half. Season if wished. Pour the sauce over the lamb chops and serve.

Shoulder of lamb with sorrel

1 shoulder of lamb, boned out and with any excess fat removed
½ oz (13 gr) butter
1 medium onion, finely chopped
8 oz (225 gr) mushrooms, half finely chopped, half sliced

12 sorrel leaves, finely chopped
2 tablespoons chopped parsley
2 tablespoons chopped watercress
¼ pint (1·5 dl) stock
½ pint (3 dl) brown sauce (page 12)

Preheat the oven to Reg 4/350°F, 180°C.
Melt the butter in a frying pan on a low heat and cook the onions in this until they are soft. Raise the heat and add the

chopped mushrooms to the pan. Cook for a further two minutes. Remove the pan from the heat and mix in the sorrel, parsley, watercress and seasoning. Spread this mixture over the cut surface of the lamb. Roll up the joint and tie it with strong thread or fine cotton string. Cook the meat in a roasting tin in the centre of the oven for 1½ hours.

Remove the lamb from the tin, carve it and keep it warm. Pour off any excess fat from the pan and then set it on top of the stove on a moderate heat. Cook the sliced mushrooms in the roasting pan for two minutes. Pour in the stock and bring it to the boil on a high heat, stirring in any residue from the bottom of the pan. Boil it until it is reduced by half. Pour in the brown sauce and blend it in well. Simmer for three minutes, stirring occasionally. Pour the sauce over the sliced lamb before serving.

Pork fillet with rosemary and sorrel

2 lb (900 gr) pork tenderloin, cut into rounds one inch (2·5 cm) thick
4 sprigs rosemary, finely chopped
½ teaspoon fine sea-salt
½ teaspoon freshly ground black pepper
1 oz (25 gr) butter
1 good handful sorrel leaves, finely chopped
1 wineglass white wine
1 wineglass stock
4 fluid oz (1 dl) double cream

Grind the rosemary with a pestle and mortar with the salt and pepper. Spread this mixture over both sides of the pork slices and leave them for four hours.

Melt the butter on a high heat in a heavy sauté or frying pan. Brown the pork slices in this on both sides, lower the heat and continue to cook until they are done. Remove them and set them aside to keep warm. Stir the sorrel into the pan and let it bubble. Raise the heat and pour in the wine and stock. Boil them until they are reduced by half, scraping in any residue from the bottom of the pan. Stir in the cream, bring it to the boil and pour the sauce over the pork.

This recipe could also be used for pork chops if tenderloin is difficult to obtain. The amounts of wine, stock and cream should then be cut down a little as chops don't need quite so much sauce.

Roast lamb with sorrel

1 best end of neck or loin of lamb, boned
thyme and/or marjoram
10 sorrel leaves, chopped

Preheat the oven to Reg 4/350°F, 180°C.
Strew the thyme and/or marjoram and some salt and pepper over the cut surface of the lamb. Lay the sorrel on top and roll and tie the joint. Roast as usual.

Buttered sorrel eggs

4 small hard-boiled eggs, finely chopped
16 large sorrel leaves, chopped
4 oz (100 gr) butter

Melt the butter on a moderate heat in a small frying pan. Add the sorrel leaves and cook them until they bubble. Stir in the eggs. Season. Take the pan off the heat and press the mixture into individual pots (soufflé dishes or ramekins). Chill until firm and serve with brown toast but no more butter.

Herring roes like caviar

6 oz (150 gr) herring roes, hard preferably but soft if necessary
1 oz (25 gr) butter
1 small onion, finely chopped
12 large sorrel leaves, chopped
juice of ½ lemon

Chop the roes very finely until they are mushy. Melt the butter on a low heat in a small frying pan and cook the onion gently in this until it is just beginning to brown. Raise the heat and stir in the sorrel and roes. Continue to cook, still stirring, until the roes are firm. Mix in the lemon juice and season. Put into small pots and serve chilled with brown toast.

Hot bacon and mushroom salad

4 oz (100 gr) lean bacon, chopped small
4 oz (100 gr) flat mushrooms, finely chopped
1 clove garlic, finely chopped
8 sorrel leaves, chopped
2 tablespoons wine vinegar
shredded lettuce for serving

Arrange the lettuce in four individual salad bowls or one large one. Lightly grease a heavy frying pan and set it on a moderate heat. Put in the bacon and as soon as the fat begins to run add the garlic and cook until the bacon is brown. Add the mushrooms and sorrel to the pan and continue to cook, stirring until the sorrel is limp. Raise the heat to high and stir in the wine vinegar and seasoning. Bring the mixture quickly to the boil, and immediately arrange it over the chopped lettuce and serve as a first course.

෴   ෴   ෴

Nearly all the herbs become really prolific in May, with masses of fresh green leaves, so now is the time to pick them by the handful and use them in as many different ways as possible. One of my favourites is the feathery fennel, which, with its slight flavour of liquorice, goes very well with pork or fish.

Pork with orange and fennel

1½ lb (675 gr) lean boneless pork, cut into half-inch (1·3 cm) cubes
8 oz (225 gr) lean bacon, cut into small pieces
½ oz (13 gr) lard
juice of 2 large oranges
3 tablespoons chopped fennel leaves

Melt the lard in a heavy sauté pan on a high heat and brown the pork and bacon in this, stirring it around until all the liquid which appears at first is evaporated and the pieces of meat are beginning to brown. Pour in the orange juice and bring it to the boil, scraping in all the pan residue. Stir in the chopped fennel. Season, cover immediately, lower the heat and cook for 20 minutes.

White fish with shrimp sauce

2 lb (900 gr) white fish (coley, cod or haddock), skinned
juice of 1½ lemons
1 oz (25 gr) butter
1 heaped tablespoon flour
½ pint (3 dl) shrimps, shelled
1 tablespoon chopped fennel

½ pint (3 dl) fish stock, made from the skin of the fish and a few of the prawn shells simmered with an onion, a carrot, a stick of celery and a bouquet garni

Cut the fish into serving pieces. Put the pieces into a buttered ovenproof dish, sprinkle over the juice of one of the lemons and leave to stand for 30 minutes.

Preheat the oven to Reg 4/350°F, 180°C. Cover the fish with a butter paper, season, and bake it in the centre of the oven for 20 minutes.

Meanwhile make the sauce. Melt the butter in a saucepan on a moderate heat, stir in the flour and, off the heat, blend in the fish stock. Replace it on the heat, bring to the boil and stir in the shrimps, fennel and the juice of the remaining half lemon. Take the fish from the oven and set it on a warmed serving dish. Stir a little of the cooking juices into the sauce, but take care not to let it become too thin. Pour the sauce over the fish before serving.

You can also make a simpler fennel sauce as you would make a parsley sauce, substituting fennel for parsley or using a mixture of the two. If you are going to have a green salad with your fish, use fennel as the main flavouring in the salad.

ଓଃ   ଓଃ   ଓଃ

Lovage is a little-known, celery-flavoured herb which almost shoots out of the ground in May. During the summer months when celery is scarce a few lovage leaves added to stock will make a good substitute; do use only a few, though, as it is very strong, and too much will give a peculiarly bitter taste.

With the contrasting blandness of potatoes, lovage makes a very good soup.

Lovage soup

2 oz (50 gr) chopped lovage leaves, without any stalks
1 large onion, thinly sliced

6 oz (150 gr) old potatoes, peeled and thinly sliced
1½ pints (9 dl) stock
5 fluid oz (1·5 dl) double cream

Put the lovage, onion and potatoes into a pan with the stock. Cover, bring to the boil and simmer for 30 minutes. Cool slightly and work in the blender. Reheat, check the seasoning, and stir in the cream just before serving.

Lovage and chicken also go together well because of the mild flavour of chicken.

Chicken and lovage

a 3-3½ lb (1·450-1·7 kg) roasting chicken
1 onion
1 carrot
a few black peppercorns
a good bunch of lovage
1 oz (25 gr) butter

2 tablespoons chopped lovage leaves
1 tablespoon flour
grated rind and juice of 2 small oranges
4 tablespoons double cream
1 bunch watercress
2 boxes mustard and cress

Put the chicken in a large saucepan with the onion, carrot, peppercorns and the bunch of lovage. Cover with water to the thighs and poach it gently for an hour. Remove the chicken and keep it warm.

In a small saucepan, melt the butter on a moderate heat. Add the chopped lovage and cook it until it is tender. Blend in the flour and half a pint (3 dl) of the stock in which the chicken was cooked and bring to the boil, stirring. Stir in the orange rind

and juice and the cream. Season. Keep the sauce warm but do
not let it boil again.

Joint the chickens and lay the joints on a bed of mixed chopped cresses. Pour the sauce over the top and serve immediately.

ஜ   ஜ   ஜ

It is often very difficult to find a good, sound English onion in
May. They have been out of the earth for too long and many are
rotten before you buy them. Onions are an indispensable vegetable, but if you cannot buy sound ones or your supplies have
run out, spring onions can sometimes fill the gap. They have
been in the shops for a couple of months by now, but the earlier
ones are thin and wiry. In May the white parts fill out and become rounder and the green parts are still crisp. They are
delicious with fresh bread and cheese and also with cold pork
and ham. As they have a less stinging effect than large onions
when eaten raw they can also enhance lighter flavours, such as
boiled eggs, in a salad. They can be chopped and used like a
herb in other egg dishes, such as omelettes or soufflés, or to en-
liven old potatoes. Toss plain boiled potatoes in a mixture of
chopped sage and spring onions and melted butter, or mix some
chopped spring onions into mashed potatoes.

The combination of spring onions and cheese makes an unusual
soup.

Cheese and onion soup

16 medium spring onions, finely   1½ pints (9 dl) stock
  chopped   juice of 1 lemon
1 oz (25 gr) butter   4 oz (100 gr) curd cheese
1 level tablespoon flour

Melt the butter in a saucepan on a low heat and cook the onions
slowly until they are beginning to soften. Stir in the flour and
blend in the stock. Bring to the boil, stirring. Pour in the lemon
juice and simmer for ten minutes. Cream the cheese in a bowl
and blend in a little of the hot soup. Continue to blend it in until

all the liquid is added and the soup is smooth. Return it to the saucepan to reheat, but do not allow it to boil.

Spring onions can be substituted for large ones when cooking meat, though you would need a fair number to provide enough flavour in a casserole. Spring onions can also be grilled with meat, added to various kinds of stuffing, or mixed into sauces.

Pork with fennel and spring onions

2 lb (900 gr) lean boneless pork in one-inch (2·5 cm) cubes
½ oz (13 gr) lard or pork dripping
1 large clove garlic, finely chopped
1 dessertspoon made English mustard

4 tablespoons wine vinegar
4 tablespoons stock
12 large spring onions, chopped
2 tablespoons chopped fennel

Heat the fat on a high heat in a heavy sauté pan or wide-bottomed casserole. Add the garlic and the pork cubes and cook, stirring about, until they are golden brown. Do them in two batches if necessary. Blend together the mustard, vinegar and stock, and when all the pork is browned, stir in this mixture, continuing to stir until it boils. Mix in the chopped onions and fennel, season, cover tightly, and cook on a very low heat for 50 minutes, stirring after the first 30 minutes to make sure the meat is not sticking.

Braised skirt with spring onions

1½ lb (675 gr) beef skirt, cut into two fairly thin, equal-sized slices
2 bunches spring onions
1 oz (25 gr) butter

1 level tablespoon flour
1 wineglass sherry
1 wineglass stock
12 flat mushrooms

Preheat the oven to Reg 4/350°F, 180°C.
Trim all the skin and pieces of fat from the meat. Lay the onions, including the green parts, all over one of the pieces of meat, putting alternate white and green parts in one direction. If the onions are very fat, split them in half lengthways. Lay the other piece of meat on top like a sandwich and tie strong thread round

the pieces both across and lengthways. Melt the butter in a heavy flameproof casserole on a high heat and brown the meat parcel on both sides. Remove the meat and set it aside. Stir in the flour and cook it until it is russet brown. Blend in the sherry and stock and bring to the boil, stirring. Season. Replace the meat, cover the casserole, and cook it in the oven for an hour, adding the whole mushrooms for the last 15 minutes. Remove the thread from the beef sandwich and carve it in thick slices across the onions. Serve it with the sauce poured over it.

If it is difficult to obtain two large, matching slices, use four smaller slices and make two separate sandwiches.

ஃ   ஃ   ஃ

Throughout May English tomatoes become a little cheaper, but there are still a good many in the shops from the Canary Islands and Spain. Often the riper, softer ones are sold off cheaply as 'frying tomatoes'. I buy as many of these as I can although I rarely actually fry them. Instead I use them for soups, sauces and stews.

Tomato and Chorizo soup

1 lb (450 gr) ripe tomatoes, peeled and chopped, but not seeded
½ oz (13 gr) butter
4 oz (100 gr) Chorizo sausage (or Italian or Polish equivalent), cut in half lengthways and thinly sliced

1 large clove garlic, crushed with salt
1 tablespoon tomato purée
1 pint (6 dl) stock
juice of 1 medium orange

Melt the butter in a saucepan on a low heat and cook the chopped sausage in this for two minutes. Stir in the tomatoes, cover the pan and cook until the tomatoes are pulpy. Mash them well down, stir in the garlic, tomato purée and stock and bring to the boil. Simmer for ten minutes. Stir in the orange juice, check the seasoning, and reheat.

A variation of this soup can be made by using four table-spoons of chopped mixed herbs instead of the sausages, omitting the garlic, and using a wineglass of sherry instead of the orange juice.

Hot tomato sauce for sausages

½ lb (225 gr) ripe tomatoes, skinned and chopped, but not seeded
1 small onion, finely chopped
½ oz (13 gr) butter

1 teaspoon paprika
a pinch of cayenne pepper
1½ tablespoons mixed chopped herbs

Simmer the onion in the butter with the paprika and cayenne pepper until it is soft. Add the tomatoes, herbs and seasoning to the pan. Cover and cook on a low heat for ten minutes, by which time the sauce will be thick and pulpy.

This hot spicy sauce goes well with any kind of grilled sausages.

Tomato sauce for grilled meat, fish or stuffed pancakes

½ lb (225 gr) ripe tomatoes
1 oz (25 gr) butter
1 small onion, thinly sliced
1 tablespoon flour
½ pint (3 dl) stock
bouquet garni

pared rind and juice of ½ lemon
1 tablespoon chopped parsley
either 1 large pickled gherkin, finely chopped
or 1 tablespoon chopped capers

Melt the butter on a low heat and gently cook the onion in this until it is soft. Wipe the tomatoes and cut them in quarters. When the onion is ready, stir in the flour, blend in the stock, and bring to simmering point, stirring. Add the tomatoes, the bouquet garni, seasoning, and the rind and juice of the lemon to the pan. Cover, and simmer for 30 minutes. Strain the sauce through a sieve, pressing down and rubbing slightly to get as much tomato pulp through as possible. Return the sauce to the rinsed pan and add the parsley and the chopped capers or gherkin before reheating.

The capers are particularly suitable with lamb or fish, and the gherkin with beef.

Sauté of beef with tomatoes and herbs

1½ lb (675 gr) beef skirt cut into
  one-inch (2·5 cm) cubes
2 tablespoons olive oil
½ oz (13 gr) butter
1 large onion, finely chopped
1 tablespoon flour
1 wineglass stock
1 wineglass white wine

1 lb (450 gr) ripe tomatoes,
  skinned, seeded and chopped
1 large clove garlic, crushed with
  salt
2 tablespoons chopped parsley
1 tablespoon chopped thyme
1 tablespoon chopped marjoram
2 bayleaves

Heat the oil in a heavy sauté pan on a high heat. Add the butter
and when the foam subsides brown the pieces of meat all over
in this. Remove and set aside. Lower the heat right down, add
the onion, and cook it until it is soft. Stir in the flour and cook
it until it is a russet brown. Stir in the stock and wine, blending
well. Raise the heat a little and bring the liquid to the boil. Stir
in the garlic, tomatoes, herbs and seasoning. Bring to the boil
again and mix in the browned meat. Cover, and simmer gently
for an hour, removing the bayleaves before serving.

Stuffed whiting niçoise

4 whiting
1 oz (25 gr) butter
4 oz (100 gr) finely chopped onion
4 tablespoons finely chopped
  mushrooms
juice of 1 lemon
4 tablespoons finely chopped
  parsley

2 tablespoons olive oil
1 large clove garlic, finely
  chopped
1 lb (450 gr) ripe tomatoes,
  skinned, seeded and chopped
1 wineglass dry white wine
a few sprigs of thyme
12 black olives, halved and stoned

Remove the heads and fins from the whiting. Slit them down the
belly, clean them and remove the backbones, but keep them
joined down the back.

    Melt the butter in a small frying pan on a low heat and cook
the onion in this until it is soft. Raise the heat, add the mushrooms, and cook them briskly for two minutes. Remove the pan
from the heat and stir in the lemon juice and parsley. Put the
pan back on the heat and stir it until most of the juice has been
absorbed.

Open out the whiting and lay them down flat. Divide the mixture into four and spread it over one half of each fish. Fold over the other half, reshape the fish and lay them in a wide, shallow, lidded casserole. Preheat the oven to Reg 6/400°F, 200°C.

Heat the olive oil in a small pan on a moderate heat. Add the chopped garlic and cook it until it is on the point of turning brown. Put in the chopped tomatoes and cook, stirring and pressing until they are reduced to a purée. Pour in the white wine and boil briskly until the sauce is thick. Add the sprigs of thyme and the olives. Season. Spoon this sauce over the fish, cover, and cook in the oven for 25 minutes. Remove the thyme before serving. Serve with pasta and a green salad.

Grilled pork chops with tomatoes and spring onions

4 pork chops	12 spring onions, chopped
1 tablespoon tomato purée	1 lb (450 gr) ripe tomatoes,
1 tablespoon Dijon mustard	skinned and sliced

Preheat the grill to high.

Mix the tomato purée with the mustard and spread half of this mixture over one side of the chops. Lay the chops on the grill pan, mustard side up. Grill until that side is completely done, lowering the height of the pan if necessary, but keeping the temperature high. Turn the chops over and spread the remaining mustard mixture on the other side. Put them back under the high grill. When they are almost done, scatter the chopped onions over the top and replace them to finish cooking.

When the chops are done, smother them with the tomato slices and put them back under the grill until the tomatoes are melting into them.

Vegetables available in June

asparagus – until Midsummer Day

beans, broad – the first small tender ones come early in the
  month

beans, green – Spanish and Cypriot, very tender but expensive

beetroot – the first bunches of baby beetroot are available at the
  end of the month.

cabbage – the first Primo summer cabbage come into the shops
  in the second week

carrots – by the end of the month the first bunches of baby new
  carrots appear in the shops

cauliflowers – not many about

celery – English celery is available again towards the end of the
  month but is expensive

spring onions – very good, the bulbous ends are large and
  tender

peas – the first ones reach the shops by the middle of the month

peppers – become cheaper in June as they come from the
  Channel Islands

potatoes – plentiful supplies, with English ones available for
  most of the month

radishes – good all through the month

tomatoes – English ones become sweeter and cheaper as the
  month progresses

watercress – this flowers in June and in hot weather runs to seed

Fruit available in June

apples and pears – French and South African

cooking apples – even English Bramleys are soft now

apricots – available throughout the month, but rather small and
  hard at first

cherries – French ones are in the shops all through June;
  English ones should arrive in the last week

citrus fruits – South African and not very juicy from now right
  through the summer

gooseberries – the first English summer fruit
peaches – imported and rather small and hard at first
raspberries – these are quite a scarce fruit now – they come in
    during the last week
strawberries – are still expensive at first but become cheaper and
    more plentiful.

Fresh herbs available in June

bay
chervil – grows up well towards the end of the month
chives – still a good thick crop and if they have not all been
    picked off they will produce their round blue flowers now
fennel – lots of feathery leaves
lovage – this becomes rampant towards the end of the month
    and needs constant cutting back.
marjoram – the stems are long and tender and the leaves large
mint – starts to grow rapidly
parsley – still growing steadily
rosemary – very tender aromatic leaves
sage – a great deal of new tender growth
savory – long tender stems and soft leaves
tarragon – just about grows big enough to be used by the end
    of the month
thyme – very tender stems and leaves

           ಜ   ಜ   ಜ

By the beginning of June, summer weather should have arrived
for good and the morning and evening as well as the middle of
the day will be much warmer. A whole new atmosphere seems
to set in and I am always so glad when the new vegetables start
coming into the shops one after the other, and we can forget
about the tired old ones.

English new potatoes only just make it by the beginning of the
month, when from the warmer, more sheltered local farms the
first baby new ones arrive in the shops. According to my farmer
friend we should consider ourselves very lucky if they are there

by the first day in June, but certainly by the end of the first week supplies should start. And how grateful I always am for them! Although new ones have been coming for two months now from places gradually nearer and nearer to home, there is nothing like the first local ones. They are, of course, delicious boiled and served quite simply with butter and parsley, but there are many different dishes you can make with them.

New potatoes with cheese and chervil

1½ lb (675 gr) baby new potatoes
1 oz (25 gr) butter
2 tablespoons chopped chervil or parsley
2 tablespoons grated Cheddar cheese

Boil the washed new potatoes in their skins until they are tender. Toss them in the melted butter and on a very low heat stir in the cheese, chervil and seasoning. Take off the heat as soon as the cheese has melted.

New potatoes with fennel

1½ lb (675 gr) new potatoes, large or small
2 oz (50 gr) butter
2 tablespoons chopped fennel

Boil the washed potatoes in their skins in salted water and drain. Slice them into rounds, keeping the skins on, while they are still warm. Melt the butter in a saucepan on a low heat. Carefully mix in the potato slices and the fennel, taking care not to break up the potatoes too much.

Parmesan potatoes

1½ lb (675 gr) new potatoes
½ oz (13 gr) melted butter
1 tablespoon grated Parmesan cheese

Boil the potatoes in their skins in salted water until they are just tender. Skin them while they are still warm. Cut them in half lengthways and brush them in melted butter. Preheat the grill to high and grill the potatoes, cut side up so that they turn golden brown. Turn the potatoes over and replace under the grill.

When they are almost done, sprinkle over some grated Parmesan cheese and replace until they brown.

These are good either hot, or cold with picnics.

Spiced yellow potatoes

1½ lb (675 gr) new potatoes   a pinch cayenne pepper
1½ oz (38 gr) butter   1 clove garlic, finely chopped
1 dessertspoon turmeric

Boil the potatoes in their skins in salted water till they are just tender. Drain them and peel them while they are still warm. Melt the butter on a low heat in the saucepan, stir in the spices and garlic and cook for five minutes, stirring. Stir in the potatoes. Cover, and set on the lowest possible heat for five minutes, shaking occasionally to prevent the potatoes from sticking or browning.

Potato salads are always best made with new potatoes. Here are two which, if the weather should suddenly take a turn for the worse and you have planned a cold meal, are equally good served hot to cheer up cold meats.

Potato and mustard cream salad

1 lb (450 gr) new potatoes   ½ pint (3 dl) milk
1 oz (25 gr) butter   juice of 1 lemon
1 dessertspoon dry mustard   2 tablespoons double cream
  powder   6 spring onions, chopped
1 tablespoon flour

Boil the potatoes in their skins in salted water until they are just tender. Peel and slice them while they are still warm. Melt the butter on a moderate heat and stir in the mustard powder and flour. Blend in the milk and stir until the sauce is bubbly. Off the heat, stir in the lemon juice and cream. Carefully mix in the sliced potatoes and the spring onions with a wooden spoon. Either reheat without boiling, or let the salad cool completely and serve it slightly chilled.

Potato salad in sour cream

1 lb (450 gr) new potatoes
4 tablespoons sour cream
juice of 1 lemon
1 tablespoon chopped mint

Boil the potatoes in their skins in salted water and peel them while they are still warm. Slice them fairly thickly. Gently warm the cream and lemon juice together on a low heat. Stir in the potatoes and mint and heat through without boiling. Serve the salad hot, or let it cool completely.

If the idea of a hot salad appeals to you, then here is another but this one is not really suited to being served cold.

Hot potato salad with tomato dressing

1½ lb (675 gr) new potatoes
5 tablespoons olive oil
3 tablespoons wine vinegar
1 dessertspoon tomato purée
1 tablespoon chopped chives

Boil the potatoes in their skins in salted water and peel and slice them when they are still warm. Put them back into the saucepan on the lowest possible heat. Combine all the ingredients of the dressing together and mix them carefully into the sliced potatoes. Heat very gently and serve hot.

Roast potatoes need not be old ones. Roasted new potatoes are just as good in their own way, either blanched first or put straight in the oven.

Roast new potatoes in dripping

1 lb (450 gr) small new potatoes
4 tablespoons good beef dripping
6 small onions, quartered

Preheat the oven to Reg 6/400°F, 200°C.
Put the dripping in a large roasting pan in the oven until it is smoking hot. Scrape the potatoes. Roll them in the dripping until they have a good covering of fat. Add the onion quarters, first turning them over in the fat until they are coated as well. Return the pan to the oven for an hour by which time the potatoes and onions should be golden brown. Turn them occasionally. Drain the onions and potatoes on absorbent paper, season, and serve them together in a dish.

Oven-browned potatoes and onions

1½ lb (675 gr) medium new potatoes
1 oz (25 gr) melted butter
1 medium onion, finely chopped
2 tablespoons chopped mint

Preheat the oven to Reg 6/400°F, 200°C or Reg 5/350°F, 180°C (according to what else you are cooking at the same time) and butter a shallow ovenproof dish.

Put the potatoes into cold, salted water, bring them to the boil and boil them briskly for three minutes. Drain them, and while they are still hot, scrape off the skins with a blunt knife, damaging the smooth surface as little as possible. Cut them in half lengthways, lay them in the dish, season them and brush them with the melted butter. Strew the onion over them. Bake them in the oven for an hour at the higher temperature or an hour and a half at the lower temperature. Scatter the chopped mint over them for the last three minutes.

Paprika new potatoes

1 lb (450 gr) small new potatoes
1 oz (25 gr) melted butter
paprika

Preheat the oven to Reg 4/350°F, 180°C.
Blanch and peel some small new potatoes as in the previous recipe. Cut them in half lengthways. Score the rounded surfaces

lengthways with a sharp knife in lines ⅛-inch (3 mm) apart. Lay them in a buttered ovenproof dish, season them and brush them with melted butter. Put them into the oven for 30 minutes. Dust the tops with paprika and return them to the oven for a further ten minutes.

They are best served hot, but they can also be taken, cold, on picnics.

Casserole of potatoes with fennel and spring onions

about 24 baby new potatoes, scraped
2 oz (50 gr) butter
2 tablespoons chopped fennel
8 spring onions, chopped

Preheat the oven to Reg 4/350°F, 180°C.
Melt the butter in a flameproof casserole on a moderate heat. Lightly brown the potatoes in this, uncovered, on all sides. Put them into the oven, covered, for 30 minutes. Shake the casserole, add the fennel, spring onions and seasoning to the potatoes, and put them back into the oven for ten minutes. Serve the potatoes with the butter and herbs spooned over the top.

Instead of being boiled or baked, new potatoes can be glazed in stock, or another liquid, such as beer.

New potatoes in beer

1½ lb (675 gr) small new potatoes, scraped
2 oz (50 gr) butter
1 bunch spring onions, chopped
½ pint (3 dl) bitter beer

Melt the butter in a saucepan on a low heat. Cook the spring onions in this until they are just soft. Stir in the potatoes and pour in the beer. Bring to boiling point, cover and simmer gently for 15 minutes. Raise the heat to moderate and continue cooking until all the liquid is absorbed and the potatoes are glazed. This should take about 15 minutes. Lower the heat a little if it happens too quickly.

In the herb garden mint grows up at just the right time to go with new potatoes. Boil them with a sprig of it and serve them with chopped mint and melted butter, with a little parsley mixed in as well. Or try this pilaf.

Potato and mint pilaf

12 small new potatoes
2 oz (50 gr) butter
6 oz (150 gr) long-grain rice

2 tablespoons chopped mint
stock to cover about ¾ pint
  (4·5 dl))

Dice the scraped potatoes into quarter-inch (6 mm) dice. Melt the butter in a narrow, high-sided saucepan on a moderate heat. Add the rice and the potato dice and stir for about two minutes until they are well coated with butter. Stir in the mint, season, and just cover with stock. Put on the lid and simmer on the lowest possible heat for about 30 minutes when all the stock should be absorbed and the rice soft. Check and stir from time to time adding a little more stock if necessary.

⸙   ⸙   ⸙

New potatoes are followed at the end of the first week of June by broad beans. When they are young and really sweet, you can serve them raw in salads and with cold meats.

Pork and broad bean salad

a 2 lb (900 gr) joint of lean end of
  belly of pork, boned and with
  the rind removed
12 allspice berries
12 black peppercorns
pinch salt
1 clove garlic, chopped
1 teaspoon chopped rosemary
2 tablespoons chopped savory
2 lb (900 gr) broad beans, weighed
  in their shells

for the dressing:
4 tablespoons olive oil
1 tablespoon wine vinegar
1 tablespoon tomato purée
1 tablespoon soy sauce

Preheat the oven to Reg 4/350°F, 180°C.

Crush the allspice, peppercorns, garlic and salt together in a pestle and mortar, and rub them over the cut surface of the pork. Scatter the rosemary and half the savory over, roll the joint and tie it with strong thread. Put it in a roasting tin in the centre of the oven for 1½ hours. Remove it, let it cool completely, and then dice the pork into ½-inch (1·25 cm) pieces.

Shell the beans and mix them with the pork and the remaining savory. Blend the oil and vinegar and beat in the tomato purée and soy sauce. Coat the beans and pork in the dressing and let the salad stand for 30 minutes before serving.

When they are young and tiny, broad beans are best cooked with a knob of butter, a little chopped parsley and just enough stock to cover them. Simmer them gently, covered, for 20 minutes, so that most of the liquid is absorbed and the beans are plump, tender and shiny. Alternatively you can simmer them only in butter, and just as they are tender stir in some scalded cream and pepper. This is a very extravagant recipe, but broad beans are an extravagant vegetable anyway as you have to buy so many pods to obtain so few beans. So it's a good idea to cook them with your meat or fish or incorporate them in some way into the sauce.

Beef and bean goulash

2 lb (900 gr) stewing beef, cut into one-inch (2·5 cm) cubes	¼ pint (1·5 dl) stock
1½ oz (38 gr) butter	1 tablespoon chopped marjoram
2 medium onions, thinly sliced	1 tablespoon chopped savory
1 tablespoon paprika	2 lb (900 gr) broad beans, weighed in their shells
1 wineglass white wine	

Preheat the oven to Reg 4/350°F, 180°C.

Melt the butter on a high heat in a heavy flameproof casserole. Brown the pieces of beef all over in this. Remove them and set aside. Lower the heat and take the pan away for a minute to let the butter cool a little. Stir in the sliced onions and paprika and cook them very slowly until the onions are soft, stirring occasionally. Blend in the wine and stock. Raise the heat and bring them to the boil, stirring. Add the beef, herbs and seasoning to the casserole and put it into the oven for an hour. Stir in the shelled beans and return the dish to the oven for a further 30 minutes.

Pork with summer vegetables

2 lb (900 gr) lean, boneless pork, cut in ¾-inch (2 cm) dice
1 oz (25 gr) butter, *or*
  2 tablespoons melted pork fat
12 small spring onions, chopped
8 new carrots, sliced very thin

2 lb (900 gr) broad beans, weighed in their shells
1 lb (450 gr) peas, weighed in their shells
½ pint (3 dl) dry cider

Melt the butter or heat the fat in a wide-bottomed flameproof casserole. Brown the pieces of meat all over and set them aside. Lower the heat and cook the onions and carrots gently until the onions are beginning to soften. Stir in the shelled beans and peas until they are well coated with butter. Pour in the cider and bring it to the boil. Season. Replace the pork, cover the casserole tightly, and cook on the lowest heat possible for 30 minutes. Serve with buttered new potatoes.

White fish and broad beans

1½ lb (675 gr) white fish (cod, coley or haddock), skinned
juice of 1 lemon
2 bayleaves
a few black peppercorns
2 lb (900 gr) broad beans, weighed in their shells

2 oz (50 gr) butter
1½ tablespoons flour
¾ pint (4·5 dl) fish stock, made from the skin
2 tablespoons chopped parsley
2 hard-boiled eggs, finely chopped
1 dessertspoon anchovy essence

Cut the fish into even-sized pieces and lay it in a buttered oven-proof dish. Sprinkle over the lemon juice and peppercorns and the bayleaves torn into small pieces. Leave it to stand for at least ½ hour. Preheat the oven to Reg 4/350°F, 180°C, and bake it in the centre for 20 minutes, covered with foil or a butter paper.

Meanwhile, shell the beans and cook them, covered, in the butter in a saucepan on a very low heat until they are just tender. Stir in the flour and blend in the stock. Simmer for ten minutes. Just before serving the sauce stir in the parsley, chopped eggs and anchovy essence. Arrange the fish on a warmed serving dish and pour the sauce over it.

As broad beans get older and larger, they lose the delicate flavour of the new baby ones. They can then be used to make a tasty soup.

Bean and ham soup

1 lb (450 gr) broad beans, weighed in their shells
1½ pints (9 dl) ham stock
½ oz (13 gr) butter
1 tablespoon flour
2 tablespoons ham, chopped very small

Shell the beans and put them into a pan with the stock and about six of the best bean pods. Bring to the boil and simmer, covered, for 30 minutes. Strain, and discard the pods. Put the beans and a quarter of the liquid in the blender and work until smooth. Mix with the remaining liquid. Melt the butter on a moderate heat, blend in the flour and stir until it bubbles. Off the heat, blend in the bean liquid. Return to the heat, check the seasoning, bring the soup to the boil and simmer it for two minutes, stirring. Stir in the ham and serve immediately.

Old broad beans can also be puréed and used in the following ways.

Lamb with broad bean stuffing

2-2½ lb (0·9-1·125 kg) loin of lamb, chined and boned
2 lb (900 gr) broad beans, weighed in their shells
2½ oz (65 gr) butter
1 small onion, finely chopped
4 oz (100 gr) mushrooms, finely chopped
1 tablespoon chopped marjoram
1 large wineglass white wine
1 tablespoon flour
¼ pint (1·5 dl) stock
2 tablespoons white wine if needed

Preheat the oven to Reg 4/350°F, 180°C.
Shell the beans and cook them in boiling salted water until they are soft. Drain them well and pound them to a paste with a pestle and mortar or a wooden spoon. Melt 2 oz (50 gr) of the butter on a low heat and cook the onion gently in this until it is just beginning to soften. Raise the heat, add the mushrooms, and cook briskly for two minutes. Beat the mushrooms and onions into the beans, together with the marjoram. Season. Spread this mixture over the cut surface of the lamb. Roll up the meat and tie it with strong thread or fine cotton string. Melt the remaining butter on a high heat in a heavy flameproof casserole and brown the meat all over in this. Pour in all but two tablespoons of the wine and let it bubble. Cover and put it into the oven for 1¼ hours. Remove the lamb from the casserole, carve it and keep it warm.

Pour off any juices that are in the casserole and skim them. Return the fat to the pan and blend in the flour. Stir in the stock, scraping in any pieces of stuffing from the bottom of the casserole. Add the juices from the pan and the remaining white wine if there is only a very little liquid remaining. Pour the sauce over the lamb before serving.

Broad bean loaf

2 lb (900 gr) broad beans, weighed in their shells
½ lb (225 gr) good sausage meat
1 small onion, finely chopped
½ oz (13 gr) butter
1 tablespoon mixed chopped sage and savory
2 extra sprigs savory
2 hard-boiled eggs

Preheat the oven to Reg 4/350°F, 180°C.
Boil the shelled beans in salted water until they are tender. Drain and refresh them and pound them to a purée. Thoroughly mix the sausage meat into the beans. Cook the onion in the butter until it is soft and mix it into the bean mixture, together with the herbs and seasoning.

Put a layer of this mixture about half an inch (1·25 cm) thick in the bottom of a 1 lb (450 gr) terrine or loaf tin. Lay the eggs on the top with space all around. Pack in the rest of the loaf mixture so it surrounds and covers the eggs. Press the savory sprigs decoratively on to the top. Stand the loaf tin in a baking tin of water and put it into the centre of the oven for an hour. Cool completely before removing it from the tin.

This makes a very good lunch, supper or picnic dish.

Broad bean pâté

2 lb (900 gr) broad beans, weighed in their shells
4 oz (100 gr) curd cheese
2 tablespoons chopped parsley
juice of ½ lemon

Cook the shelled beans in boiling salted water until they are soft. Drain thoroughly. Pound them to a paste with a pestle and mortar or a wooden spoon.

Gradually beat in the cheese and parsley and finally the lemon juice to taste. Season. Press the pâté into an earthenware bowl and chill. Serve it cold with brown toast.

This is very good made with older beans, but even better if the beans are young, if you can spare them, because of their more delicate flavour.

಼ಣ   ಼ಣ   ಼ಣ

The first peaches come into the shops in June – a sure sign that summer is here. As well as making a beautiful sweet simply steeped in white wine they can make an unusual addition to summer salads. Here's one using broad beans again.

Lamb, broad bean and peach salad

1½ lb (675 gr) cold roast lamb, cut into slices	4 tablespoons olive oil juice of ½ lemon
2 lb (900 gr) broad beans (weighed in their shells)	1 tablespoon chopped mint 1 tablespoon chopped chives
1 sprig of mint	1 tablespoon chopped parsley
4 tablespoons white wine	4 small or 2 large peaches

Shell the beans and cook them for 10 minutes in boiling salted water with the sprig of mint and two of the pods for flavour. Drain them well, refresh them and drain again.

Blend the oil, wine and lemon juice together and mix in the chopped herbs. Stir half this dressing into the beans while they are still warm.

Scald and skin the peaches and cut them into slices. Add them to the beans when the latter are completely cool. Arrange the lamb down the centre of a serving plate with the salad on either side, and spoon the remaining dressing over the lamb.

If you are roasting a piece of lamb specially for this salad, as soon as it comes out of the oven pour off all the juices in the pan and skim them of most of the fat. Then mix them into the dressing you have reserved for the lamb.

The next salad, which can accompany ham, fish or chicken, makes good use of the very early, rather unripe peaches.

Peach and sour cream salad

4 medium-sized firm peaches
2 lettuce hearts or 1 lettuce
1 dessertspoon curry powder
1 teaspoon soft brown sugar

2 tablespoons lemon juice
4 tablespoons sour cream
1 clove garlic, very finely chopped

Shred the lettuce and arrange it either on one large serving dish or on four individual plates. Stone the peaches, slice them and cut the slices into half-inch (1·25 cm) pieces. Put the curry powder, sugar, lemon juice, garlic and seasoning in a bowl and work in the sour cream. Turn the pieces of peach over in the dressing and pile them on top of the lettuce.

This ham and cottage cheese dish, also with curry powder, makes a good lunch or a light first course.

Ham, cheese and peach curry

8 oz (225 gr) lean ham, cut into
   half-inch (1·25 cm) dice
juice of 1 lemon
1 dessertspoon curry powder

2 peaches, peeled and diced
8 oz (225 gr) plain cottage cheese
2 tablespoons chopped chives

Mix the lemon juice and curry powder in a bowl and gradually beat in the cottage cheese. Mix in the ham, peaches and chives. Season, and serve on a bed of chopped lettuce.

Two more first course ideas now, each using a different kind of cheese.

Peaches and cream cheese salad

4 peaches, skinned and halved
8 oz (225 gr) cream cheese
juice of 2 lemons
2 tablespoons chopped fennel

Blend the lemon juice gradually into the cheese and beat in the fennel. Either pile the mixture on top of the peach halves, or use it to sandwich them together.

Peach boats

4 medium peaches, skinned and   juice of 1 lemon
  chopped   8 sticks celery
4 oz (100 gr) curd cheese   a little chopped tarragon

Blend the cheese with the lemon juice, season, and stir in the pieces of peach with a metal spoon. Make boats from the wide bottom ends of the celery and pile the peach mixture into them. Sprinkle the chopped tarragon on top.

   If you cannot obtain celery, pile the salad on to lettuce leaves instead. Tarragon should just be ready by the end of June.

83   83   83

The most widely available English fruit in the shops in June are gooseberries, which are traditionally flavoured with a sprig of elder flowers and made into tarts and raised pies. Growing in our garden when I was a child was what seemed to me a whole forest of gooseberry bushes. We couldn't have gooseberry pie *every* day, and even if we preserved some, many still hung un- used on the bushes. It always seemed a shame that nobody had any idea what to do with them. Just lately, I've been experimenting, and have found that their sharpness goes well with pork, particularly useful at a time when good cooking apples are scarce.

Pork chops and gooseberries

4 lean pork chops, boned
4 lean rindless rashers bacon
8 oz (225 gr) shortcrust pastry
2 large or 4 small onions, finely
  chopped

4 tablespoons unsweetened
  gooseberry purée
4 teaspoons soft brown sugar

Preheat the oven to Reg 6/400°F, 200°C.
Roll out the pastry into four rounds, each twice as big as the chops. Set the bacon on a low heat in a heavy frying pan with only a very little fat. Cook it until it is just browning. Lay one bacon rasher on one half of each piece of pastry. Fry the chops in the same fat on a moderate heat until they are golden brown on both sides. Lay the chops on top of the bacon. Lower the heat and cook the onion in the fat until it is soft. Put the onion on top of the chops. Sweeten the gooseberry purée with the sugar and spoon it over the onions. Season. Fold over the pastry and seal the edges. Lay the pasties on a floured baking tray and brush them with milk or beaten egg. Bake them for 30 minutes.

Braised pork and gooseberries

a 2 lb (900 gr) piece loin of pork,
  boned, rolled and tied
½ oz (13 gr) butter or
  2 tablespoons pork fat
1 medium onion, finely sliced

2 slices lean bacon, diced
¼ lb (100 gr) gooseberries, topped
  and tailed and chopped
¼ pint (1·5 dl) dry cider

Preheat the oven to Reg 4/350°F, 180°C.
Heat the butter or fat in a heavy flameproof casserole and brown the pork all over. Remove it and lower the heat. Add the onion and bacon to the casserole and cook them gently until the onion is soft. Stir in the gooseberries and the cider. Raise the heat a

little and bring them to the boil. Replace the pork. Season, cover and put into the oven for 1¼ hours. Carve the pork and arrange it on a warmed serving dish. Boil the sauce up to reduce it a little and spoon it over the pork to serve.

Gooseberries traditionally accompany mackerel and go well with its oily texture.

Baked spiced mackerel and gooseberries

4 small mackerel
½ lb (225 gr) gooseberries, topped and tailed and thinly sliced
¼ pint (1·5 dl) dry cider
2 one-inch (2·5 cm) pieces of cinnamon

2 blades mace
6 allspice berries
pepper

for serving:
shredded lettuce
1 bunch radishes

Preheat the oven to Reg 4/350°F, 180°C.
Fillet the mackerel and lay them in an ovenproof dish. Scatter the gooseberries over them. Pour over the cider and add the spices to the dish, well spread about. Cover with foil, and cook in the centre of the oven for 30 minutes.

Discard the spices. Lift out the mackerel and gooseberries and set them on a warmed serving dish. Surround them with the shredded lettuce and decorate with the bright red halves of radishes.

Mackerel with gooseberry sauce

2 large or 4 small mackerel
grated nutmeg
1 cinnamon stick, broken in two
1 medium onion, thinly sliced

½ lb (225 gr) gooseberries, chopped
¼ pint (1.5 dl) dry cider

Preheat the oven to Reg 4/350°F, 180°C. Lightly oil a flat ovenproof dish.

Fillet the mackerel, and halve each fillet if they are large ones.
Lay the fillets in the dish, grate over some nutmeg, and add
the cinnamon. Scatter the sliced onion over, and strew the
gooseberries on top of the onion. Pour in the cider, cover the
dish with foil, and put it in the centre of the oven for 30
minutes. Then, allow the whole lot to cool in the dish.

Brush all the pieces from the mackerel and lay the fillets in a
serving dish. Remove the cinnamon sticks and rub the remaining
contents of the dish through a sieve. Stir it together to make a
smooth, creamy sauce. Check the seasoning and spoon it over
the mackerel to serve.

In these quantities, this makes a light dish for lunch or a
summer evening salad. If you would prefer to serve it as a first
course, simply halve the quantities and use a small onion.

෯   ෯   ෯

June is a prolific month in the herb garden, and herbs are an
important part of the pâtés and meat loaves which are so delicious for summer salads and picnics. Two of these recipes are
made with ham and one with beef.

Ham and chicken pâté

12 oz (325 gr) cooked ham, finely
minced
6 oz (150 gr) cooked chicken,
finely minced
4 oz (100 gr) butter
1 large onion, finely chopped

1 tablespoon chopped parsley
1 tablespoon chopped thyme
¼ teaspoon ground mace
4 tablespoons sherry
few drops of Tabasco sauce to
taste

Melt 1 oz (25 gr) of the butter in a frying pan on a low heat and
cook the onion in this until it is soft. Put in the rest of the butter
and let it melt. Take the pan off the heat and work in the ham
and chicken. Put the mixture into a blender and work it until it
is smooth. Turn it into a mixing bowl and beat in the herbs,
mace, sherry and Tabasco. Check the seasoning, press the mixture into an earthenware dish and put it into the refrigerator for
at least two hours before serving.

Simple ham loaf

1 lb (450 gr) cooked ham (including a little fat)	2 tablespoons chopped parsley
½ teaspoon ground mace	1 tablespoon chopped marjoram
8 crushed juniper berries	1 tablespoon chopped savory
	2 eggs, beaten

Preheat the oven to Reg 4/350°F, 180°C.

Put the ham twice through the fine blade of a mincer and thoroughly mix in the rest of the ingredients. Pack the mixture into an earthenware terrine and bake it in a bain marie in the oven for an hour. Set a weight on top while it is cooling. When it is cool, loosen the sides with a knife and turn it out to serve.

Potted beef

1½ lb (675 gr) braising steak	1 small onion
6 cloves, or ¼ teaspoon ground cloves	1 carrot
	pinch ground mace
6 allspice berries, or ¼ teaspoon ground allspice	2 bayleaves

Preheat the oven to Reg 4/350°F, 180°C.

Cut any fat from the meat and put it into an earthenware casserole. Set this in a bain marie and put it in the oven while you are preparing the other ingredients. Grind the cloves and allspice berries together. Cut the lean meat into small dice. Peel and halve the onion. Scrub the carrot and halve it lengthways.

Take the casserole from the oven and stir in the meat, vegetables and spices and tuck in the bayleaves. Put it back into the bain marie for 1½ hours. Strain the contents of the casserole and reserve the juices. Discard the onion, carrot and bayleaf. Pound the meat either with a large pestle and mortar or in a bowl with a wooden spoon, and work in the reserved juices. Press the beef into a small terrine, cover it with greaseproof paper and set a weight on top. Let it stand like this in a cool place for at least three hours before serving.

Fish can also make light pâtés for the summer.

Striped fish pâté

for the white layers:

½ lb (225 gr) fresh cod fillet, skinned

1 oz (25 gr) butter

1 small onion, finely chopped

1 small clove garlic, finely chopped

2 teaspoons anchovy essence

1 tablespoon chopped parsley

juice of ¼ lemon

for the yellow layers:

½ lb (225 gr) smoked cod fillet

1 bayleaf

1 slice of onion

a few black peppercorns

sprig of lemon thyme

sprig of fennel

1 tablespoon chopped parsley and fennel mixed

1 oz (25 gr) melted butter

few drops of Tabasco sauce

juice of ¼ lemon

To make the white layers, melt the butter in a frying pan on a low heat and cook the onion and garlic gently until the onion is soft. Chop the cod very finely. Raise the heat under the pan, put in the cod and cook it briskly for about three minutes, stirring. Immediately remove it from the heat and let it cool slightly. Put it into a blender with the anchovy essence, parsley and lemon juice and work it until it is smooth.

To make the yellow layers, put the smoked cod into a shallow pan or frying pan with the bayleaf, onion, peppercorns and sprigs of thyme and fennel. Cover it with water and put on the lid. Bring the fish gently to the boil and let it simmer for seven minutes.

Drain the fish well, skin and flake it. Pound it or work it in a blender with the chopped herbs, melted butter, Tabasco and lemon juice.

To complete the pâté, chill both mixtures until they are almost firm. Divide the yellow mixture into three and the white into two. Pack the mixtures in layers in a small terrine or straight-sided dish, starting and ending with yellow. Chill the pâté again until it is really firm.

Vegetables available in July

beans, broad – these are still good at first, but become rather
  large and tough towards the end of the month
beans, green – later in the month the first home-grown French
  beans come into the shops
cabbage, primo – fresh and crisp
carrots – the home-grown bunches have the best flavour
cauliflowers – this isn't really a cauliflower month but they are
  quite widely available
celery – very scarce, and nearly all foreign
courgettes – English ones arrive in the last two weeks
marrows – the first small ones by the middle of the month
peas – small and tender at first, larger and less sweet later
peppers – green peppers are now English and almost half the
  price they were in the winter
potatoes – all new now
radishes – large and crisp
spinach – still available and good if you can find it
tomatoes – English ones are becoming really plentiful
turnips – round white baby ones in bunches are available all
  through the month

Fruit available in July

apples and pears – French or South African
apricots – now larger and sweeter than in June
blackcurrants – sometimes difficult to obtain in shops
cherries – the English crop arrives in July
citrus fruit – not at all good now, sometimes soft and bad and
  sometimes very dry
gooseberries – small ones for cooking and larger dessert ones
  available all through the month
peaches – bigger and sweeter now than in June and better for
  sweet dishes
raspberries – at the peak of their rather short season
redcurrants – widely available throughout the month
strawberries – in marvellous abundance

Fresh herbs available in July

All the herbs listed here flourish in July

basil	marjoram
bay	mint
chervil	parsley
chives	rosemary
coriander	sage
dill	savory
fennel	tarragon
lovage	thyme and lemon thyme

ಜ   ಜ   ಜ

July is always an exciting and exhilarating month for food. New vegetables and fruits are everywhere and never, even at Christmas, are the greengrocers' displays more colourful.

Strawberries are the most popular as well as the most plentiful of all fruits in July. They are heaped up in overflowing piles on shop counters and market stalls, and all over the countryside, but especially in the South, big signs invite you to pick your own in the strawberry fields. I love these expeditions and even if I am picking the fruit to serve loads of people at a party or for jam, I always compulsively pick far more than I need, simply because the fruit is so abundant and fresh and beautiful. If you have large quantities of cheap strawberries, it is worth sacrificing a few to experiment with. Used carefully, and blended appropriately, they can make unusual first course salads.

Strawberry and yoghurt salad

1 lb (450 gr) strawberries, halved or quartered according to size
juice of ½ lemon, or more
5 fluid oz (1·5 dl) plain yoghurt
1 clove garlic, finely chopped

Quarter or halve the strawberries, depending on their size. Mix the lemon juice with the yoghurt. Add the garlic, season if you want to, and spoon the dressing over the strawberries.

Strawberry and grapefruit salad

½ lb (225 gr) strawberries, halved
2 grapefruit, with each segment
  cut into four
French dressing

1 large clove garlic, crushed
1 tablespoon chopped mixed
  herbs

Add the garlic, herbs and black pepper to the French dressing, and mix the grapefruit and strawberries into it.

Strawberry and prawn salad

½ lb (225 gr) strawberries, halved
  or quartered depending on
  their size
½ lb (225 gr) shelled prawns
4 tablespoons olive oil
juice of 1 lemon

1 dessertspoon paprika
1 teaspoon Tabasco sauce, or a
  pinch of cayenne pepper
shredded round lettuce and lemon
  slices for serving

Mix the prawns and strawberries together. Blend together all the other ingredients to make the dressing. Mix the dressing into the prawns and strawberries and chill slightly. Serve on the lettuce, garnished with the thin slices of lemon.

❀   ❀   ❀

It is not so unusual to use redcurrants in savoury dishes, especially in the form of redcurrant jelly. In July lemons, which counteract the fattiness of lamb so well, are not very juicy, and good cooking apples for pork are not readily available. But redcurrants can make sharp sauces for either meat, and can also be cooked in the pot with them.

Pork, potatoes and redcurrants

4 pork chops
2 tablespoons melted pork fat, or
  ½ oz (13 gr) butter
1 lb (450 gr) small new potatoes,
  scraped
1 large onion, chopped

1 clove garlic, chopped
½ lb (225 gr) redcurrants
2 sprigs rosemary, chopped
1 wineglass red wine
1 wineglass stock

Preheat the oven to Reg 4/350°F, 180°C.
Heat the fat in a flameproof casserole on a moderate heat and brown the chops in this on both sides. Remove the chops and set them aside. Put the potatoes into the casserole and brown them all over, uncovered. Take them out and set them aside with the chops. Lower the heat, put in the onion and garlic and cook until the onion is soft. Stir in the redcurrants, rosemary, wine and stock. Bring them to the boil and replace the chops and potatoes. Season if necessary, cover the casserole and put it into the oven for 45 minutes.

Take out the chops and potatoes and arrange them on a serving dish. Strain the sauce from the casserole through a sieve, pressing down hard and rubbing slightly. Reheat the sauce and serve it separately.

Shoulder of lamb with redcurrant sauce

1 shoulder of lamb, boned	1 large onion, chopped
2 tablespoons chopped marjoram	½ lb (225 gr) redcurrants
4 tablespoons chopped mint	2 wineglasses red wine
2 tablespoons melted lamb fat or ½ oz (13 gr) butter	½ oz (13 gr) kneaded butter

Preheat the oven to Reg 4/350°F, 180°C.
Scatter the marjoram and half the mint over the cut surface of the lamb. Roll it up and tie it with strong thread or fine cotton string. Heat the butter or fat on a high heat in a heavy, flameproof casserole and brown the joint all over. Remove it and set it aside. Lower the heat, put in the onion, and cook gently until it is soft. Stir in the currants and wine and bring them to the boil. Season. Replace the lamb, cover the casserole, and put it into the oven for an hour. Remove the lamb, carve it and keep it warm. Strain the sauce from the casserole through a sieve, pressing down hard. Return it to the casserole and bring it to the boil. Whisk in as much kneaded butter as required and stir in the remaining mint. Serve the sauce and the meat separately.

A delicious pâté can be made by blending redcurrants with chicken livers.

Redcurrant and chicken liver pâté

½ lb (225 gr) redcurrants, stringed
½ lb (225 gr) chicken livers,
  chopped small
3 oz (75 gr) softened butter

1 large onion, finely chopped
1 clove garlic, finely chopped
8 crushed juniper berries

Melt half the butter on a low heat in a small frying pan. Cook the onion and garlic in this until the onion is soft. Raise the heat and stir in the livers and redcurrants. Cook them briskly for three minutes, stirring. Remove the pan from the heat, and when the liver mixture is cool, work it in the blender until it is smooth. Put it in a bowl and beat in the rest of the softened butter and the crushed juniper berries and seasoning. Pack it into an earthenware pot and chill until it is firm.

If the pâté is to be kept for longer than a day, cover the top with clarified butter.

ಚಿ   ಚಿ   ಚಿ

Raspberries are another delicious soft fruit which are part of the greengrocer's summer display. If you can only buy a few, then serve them with whipped cream or yoghurt as a sweet, and with honey instead of sugar, but if you are lucky enough to be able to pick or, even better, grow your own, and have plenty to spare, try using them in summer salads.

Shrimps are fiddly things to peel, but round about raspberry time they are as big as they will ever be so it's worth taking advantage of this. They have a more delicate flavour than the bigger prawns, and what's more they are cheaper!

Raspberry, shrimp and cheese salad

½ lb (225 gr) raspberries
1 pint (6 dl) shrimps
8 oz (225 gr) cottage cheese
juice of ½ lemon

2 teaspoons anchovy essence
1 tablespoon chives
shredded lettuce for serving

Blend the cheese, lemon juice and anchovy essence together and mix in the shelled shrimps and the chives. Carefully fold in the raspberries, so as not to break them up. Serve the salad on a bed of shredded lettuce.

This quantity will feed two people as a main course for lunch or a light evening meal, or four as an hors d'oeuvre or with another cold salad dish as a main course.

Here is another recipe including cottage cheese, which will make a light lunch dish for four.

Chicken, cheese and raspberry salad

half a 3-3½ lb (1·3-1·5 kg) roasting chicken
2 tablespoons olive oil
salt, pepper
grated rind of 1 lemon
1 tablespoon chopped lemon thyme or thyme
for the salad:

½ lb (225 gr) cottage cheese	1 tablespoon chopped lemon
½ lb (225 gr) raspberries	thyme
1 dessertspoon Dijon mustard	1 large green pepper, seeded and
juice of ½ lemon	chopped

Preheat the grill to high.
Cut the chicken into joints, bone them and cut the meat into pieces about two inches (5 cm) square. Brush the pieces with olive oil and sprinkle them with salt, black pepper and lemon rind. Lay the chicken pieces on the hot grill rack, skin-side down and scatter over half a tablespoon of the lemon thyme. Cook the chicken pieces until the side nearest the heat is golden. Turn them over, scatter over the other half tablespoon of lemon thyme and grill the other side. Set them aside to cool completely, and dice them.

Blend the mustard and lemon juice into the cheese and mix in the lemon thyme, green pepper and chicken. Then carefully mix in the raspberries.

Serve this salad, like the previous one, on a bed of lettuce, or better still pack it into a box and go off on a picnic.

Here is another chicken salad, suitable for a more formal meal.

Marinated chicken and raspberry salad

a 3½ lb (1·5 kg) roasting chicken, jointed
for the chicken marinade:

8 juniper berries	½ lb (225 gr) raspberries
8 allspice berries	1 glass red wine
4 cloves	2 tablespoons olive oil

for the raspberry marinade:

1 tablespoon chopped mint	1 glass red wine

Crush the spices together and mix them with the wine and olive oil in a fairly deep, flat dish. Turn the chicken pieces in this marinade and leave them cut side down to stand at room temperature for at least four hours.

At the same time put the raspberries and mint into another bowl and pour in the wine.

When you are ready to cook the chicken, preheat the grill to high. Take the chicken joints from the marinade and shake them gently to remove any excess liquid. Lay them on the hot grill rack, skin-side down, and cook them as close to the heat as possible until they are golden brown. Turn them over and brown the other side. Remove the rack from the grill and place the joints in the bottom of the pan. Spoon over all the chicken marinade and continue to cook the chicken, basting it frequently and turning, until the juices run clear when the meat is pierced. Remove it from the grill and let it cool.

Reserve any juices that are in the pan and mix them into the marinating raspberries. When the chicken is quite cold, arrange it on the lettuce in a serving dish and spoon over the raspberries, together with all the marinade and pan juices.

If you like blue cheese, this recipe makes an unusual hors d'oeuvre, or you could serve it after the main dish as a combination of sweet and cheese courses.

Raspberry and blue cheese salad

8 oz (225 gr) raspberries	4 oz (100 gr) soft blue cheese
4 tablespoons mayonnaise	thinly sliced cucumber

Grate the blue cheese into the mayonnaise and beat them well together. Carefully mix in the raspberries. Serve it on individual plates, surrounded by thin slices of cucumber.

For a hot meal, raspberries can make a spicy sauce for pork chops.

Grilled pork chops with raspberry and cider sauce

4 loin pork chops
6 allspice berries
6 juniper berries
for the sauce:
½ lb (225 gr) raspberries
½ pint (3 dl) dry cider
1 tablespoon red wine vinegar

10 black peppercorns
1 large clove garlic, chopped

4 juniper berries
4 allspice berries
4 black peppercorns
1 small onion, thinly sliced

First prepare the coating for the chops. Crush the allspice, juniper, peppercorns, garlic and a pinch of sea salt together with a pestle and mortar, and spread them on both sides of the chops. Let them stand for two hours at room temperature.

Meanwhile make the sauce. Set aside 12 raspberries, and put the rest with all the other ingredients for the sauce in a saucepan. Bring them gently to the boil, cover them and let them simmer for 15 minutes. Rub them through a sieve.

When you are ready to cook the chops, preheat the grill to high and cook them as close to the heat as you can, until they are golden brown and just cooked through. Remove the grill rack and put the chops in the bottom of the pan. Pour over the sauce and put in the reserved raspberries. Put the chops back under the grill for five minutes, basting occasionally and making sure the sauce doesn't reduce too quickly. Serve the chops on a warmed serving dish with the raspberries and the sauce spooned over them.

Raspberries also make a delicious pickle to serve with meat, particularly with cold lamb or pork.

Pickled raspberries

1 lb (450 gr) raspberries	1 dessertspoon allspice berries
½ pint (3 dl) red wine vinegar	1 teaspoon juniper berries
2-inch (5 cm) piece of cinnamon	a piece of bruised ginger root
stick	1 tablespoon clear honey

Put the vinegar and spices into an enamel saucepan. Bring them
to the boil and let them simmer for 10 minutes. Strain the vinegar
and put it back in the pan. Add the honey, and stir it on a low
heat until it dissolves. Have the raspberries ready in a bowl.
Pour the hot vinegar over them and leave them until they are
quite cool. Lift the raspberries out with a perforated spoon and
put them into screw-topped jars. Cover them with vinegar and
leave them for at least a week before opening.

ఴ   ఴ   ఴ

Cherries have always had at least one savoury association – with
duck. There are many recipes for duck with cherries, most of
them hot, with a rich sauce, so here for a special dinner or lunch
on a hot July day is a lighter, cold one.

Stuffed duck with cherries

a 4-4½ lb (1·8-2 kg) duck	1 tablespoon chopped mint
1 lb (450 gr) fairly lean belly of	1 tablespoon chopped parsley
pork	1 pinch ground mace
¼ lb (100 gr) red cherries	1 pinch ground cloves
grated rind of 1 lemon and juice	
of ½ lemon	

Preheat the oven to Reg 4/350°F, 180°C.
Bone out the duck completely and mince the pork. Stone and
chop the cherries, leaving a few aside for decoration. Mix the
pork thoroughly with the cherries, lemon rind and juice, herbs,
spices and seasoning. Stuff the duck with this mixture, reshape,
it and sew it up with trussing string or strong thread. Put the
duck into a baking tray, cover it with foil and cook it in the
centre of the oven for 1½ hours. Pour off most of the fat, remove

the foil, and put it back in the oven for 30 minutes to brown.

Cool the duck completely, preferably leaving it overnight. Pour the fat and juices from the tin into a bowl and put them in the refrigerator to separate and set completely, also overnight if possible.

When you are ready to glaze the duck, separate all the fat, and use the jelly from underneath for the glaze. There should be enough for several layers. Put the jelly into a small bowl in a saucepan of simmering water and leave it on a low heat until it melts. Stand the duck on a serving dish and brush it all over once with the glaze. Stone the remaining cherries and slice them crossways. Arrange them in a pattern on the duck, sticking them on to the glaze. When the first coating has completely dried, brush the duck again, going over the cherries as well.

The duck can be served with the following sauce.

Cherry sauce

6 oz (150 gr) red cherries, stoned and chopped
3 tablespoons red wine
2 tablespoons redcurrant jelly
1 tablespoon chopped mint

Put the wine and jelly into a saucepan and heat them together gently until the jelly has melted. Stir in the cherries. Cool the sauce and stir in the mint when it is cold but still liquid. Turn it into a sauceboat and leave it until it is lightly set.

As well as making a good accompaniment to the stuffed duck, this sauce can be served with plain roast duck or chicken.

If you have any of the stuffed duck left over, it can appear again the next day as a first course.

Cherry and duck salad

8 oz (225 gr) cold duck, diced
½ lb (225 gr) cherries (black or
  red), stoned and chopped
2 tablespoons chopped mint

4 tablespoons thick mayonnaise
chopped cress or lettuce for
  serving

Mix the duck and cherries with the mint and mayonnaise. Serve on a bed of cress or lettuce.

You can also make a cherry salad with chicken. Substitute tarragon for the mint and use black cherries if possible. Or you can serve it with hard boiled eggs, using chives and black cherries.

Black cherry soup

1 lb (450 gr) black cherries, stoned
  and chopped
16 black cherries for garnish,
  stoned and quartered
1 oz (25 gr) butter
1 medium onion, thinly sliced
1 tablespoon flour
1½ pints (9 dl) stock
2 strips lemon rind
2 egg yolks

Melt the butter on a low heat and cook the onion slowly in this until it is soft. Blend in the flour and stock. Stir in the chopped cherries and lemon rind. Bring to the boil, stirring, and simmer gently for 20 minutes. Strain the mixture through a sieve, pressing down and rubbing hard to extract as much pulp as possible. Work the egg yolks together in a bowl and gradually blend in a little of the hot cherry liquid. Mix this into the rest and return to the rinsed-out pan. Gently reheat without boiling. Add the raw halved cherries to the soup bowls just before serving.

83　　83　　83

Another stoned fruit which we can buy right through July is the apricot. Most of them now come from America but they have been grown for a long time in the Cotswold area of England. They used to be thinned out at about the same time that the hams were cooked for sheep-shearing suppers, and so in an age in which nothing was wasted, they became a natural accompaniment to ham.

Honey-roast ham with apricots

a 2 lb (900 gr) piece hock

for boiling the ham:
1 carrot
1 onion
1 stick celery
bouquet garni
a few black peppercorns and
   cloves

8 apricots, stoned and quartered
1 medium onion, thinly sliced
1 small head celery, cut into
   one-inch (2·5 cm) lengths
1 oz (25 gr) butter
¼ pint (1·5 dl) stock (not from the
   ham or it will be too salty)
2 tablespoons honey

Soak the ham overnight. Put it into a saucepan with the carrot, onion, stick of celery, bouquet garni, peppercorns and cloves. Cover the ham with water and bring it to the boil. Skim, and simmer gently for an hour.

Preheat the oven to Reg 4/350°F, 180°C. Lift out the ham, remove the rind and let it cool slightly.

Melt the butter in a large flameproof casserole on a low heat. Put in the onion and celery and cook them gently until they are beginning to soften. Pour in the stock. Spread the honey all over the ham. Set the ham on top of the vegetables, put in the apricots and put the uncovered casserole into the oven for an hour.

To serve, carve the ham and arrange it on a warm serving dish. Moisten it with a little of the stock. Put the apricots on top of the ham and the celery and onion down the side.

Apricots stuffed with ham make an attractive salad.

Stuffed apricots with ham

4 fairly ripe apricots, stoned and halved
4 oz (100 gr) lean ham
4 oz (100 gr) either cream cheese or curd cheese
chopped lettuce and cress for serving

Either cut the ham into tiny pieces or mince it, and blend it with the cheese. Sandwich large amounts between the apricot halves and serve arranged on the lettuce and cress bed.

As they are fairly sharp, apricots can be cooked with fresh pork as well as ham; they can also be cooked with cabbage as an accompaniment to roast pork.

Pork chops and apricots

4 pork chops, trimmed
2 tablespoons melted pork fat *or* ½ oz (13 gr) butter
1 large onion, sliced

4 sticks celery, diced
1 clove garlic, finely chopped
¼ pint (1·5 dl) dry cider
8 apricots, stoned and quartered

Heat the fat in a large frying pan on a high heat and brown the chops on both sides in this. Lower the heat and add the onion, celery and garlic and cook them until they are soft. Pour in the cider and bring it to the boil on a slightly higher heat. Put the chops back in the pan with the apricot quarters on top, season, cover and simmer gently for 35 minutes.

╗ ╗ ╗

Primo cabbage is a lovely fresh-tasting leaf vegetable for the summer, and is available all through July. You can serve it hot or cold.

Marinated fish salad with primo cabbage

1½ lb (675 gr) white fish (cod, coley, haddock), skinned
2 kipper fillets, skinned
6 oz (150 gr) button mushrooms, sliced

3 tablespoons olive oil
grated rind and juice of 1 lemon
1 small onion, finely chopped
black pepper
½ primo cabbage (without the outer leaves), shredded

½ cucumber
1 dessertspoon lemon juice
5 tablespoons mayonnaise
2 tablespoons chopped fennel leaves

Mix the oil, lemon rind and juice, onion and pepper together, and put in a flat dish. Remove bones from the white fish and the kipper fillets. Put the fish and the mushrooms in the marinade, laying the fish cut side down and brushing the top as well. Leave for four hours, turning occasionally.

While the fish is marinating, cook the cabbage. Blanch it in boiling salted water for two minutes only. Drain and refresh it with cold water and leave it to get quite cold.

Preheat the oven to Reg 4/350°F, 180°C. Take the white fish from the marinade, brushing off all the pieces of onion. Lay it in a lightly greased ovenproof dish and cook it in the oven until it is just done (10 minutes for thin pieces, 15 minutes if they are thicker). Remove it from the oven and allow it to cool completely. Cut the kippers into small strips without cooking them, flake the white fish when cool and mix both with the mushrooms from the marinade, and about one tablespoon of the chopped onion.

Peel the cucumber and cut it into quarters lengthways. Take out the seeds and chop it into half-inch pieces. Toss the cucumber with the cabbage and lemon juice. Mix the mayonnaise into the fish and mushrooms and pile them on top of the cabbage and cucumber. Strew the fennel over the top.

Primo cabbage and apricots

1 primo cabbage, with the outer
  leaves discarded, shredded
1 oz (25 gr) butter
6 apricots, quartered and stoned
1 medium onion, sliced
¼ pint (1·5 dl) stock

Preheat the oven to Reg 4/350°F, 180°C.
In a heavy flameproof casserole, melt the butter on a low heat and cook the onion slowly in this until it is soft. Stir the cabbage and apricots into the onion. Pour in the stock and bring it to the boil. Cover the casserole and put it into the oven for 45 minutes.

Primo cabbage and green peppers

½ primo cabbage (or 1 very small
  one), shredded
2 tablespoons olive oil
1 green pepper, finely diced
6 spring onions, finely chopped
1 clove garlic, finely chopped

Gently heat the olive oil on a very low heat in a heavy saucepan. Stir in the vegetables and two tablespoons of cold water. Cover tightly and cook on the same low heat for 30 minutes, shaking the pan occasionally and checking towards the end that the cabbage is not sticking. Only if really necessary add more water by the tablespoon.

Primo cabbage with cucumber and tomatoes

1 primo cabbage, shredded	½ lb (225 gr) firm tomatoes,
2 tablespoons olive oil	skinned, deseeded and roughly
½ cucumber, sliced but not peeled	chopped
1 clove garlic, finely chopped	a little sour cream (optional)

Put the olive oil in the bottom of a heavy saucepan, and add the cabbage, the cucumber and the garlic. Season. Cover the pan tightly and set it on a low heat with no other liquid for 20 minutes, shaking occasionally. Stir the tomatoes into the saucepan and heat them through without letting them get mushy.

Serve with small spoonfuls of sour cream on the top, or without.

83　　83　　83

Peas have been in the shops since the second or third week of June, but at the beginning of July they are still small and sweet. They can be simmered gently in only a little water or stock, with a knob of butter and a teaspoon of soft brown sugar, sometimes with chopped mint or parsley added. Or you can use white wine as the cooking liquid.

Buttered peas and lettuce heart

1 lb (450 gr) peas (weighed in their shells), shelled	1 large firm round lettuce heart, sliced
1 oz (25 gr) butter	1 tablespoon chopped parsley
	4 tablespoons white wine

Melt the butter in a wide saucepan on a low heat. Add the peas and cook them gently until they are just tender. When the peas are done, raise the heat and add the lettuce and parsley, Season. pour in the wine and boil to reduce it to a sticky glaze. Serve immediately.

Although they are not quite as extravagant a vegetable as broad beans, a good deal of the weight of peas that you buy is made up by the pods, and it can be rather a tedious business to shell enough to produce a whole dishful for the table. So it is a good idea to incorporate them into the main dish.

Lamb chops and green peas

4 good-sized lamb chops
1 lb (450 gr) peas (weighed in their shells)
4 flat anchovy fillets
½ oz (13 gr) butter

1 wineglass white wine
1 tablespoon chopped mint
1 tablespoon chopped parsley
4 small tomatoes for serving

Shell the peas, reserving a few good pods for flavour. Chop the anchovies and pound them to a purée. Melt the butter on a high heat in a heavy frying pan and brown the chops in this. Remove them and set aside. Quickly add the peas to the pan and stir them around to coat them with fat. Pour in the wine, bring to the boil and reduce it a little. Stir in the anchovies, mint, parsley and seasoning. Replace the chops and tuck in the pea pods. Cover tightly and cook on the lowest possible heat for 30 minutes. Discard the pea pods and serve garnished with the tomatoes, cut in half and grilled.

Veal in Marsala with peas

2 lb (900 gr) pie veal, cut into one-inch (2·5 cm) cubes
2 oz (50 gr) butter
¼ lb (225 gr) mushrooms, quartered

2 wineglasses Marsala or sherry
2 lb (900 gr) peas (weighed in their shells), shelled
4 tablespoons double cream

Melt half the butter in a wide-bottomed casserole on a high heat. Brown the meat all over and set it aside. Lower the heat a little and put in the remaining butter. Cook the mushrooms for two minutes and then pour in the Marsala. Bring it to the boil, scraping in any residue in the bottom of the pan. Replace the veal, season, cover and simmer on the lowest heat possible for 45 minutes. Add the peas and continue cooking for a further 15 minutes. Stir in the cream and heat through. Serve with buttered noodles.

Turmeric beef with peas

2 lb (900 gr) stewing beef, cut in one-inch (2·5 cm) cubes
1½ oz (38 gr) butter or beef dripping
2 medium onions, sliced
2 level teaspoons turmeric

¾ pint (4·5 dl) stock
2 lb peas (weighed in their shells), shelled
4 tablespoons sour cream
juice of 1 lemon

Preheat the oven to Reg 4/350°F, 180°C.
Melt the butter or dripping in a heavy flameproof casserole on a high heat. Brown the beef all over in this, and remove it from the casserole. Lower the heat and take off the casserole to cool it a little. Add the sliced onions and the turmeric to the casserole, and cook them slowly until the onions are soft. Blend in the stock and bring it to the boil, stirring. Replace the meat. Cover the casserole and put it in the centre of the oven for an hour. Add the peas to the casserole and put it back for a further 30 minutes. Stir in the cream and lemon juice, check the seasoning, and reheat without boiling.

Cod and peas in beer

4 large cod cutlets
1 medium onion, thinly sliced
1 bayleaf
nutmeg
½ pint (3 dl) bitter beer, or light ale

2 lb (900 gr) peas (weighed in their shells), shelled
1 oz (25 gr) butter
1 heaped tablespoon flour
1 dessertspoon malt vinegar

Preheat the oven to Reg 3/325°F, 170°C.
Lightly butter an ovenproof dish, and lay in the cod cutlets. Scatter over the onion slices and bayleaf, season, and grate the nutmeg over the top. Pour over the beer. Cover with a butter paper, and put into the oven for 25 minutes. Skin the fish, remove the bones and put it on a serving dish to keep warm. Strain the cooking liquid.
   Cook the peas gently in the butter for five minutes in a sauce-

pan. Stir in the flour and blend in the liquid reserved from the fish. Simmer for two minutes. Stir in the vinegar, and pour the sauce over the fish.

Here are two cold recipes for peas. Both of them are ideal for summer lunches and the meat loaf can make up part of a picnic hamper.

A cold dish of peas, ham and eggs

1 lb (450 gr) peas (weighed in their shells), shelled
4 eggs
1 tablespoon wine vinegar
a pinch of ground mace
a pinch of ground cloves
1 tablespoon chopped parsley
1 tablespoon chopped chervil (if you have no chervil, use 2 tablespoons parsley)
1 oz (25 gr) butter
6 oz (150 gr) lean ham, diced into quarter-inch (6 mm) pieces
1 small lettuce for serving

Beat the eggs with the vinegar, spices and herbs. Melt the butter in a small saucepan on a low heat. Put in the peas, cover them and let them simmer for 10 minutes. Add the cubes of ham, cover the pan again, and continue to cook for a further five minutes. Take off the lid and pour in the egg mixture. Keep stirring on the low heat until the egg solidifies like ordinary scrambled eggs. Check the seasoning and turn the mixture on to a plate to cool. Line a bowl with lettuce leaves and when the salad is cool, pile it on the top.

Beef and pea loaf

1 lb (450 gr) good minced beef
1 lb (450 gr) peas (weighed in their shells), shelled
1 large onion, finely chopped
1 oz (25 gr) butter
for the sauce:
4 tablespoons mayonnaise
4 tablespoons sour cream
grated rind of ½ lemon
1 tablespoon grated horseradish
1 tablespoon sour cream
2 tablespoons chopped parsley

2 tablespoons grated horseradish
juice of ½ lemon

Preheat the oven to Reg 4/350°F, 180°C.
Melt the butter in a small saucepan on a low heat and stir in the

peas and onion. Cover them and let them simmer for 10 minutes. Meanwhile put the beef into a large bowl and beat in the lemon rind, horseradish, sour cream and parsley. When the peas and onion are cooked thoroughly mix these into the meat as well. Pack the mixture into a 2 lb (900 gr) loaf tin and bake in the centre of the oven for an hour. Let it cool completely before turning out.

Blend all the ingredients for the sauce together. Serve the loaf cut in slices and the sauce separately.

Towards the end of July, peas grow larger and lose their original tender sweetness. This is the time to purée them down for soups or to make them into a soufflé.

Pea soufflé

1 lb (450 gr) old peas (weighed in their shells), shelled
½ pint (3 dl) stock
bouquet garni
1 oz (25 gr) butter
1 teaspoon turmeric
6 spring onions, chopped

1 tablespoon flour
1 tablespoon chopped chervil
1 tablespoon chopped coriander
(or 2 tablespoons of either of the above or 2 tablespoons parsley)
2 oz (50 gr) chopped salami
4 eggs, separated

Preheat the oven to Reg 5/375°F, 190°C and prepare a six-inch (15 cm) soufflé dish.

Put the peas into a saucepan with the stock and bouquet garni and cook, covered, on a moderate heat for 15 minutes. Work them in the blender or rub them through a sieve. Melt the butter in a saucepan on a low heat. Stir in the turmeric and spring onions and cook them until the onions are beginning to soften. Stir in the flour and take the pan off the heat. Blend in the pea liquid, replace the pan on the heat and bring the mixture to the boil, stirring. When it is thick remove it from the heat and stir in the herbs, salami and seasoning. Allow it to cool a little before beating in the egg yolks. Whip the whites until they are stiff and fold them into the rest with a metal spoon. Quickly pour the mixture into the prepared dish, and bake in the centre of the oven for 30 minutes.

If the peas have unblemished shells, it seems a pity to waste them. Two of the best pods can be added to the saucepan when cooking peas or they can be boiled with a sprig of mint with new potatoes. This soup will make good use of a large quantity of pods.

Pea-pod and bacon soup

the pods from 1-1½ lb (450-675 gr)
  peas
1½ pints (9 dl) stock
1 small onion, sliced
bouquet garni

½ oz (13 gr) butter
4 oz (100 gr) lean bacon, diced
1 small onion, finely chopped
1 tablespoon flour
2 tablespoons chopped parsley

Put the pods into a saucepan with the stock, onion and bouquet garni. Cover the pan, bring the stock to the boil and simmer for 30 minutes. Strain. Discard the onion and the bouquet garni. Scrape the flesh from the pea pods with a blunt knife and add the flesh to the stock. Melt the butter in a saucepan on a low heat. Add the bacon and onion and cook until brown. Stir in the flour and blend in the pea-pod stock. Check the seasoning. Simmer for ten minutes and add the parsley just before serving.

ಐ   ಐ   ಐ

Fresh young peas look beautiful on a plate alongside the fresh baby carrots which come into the shops in bunches at about the same time. They can be cooked separately or together, as in the following recipes.

Pea and carrot soup

¼lb (225 gr) peas (weighed in their
  shells), shelled
¼ lb (100 gr) baby carrots, sliced
  paper thin
2 oz (50 gr) butter
1 small onion, finely chopped
1 teaspoon soft brown sugar

1 tablespoon flour
1 pint (6 dl) stock
1 wineglass Marsala or sherry
2 tablespoons chopped mint
1 tablespoon chopped parsley
4 tablespoons double cream

Melt the butter on a low heat in a saucepan. Put in the peas, carrots, onion and sugar and cover. Cook them on the same low heat for 20 minutes. Stir in the flour and blend in the stock. Bring it to the boil, stirring. Stir in the Marsala. Add the herbs and seasoning and simmer, covered, for a further ten minutes. Pour the soup into individual serving dishes and swirl a tablespoon of cream into each.

Honey-glazed peas and carrots

1 lb (450 gr) peas (weighed in their shells), shelled
½ lb (225 gr) new carrots
1 tablespoon chopped mint
1 oz (25 gr) butter
¾ pint (4·5 dl) stock
1 dessertspoon honey

If the carrots are large cut them into one-inch (2·5 cm) lengths, if small leave them whole. Put them into cold salted water, bring them to the boil and cook them for one minute. Drain. Put the carrots and peas into a saucepan with the mint and butter and just cover them with the stock. Add the honey. Boil briskly, uncovered, until all the liquid is absorbed and the vegetables are glazed (10–15 minutes). Season if necessary before serving.

This can also be made only with carrots, in which case the preliminary blanching is not necessary.

Peas and carrots together again, this time with chicken: the peas inside as the stuffing and the carrots outside for flavour.

Chicken and summer vegetables

a 3-3½ lb (1·3-1·5 kg) roasting chicken
1 oz (25 gr) butter
1 wineglass white wine
1 wineglass stock
1 lb (450 gr) baby carrots
1 lb (450 gr) baby new potatoes
bouquet garni
flour
½ oz (13 gr) kneaded butter
1 tablespoon chopped parsley

for the stuffing
1 oz (25 gr) butter
1 lb (450 gr) peas (weighed in their shells), shelled
1 small onion, finely chopped
2 tablespoons granary breadcrumbs
2 tablespoons chopped parsley
1 tablespoon white wine

Preheat the oven to Reg 3/325°F, 170°C.

First make the stuffing. Melt the butter in a small saucepan on a low heat and cook the peas and onion in this, covered, until the onion is soft. Stir in the breadcrumbs, parsley and a tablespoon of wine. Season, stuff the chicken with this mixture and truss it.

Melt the other ounce of butter on a high heat in a large flameproof casserole. Brown the trussed chicken all over, taking care not to damage the skin when turning it. Pour in the wine and stock and bring it to the boil. Surround the chicken with the scraped and cleaned carrots and potatoes. If you can't fit enough vegetables into the casserole, cook some separately or cook the carrots in the pot and the potatoes separately. Season, tuck in the bouquet garni, cover and put in the centre of the oven for an hour.

Take out the casserole and raise the heat to Reg 5/375°F, 190°C. Put the chicken alone on an ovenproof dish, dredge it with flour and put it into the hot oven for 15 minutes to crisp the skin, setting the vegetables aside to keep warm. Strain the sauce from the casserole and skim it if necessary. Put it into a saucepan, bring it to the boil and thicken it slightly with the kneaded butter. Stir in the parsley.

Carve the chicken and arrange it on a dish with spoonfuls of the stuffing on it, surrounded by the carrots and potatoes. Serve the sauce separately.

Peas, carrots and lamb all go into making a delicious cold summer salad.

Jellied lamb salad

3 lb (1·3 kg) leg of lamb
bouquet garni
2 large old carrots
1 stick of celery
1 large onion
1 small turnip (if available)
2 lb (900 gr) peas (weighed in their shells), shelled, and six of the
  best pods
1 bunch new carrots, scrubbed and cut into half-inch (1·25 cm) pieces

for the jelly and the dressing:
1 oz (25 gr) gelatine
1 wineglass sherry
1 egg white for clarifying
4 whole mint leaves
1 tablespoon chopped mint
1 tablespoon chopped capers
5 fluid oz (1·5 dl) plain yoghurt
3 tablespoons mayonnaise

Put the bouquet garni, the old carrots, celery, onion, turnip and pea pods into a large saucepan or casserole big enough to hold the lamb, with enough water to cover it. Season well with salt and ground black pepper. Bring them to the boil on a moderate heat and simmer for ten minutes to flavour the liquid. Put in the leg of lamb and barely simmer for 1½ hours.

Meanwhile, tie the peas loosely in a piece of muslin or a muslin bag. Put them into the pan for the last 20 minutes of cooking. Lift out the lamb and the bag of peas. Put in the baby carrots and cook them until they are tender (about 25 minutes). Strain the stock, reserving all the baby carrots, and allow the lamb and stock to cool completely. Remove all the fat from the lamb and cut the meat into half-inch (1.25 cm) dice.

Skim all the fat from the surface of the stock, and take one pint of the stock to make the jelly. Soak the gelatine in the sherry until it melts. Set the stock on a moderate heat and when it is warm stir in the gelatine. Lightly beat the egg white and beat it downwards into the stock until it boils and rises up the sides of the pan. Remove the pan from the heat and let the stock settle. Return it to the heat and boil it up again without beating. Strain it through a scalded tea cloth. It is not essential to clarify the stock like this but it does make the final dish more attractive if the jelly is crystal clear.

Lightly oil a 2 lb (900 gr) loaf tin. Pour the liquid jelly into the tin until it is about quarter of an inch (6 mm) deep and put it in the refrigerator to set. Arrange the whole mint leaves decoratively on the top of the jelly. Mix the lamb with the chopped mint and capers and fill the tin with it, pressing down a little so it is fairly tightly packed. Cover with the rest of the jelly and leave it until it is completely set, before turning out.

Mix together the yoghurt and mayonnaise. Combine the cooked peas and baby carrots and coat them in the dressing. Surround the jellied lamb with the vegetables to serve.

❁   ❁   ❁

And now some recipes for carrots on their own and in various meat dishes.

Glazed lemon carrots

1 bunch of new carrots, trimmed
½ oz (13 gr) butter
1 teaspoon soft brown sugar
½ pint (3 dl) stock
1 tablespoon chopped mint
juice of ¼ lemon

Put the carrots into a pan with the butter and sugar. Barely cover them with the stock. Bring them to the boil and cook uncovered on a moderate heat until all the liquid has been absorbed and the carrots are glazed. Stir in the mint and lemon juice, season if necessary, and simmer for a further two minutes.

Beef and carrot mould

1 lb (450 gr) shin of beef
1 bunch new carrots, scrubbed
  and cut in half-inch pieces
6 cloves
6 allspice berries
6 black peppercorns

2 blades mace
1 bayleaf
1 small onion, peeled and cut in
  half
¼ pint (1·5 dl) sherry

Preheat the oven to Reg 4/350°F, 180°C.
Remove any fat from the edges of the beef and reserve it. Cut the lean meat into half-inch (1·25 cm) cubes. Lightly grease an earthenware casserole with dripping. Put in the beef and carrots together with the spices, seasonings, bayleaf and onion and the

fat trimmings. Pour in the sherry and cook in the oven in a bain marie for 2½ hours.

Strain the contents of the casserole and remove the onion, all the pieces of fat and the spices. Put the beef and carrots into a metal mould. Pour over the strained juices and leave in the refrigerator until set. Turn out and serve with horseradish sauce.

A ring mould makes this an attractive dish – you can fill the centre with cooked peas, or any other summer vegetable.

Carrot salad

1 bunch new carrots, whole if they are very small or cut into one-inch (2·5 cm) lengths
1 sprig mint

1 tablespoon mayonnaise
1 tablespoon plain yoghurt
1 teaspoon Dijon mustard
1 teaspoon chopped capers

Boil the carrots in salted water with the sprig of mint until they are just tender. Drain them well and let them steam a little to dry. Blend the mayonnaise and yoghurt together, beat in the mustard and add the capers. Mix the carrots into the dressing while they are still warm and leave until they are quite cool.

Lamb in the pot with mint

1 shoulder of lamb, boned
3 tablespoons chopped mint and 2 whole sprigs of mint
1 oz (25 gr) butter
½ pint (3 dl) stock

1 bunch of new carrots, trimmed and left whole if small, or cut into one-inch (2·5 cm) lengths
1 lb (450 gr) very small new potatoes, scraped
1 heaped tablespoon flour
1 tablespoon chopped capers

Preheat the oven to Reg 4/350°F, 180°C.
Strew the cut surfaces of the lamb with the chopped mint. Roll up the meat and tie it with strong thread or fine cotton string. In a large flameproof casserole melt the butter on a high heat. Brown the lamb all over and pour in the stock. Bring it quickly to the boil. Tuck in the sprigs of mint, season, cover and put into the oven for 15 minutes. Add the vegetables to the pot and

put it back for an hour. Remove the vegetables and lamb and keep them warm.

Strain the stock and skim it, retaining the fat. Put one table-spoon of the fat back in the casserole on a moderate heat on top of the stove. Blend in the flour and then the skimmed juices from the casserole. Bring to the boil, stirring. Add the chopped capers and simmer for two minutes.

To serve, carve the lamb and arrange it on a warm serving dish. Pour over the sauce and arrange the vegetables round the meat.

Chervil chicken

a 3-3½ lb (1·3-1·5 kg) roasting chicken
2 wineglasses white wine
1 oz (25 gr) butter or
   3 tablespoons chicken fat
3 sprigs of chervil and
   4 tablespoons chopped chervil

1 bunch new carrots, cut into half-inch (1·25 cm) pieces
1 cauliflower broken into small florets
½ oz (13 gr) kneaded butter
1 egg yolk
1 lb (450 gr) spinach for serving, if available

Preheat the oven to Reg 4/350°F, 180°C.
Truss the chicken, putting one sprig of chervil inside. Heat the fat on a moderate heat in a large flameproof casserole. Brown the chicken all over, turning it carefully so as not to break the skin. Pour in the wine and bring it to the boil. Tuck in the remaining sprigs of chervil and arrange the carrots and cauli-flower around the chicken. Season, cover and put into the oven for 1½ hours.

Meanwhile cook the spinach and chop it finely. Arrange it on a warm serving dish as a bed for the chicken and keep it warm. Remove the chicken from the casserole and cut it into serving pieces. Arrange them on top of the spinach and keep them warm. Put the vegetables from the casserole into another serving dish to keep warm.

Strain the juices from the casserole into a saucepan and skim them if necessary. Thicken them with a very little kneaded butter and simmer for one minute, stirring. Work the egg yolk in a bowl and gradually add about four tablespoons of the hot liquid. Blend this mixture into the juices in the saucepan and reheat but do not boil. Stir in the chopped chervil and spoon the sauce over the chicken before serving. Serve the vegetables separately.

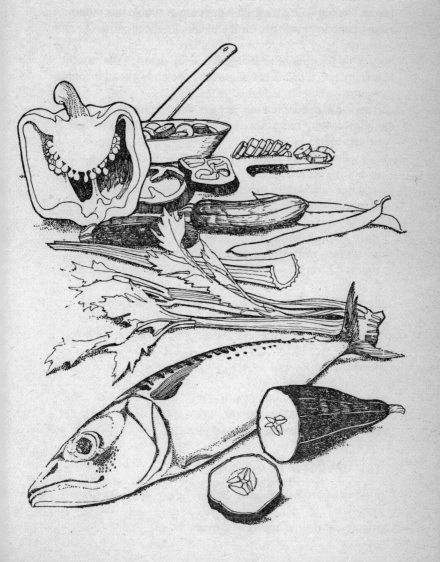

Vegetables available in August

beans, broad – very old tough ones at the beginning of the
  month
beans, French – English grown ones are available this month
beans, runner – more plentiful and usually cheaper than French
  beans
beetroot – bunches of little round ones all through the month
cabbage – green primo cabbages are crisp and firm all through
  August
carrots – still in bunches and getting slightly larger
cauliflower – not many about in August, partly because there is
  little demand
celery – the first new English celery comes into the shops at the
  end of the month
courgettes – plentiful supplies of young, tender ones
cucumbers – smooth or ridge
marrows – long ones and small round ones are in the shops all
  through the month
mushrooms – during August field mushrooms can be found
  unless it is very dry, and in some places they may be available
  in shops
onions – the new crop at last, still very small but good and
  sound
peas – none are available at the beginning of the month but
  later the second Lincolnshire crop comes into the shops;
  there are far fewer than in July
peppers – in abundance
swede – right at the end of the month
radishes – large and firm all through August
tomatoes – at their best and most plentiful

Fruit available in August

apples – the first new English eating and cooking varieties are
  ripe
apricots – at the beginning of the month only

blackberries – wild and cultivated ones are available from the middle of August

citrus fruit – very pithy and hardly worth buying

damsons – these usually are ripe enough to pick by the end of the month

gooseberries – there are still a few around in the first week

peaches – large and ripe throughout August

plums – several varieties come into the shops

Fresh herbs available in August

All the herbs should be growing fast and furiously in August

☓ ☓ ☓

August is another productive and exciting month. Its colours and flavours are the rich bright ones of the Mediterranean countries to match the hot weather and our holiday mood.

Tomatoes are plentiful throughout August, firm and sweet and really best eaten raw. The herb which complements them best is basil and if you have been successful in growing this at all (it is exceedingly difficult) you should be able to get enough in August for a few salads. The simpler the better is the rule with tomatoes – they need only a very little dressing, added just before they are served, otherwise they become too pulpy. Tomato salads can be served with the main course of the meal on their own or dressed up a little more as first courses. The next two salads with eggs make ideal starters in hot weather.

Egg and tomato salad

2 hard-boiled eggs, finely chopped
8 spring onions, chopped
1 dessertspoon Dijon mustard
8 tomatoes, sliced into rounds
2 tablespoons chopped basil, or tarragon or even parsley
olive oil

Mix the eggs with the onions and mustard, and arrange them in the centre of a dinner plate. Arrange the tomatoes round the eggs. Scatter the basil over the tomatoes, season them and dress simply with about two drops of olive oil on each tomato slice.

Egg-stuffed tomatoes

4 large firm tomatoes, skinned
4 ripe tomatoes, skinned and
  chopped
1 oz (25 gr) butter
4 eggs
4 tablespoons chopped parsley

Cut the tops off the firm tomatoes and reserve them. Scoop out all the flesh from the centres and keep for a sauce or a soup. Melt the butter in a saucepan on a moderate heat. Add the chopped ripe tomatoes and cook them until they are mushy. Beat the eggs with salt and pepper and stir them into the pan. Keep stirring them all the time until they are lightly set like scrambled eggs. Remove them from the heat immediately and allow them to cool.

Pile the egg mixture into the hollowed-out tomatoes and arrange them on a plate with any egg that is left over spooned round them. Set the caps back on top and strew over the chopped parsley. Serve slightly chilled with brown toast.

Grilled tomatoes

As a hot vegetable on their own, tomatoes are best put under a hot grill for a few minutes. Their flavour can be varied by sprinkling different chopped fresh herbs over them – thyme or rosemary if they are to go with lamb, sage for pork and tarragon for chicken.

Other possible garnishes are: chopped spring onions with a little grated Parmesan cheese; cream cheese mixed with crushed garlic and black pepper; a chopped anchovy fillet on each tomato half; chopped black or green olives. A hunt through your store cupboard will produce many more ideas.

Cooking with tomatoes is expensive for most of the year, but not in August. These next recipes call for firm tomatoes, which are just as cheap now as the squashy ones were in May.

Plaice and tomatoes

8 plaice fillets
juice of 1 lemon
8 firm tomatoes, skinned
4 tablespoons mixed chopped
  thyme and parsley
1 wineglass white wine

1 oz (25 gr) butter
1 tablespoon flour
1 dessertspoon tomato purée
2 tablespoons chopped parsley
raw tomato quarters for garnish

Skin the fillets and lay them flat. Sprinkle over the lemon juice and let them stand for 30 minutes.

Preheat the oven to Reg 4/350°F, 180°C. Deseed the tomatoes and put the seeds in a sieve over a bowl. Rub them with a wooden spoon to extract the juice and reserve it. Chop the flesh of the tomatoes. Strew each plaice fillet with the thyme and parsley. Put the chopped tomatoes on the wide end of each one and roll them up. Put the fillets in a buttered ovenproof dish with their tails tucked under. Pour over the wine, season, cover with a butter paper and put them into the oven for 15 minutes.

Remove the fillets and put them on to a serving dish to keep warm. Strain the liquid and reserve it. Melt the butter in a saucepan on a moderate heat. Stir in the flour and the tomato purée and blend in the reserved liquid and the tomato juice. Bring it to the boil and stir until it is thick and bubbly. Stir in the parsley and pour the sauce over the fish. Garnish with quartered raw tomatoes.

Mackerel with white wine and tomatoes

4 small mackerel
4 tablespoons white wine
1½ tablespoons wine vinegar
4 tablespoons chopped fennel

1 large onion, sliced into rings
1 lb (450 gr) tomatoes, skinned
  and cut into rounds

Preheat the oven to Reg 4/350°F, 180°C.
Fillet the mackerel and lay them flat on a buttered ovenproof open dish. Pour over the wine and vinegar and scatter over the fennel and onion rings. Lay the tomatoes on top of the onions. Season, and bake in the oven for 20 minutes.

Sauté of beef with tomatoes and olives

4 slices top rump, about half an
   inch (1·25 cm) thick
1½ oz (38 gr) butter
½–¾ pint (3-4·5 dl) brown sauce
   (page 12)
2 tablespoons Worcestershire
   sauce

6 firm tomatoes, skinned,
   deseeded and cut into strips
16 green olives, stoned and cut
   lengthways
2 tablespoons chopped parsley

Melt the butter in a heavy frying pan on a high heat. Brown the
beef very fast on both sides and cook it until it is tender, turning
several times and keeping the heat as high as possible. Pour off
all but a thin film of fat, keeping the meat in place. Put the pan
back on the heat and pour in the brown sauce and the Worcestershire sauce. Let it bubble a little, stirring. Lower the heat and
add the tomatoes, olives, parsley and seasoning. Serve the beef
with the sauce poured over it.

Shops and market stalls are often left with so many tomatoes at
the end of the day, particularly on Saturdays, that they have to
sell them off very cheaply indeed. I have often staggered home
with a basketful without any immediate use for them. It is also
now that those with their own crops of tomatoes in the green-
house find themselves with more fruit than they can possibly use
at the time. But tomatoes, or at least their flavour, are so important all the year round that it is well worth making them
into sauces and chutneys to last through the winter.

Spicy tomato sauce

6 lb (2·7 kg) tomatoes, wiped and
   sliced
1½ tablespoons sea salt
3 large onions, sliced

½ pint (3 dl) wine vinegar
4 oz (100 gr) molasses
1 tablespoon ground black pepper
1 teaspoon Tabasco sauce

Put the tomatoes in a large basin in layers, sprinkling them with
the salt. Leave them for two hours.
   Put all the ingredients into a preserving pan. Bring them to

the boil and cook on a low to moderate heat for two hours or until they are thick and pulpy. Put the sauce through the blender or rub it through a sieve. When it is cold put it into either sauce bottles or wine vinegar bottles and screw the lid on tightly.

Tomato, apple and pepper chutney

4 lb (1·8 kg) ripe tomatoes, skinned and halved
4 green peppers, chopped
grated rind of 2 small oranges
grated rind and juice of 2 lemons
½ pint (3 dl) white malt vinegar
5 oz (125 gr) soft brown sugar

1½ oz (38 gr) sea salt
1 teaspoon ground black pepper
1 teaspoon ground mace
1 teaspoon ground ginger
4 tart eating apples (English ones are available by the end of the month)

Put the tomato seeds into a sieve and rub them with a wooden spoon to extract all their juice. Put the tomato halves, peppers and tomato juice into a large saucepan or a preserving pan. Add all the rest of the ingredients except the apples. Peel, core and chop the apples last so they do not discolour and immediately add them to the pan and stir everything together. Bring the mixture slowly to the boil and simmer until it is rich and thick (1½–2 hours).

Put the chutney into screw-topped jars and wait until it is cold before covering it.

ෂ ෂ ෂ

We British used to be far more conservative in our eating habits than we are now, and even if we enjoyed the Mediterranean weather which (hopefully) we have in August, we didn't really give much thought to Mediterranean vegetables. However, red and green peppers or pimentoes have become more and more popular and are now grown in this country.

With courgettes, aubergines and tomatoes, they are one of the basic ingredients of ratatouille and they are also often among the ingredients threaded on to skewers for kebabs, where their crisp texture is useful for contrast.

Mackerel kebabs

2 mackerel
¼ lb (100 gr) bacon rashers, diced
¼ lb (100 gr) small mushrooms,
  quartered
1 medium onion, chopped into
  small square pieces
1 large or 2 small green peppers
  chopped into small square pieces

2 bayleaves
2 tablespoons olive oil
juice of 1 lemon
2 tablespoons chopped thyme
freshly ground black pepper
for serving:
1 lettuce, chopped
radishes

Fillet the mackerel and cut the fillets into pieces. Thread these alternately with the bacon, mushrooms, onion slices, peppers and pieces of bayleaf on to the skewers.

Mix together the olive oil and lemon juice and pour it over the kebabs. Strew the kebabs with the thyme, and plenty of pepper. Leave them to stand for two hours.

Preheat the grill to high and grill them for 10–15 minutes, turning them several times. Serve them on a bed of lettuce, garnished with the radishes.

Lamb kebabs

½ shoulder of lamb, cut into
  ¾-inch (2 cm) cubes
2 red peppers, cut into squares
1 large onion, cut into square
  pieces
¼ lb (100 gr) small mushrooms,
  quartered
2 tablespoons olive oil

grated rind and juice of 1 lemon
1 dessertspoon chopped thyme
1 clove garlic, crushed with a
  pinch of salt
cayenne pepper
5 fluid oz (1·5 dl) plain yoghurt
1 cucumber

Thread alternate pieces of lamb, pepper, onion and mushroom on to the skewers. Mix together the oil, lemon rind and juice, thyme, garlic and freshly ground pepper. Pour this over the kebabs and shake over a little cayenne pepper. Leave them to stand for four hours, turning them several times.

Preheat the grill to high. Grill the kebabs in a low position under the heat, turning them several times, until they are cooked through. Serve them on a bed of diced cucumber. Spoon over the yoghurt and sprinkle over a little more cayenne.

Without the yoghurt and the cucumber, these make an excellent picnic meal if left to get cold.

Peppers are used in many ways all over the world. The following recipes are based on methods from China, Italy, Spain and Eastern Europe.

Chinese pork with green peppers

2 lb (900 gr) lean belly of pork, finely diced	2 teaspoons ground ginger
2 tablespoons olive oil	½ teaspoon salt and ground black pepper
2 cloves garlic, chopped	1½ tablespoons cornflour
1 large onion, chopped	1 dessertspoon soy sauce
4 small green peppers, chopped	¾ pint (4·5 dl) stock

Heat the olive oil in a really large frying pan or a paëlla dish or wide-bottomed casserole on a high heat. Add the diced pork and the garlic and cook them until they are brown, moving them around in the pan all the time. Pour off any excess fat, and lower the heat. Add the chopped onion, peppers, ginger, salt and pepper. Stir them in and cook slowly for five minutes. Meanwhile blend the cournflour with the soy sauce and the stock. Pour this mixture into the pan, raise the heat a little to moderate, and keep stirring until the sauce is thick. Serve immediately with fried rice.

Pork chops, peppers and anchovies

4 pork chops	2 green peppers, deseeded and sliced
10 anchovy fillets	
1 large or 2 small cloves garlic, chopped	2 red peppers, deseeded and sliced
½ oz (13 gr) lard or pork fat	2 wineglasses red wine

Pound the anchovies and garlic together with a pestle and mortar. Melt the lard in a heavy frying pan on a moderate heat and brown the chops on both sides. Remove them and set them aside. Pour off all but a thin film of fat from the pan. Pour in the wine and bring it to the boil. Stir in the anchovies and garlic. Replace the chops and put in the peppers. Season. Cover the pan and simmer for 25 minutes.

Pork chops and red peppers

4 pork chops
½ oz (13 gr) lard or pork fat
3 red peppers (or 4 if they are very small), deseeded and sliced
6 tablespoons stock

1 wineglass white wine
2 tablespoons wine vinegar
1 large clove garlic, crushed with a pinch of salt

Melt the lard in a frying pan on a high heat. Brown the chops in this on both sides. Lower the heat and continue to fry the chops until they are half cooked. Remove them and set them aside. Add the peppers to the pan and cook them for a few minutes. Raise the heat and pour in the stock, wine and wine vinegar. Bring them to the boil, scraping in any residue from the bottom of the pan. Replace the chops and add the crushed garlic and seasoning. Lower the heat, cover and simmer for 20 minutes.

Skirt of beef with red peppers

1½ lb (675 gr) beef skirt, cut into one-inch (2·5 cm) cubes
4 tablespoons olive oil
1 large onion, finely chopped
1 large clove garlic, finely chopped
1 dessertspoon dill seeds

1 dessertspoon paprika
1 dessertspoon flour
¼ pint (1·5 dl) white wine
7 fluid oz (2 dl) stock
2 large red peppers, deseeded and sliced

Heat the oil in a sauté pan on a high heat. When it is smoking, put in the beef and brown the cubes all over. Remove the meat and lower the heat. Allow the fat to cool a little if necessary before stirring in the onion, garlic, dill and paprika. Cook them gently until the onion is soft. Stir in the flour and blend in the wine and stock. Bring to the boil, stirring, and replace the meat. Cover the pan and simmer gently for 45 minutes. Add the peppers to the pan, check the seasoning and continue cooking for a further 15 minutes.

Peppers are often stuffed with various mixtures, usually with meat to make a main dish. They can also make very attractive first courses.

Red peppers with anchovy and mushroom filling

2 medium red peppers, halved and deseeded
2 tablespoons olive oil
6 oz (150 gr) mushrooms, finely chopped
12 black olives, chopped small
4 flat anchovy fillets, finely chopped

1 clove garlic, chopped
1 tablespoon chopped mixed thyme and marjoram
juice of ½ lemon
4 thin slices Gruyère cheese, or Cheddar

Blanch the peppers in boiling salted water for three minutes. Drain them well and keep them warm. Heat the oil in a frying pan and quickly cook the mushrooms for two minutes, stirring. Stir in the olives, anchovies, garlic and herbs. Add the lemon juice and bring it to the boil. Remove the pan from the heat and put the mixture into the pepper halves. Season, and top with the slices of cheese. Grill them under a high heat until the cheese has melted.

Green peppers stuffed with spicy cheese

2 small green peppers, halved and deseeded
4 oz (100 gr) curd cheese
1 teaspoon paprika
a few drops Tabasco sauce, or a pinch of cayenne

4 tablespoons chopped chervil or parsley
4 firm tomatoes, skinned, deseeded and chopped very small

Blend the cheese with the paprika, Tabasco and chervil. Add the tomatoes to the cheese mixture, season and pile the mixture into the halved peppers.

ひ   ひ   ひ

Courgettes, or baby marrows, are one of my favourite vegetables, succulent but not pulpy or watery and with a much more definite flavour of their own than large marrows.

Sautéed courgettes with Parmesan cheese

1½ lb (675 gr) courgettes, sliced into half-inch (1·25 cm) rounds
1 oz (25 gr) butter
2 tablespoons grated Parmesan cheese

Sauté the courgettes gently in the butter until one side is just brown. Turn them over and immediately sprinkle on some Parmesan cheese so that while the other side is browning it can melt on the flesh. Season with plenty of salt and black pepper.

Here are two ways of grilling courgettes.

Grilled courgette slices

1½ lb (675 gr) small courgettes, cut in four lengthways slices
a little melted butter
2 tablespoons grated cheese
2 tablespoons chopped chives

Season the courgette slices, brush them with the melted butter and put them under a preheated grill until they are golden brown on one side. Turn them over and scatter over the grated cheese and chives. Put them back under the grill until the cheese is melted and bubbly.

Grilled courgettes with mustard

1 lb (675 gr) small courgettes, cut in half lengthways
a little melted butter
1 tablespoon Meaux mustard, or 1 dessertspoon Dijon mustard

Brush the courgettes with melted butter and put them cut side down on a heated grill pan. Put them under a high heat until they are just beginning to brown. Turn them over, season them, and spread them with the mustard. Put them back under the grill until they are golden.

Parmesan cheese can be used with the Dijon mustard but Meaux mustard is best used alone.

Courgettes can also be baked in the oven – a good idea if you are going to serve them with roast or braised meat.

Baked courgettes

6 courgettes, cut in half-inch (1·25 cm) diagonal slices
juice of 1 lemon
4 tablespoons mixed chopped herbs

Preheat the oven to Reg 4/350°F, 180°C and thickly butter a large ovenproof dish.
Lay the courgettes in the dish and season them. Sprinkle over the lemon juice and strew over the herbs. Cover with foil and bake in the oven for an hour.

Courgettes stuffed with herbs

4 medium courgettes
2 tablespoons mixed chopped herbs
2 tablespoons grated Parmesan cheese

Preheat the oven to Reg 5/375°F, 190°C and coat a piece of foil with oil.
Wrap the courgettes in the foil, and put them into the oven for 30 minutes. When they are cooked cut them in half lengthways. Scoop out the centre flesh, chop it finely and mix it with the herbs. Put the mixture back into the shells, season, and scatter the cheese over them. Put them into a lightly greased ovenproof dish and return them to the oven until the cheese has melted.

The vegetables that go best with courgettes are tomatoes, mushrooms and onions, either all together or separately.

Courgettes with tomatoes

6 courgettes, peeled and cut in four lengthways
½ lb (225 gr) tomatoes, skinned, deseeded and chopped
1 oz (25 gr) butter   1 clove garlic, chopped

Heat the butter in a frying pan on a low heat and sauté the courgettes until they are just tender (10 minutes). Raise the heat, add the tomatoes, garlic and seasoning to the pan and cook them until the tomatoes are pulpy.

Courgettes and mushrooms

6 small courgettes, sliced
¼ lb (100 gr) mushrooms, sliced
1½ oz (38 gr) butter

juice of ½ lemon
2 tablespoons chopped parsley

Put all the ingredients into a heavy sauté pan, season, cover and set on a low heat for 15 minutes.

Sauté of courgettes and onions

6 small courgettes, sliced into
    quarter-inch (6 mm) rounds
1 medium onion, thinly sliced
1 clove garlic, chopped

2 tablespoons chopped parsley
1 oz (25 gr) butter
¼ pint (1·5 dl) boiling water

Melt the butter on a low heat in a frying pan and sauté the onion and garlic until the onion is soft. Add the courgettes and stir them around until they are coated with butter. Season, cover, raise the heat a little, and cook until both the courgettes and onions are golden.

Uncover and raise the heat to high. Pour in the boiling water and add the parsley. Cook rapidly, until all the moisture is absorbed.

Courgettes cooked with onions can also be used as the basis of a very tasty omelette which can be served either hot as a lunch or supper dish or cold for a picnic.

Courgette omelette

6 courgettes, cooked with onions, as above
a little diced cold ham or chicken (optional)
6 eggs

Allow the courgettes and onions to cool. Beat the eggs in a bowl and stir in the courgettes and the meat if you are using it. Heat a little oil in an omelette pan on a moderate heat and stir in the mixture, spreading it evenly round the pan. Continue to cook, scraping up the edges to let as much of the mixture as possible run under to the heat.

When the omelette is almost firm, put the pan under a high grill for a few minutes. Sprinkle over some Parmesan cheese and continue to cook it until it is golden brown.

৪৪   ৪৪   ৪৪

Imported French beans are available through most of the summer, and English grown ones are in the shops in late July and August. They are best cooked in a saucepan with chopped thyme or savory, a tiny pinch of salt and an inch of water, covered and set on a low heat for 20 minutes. Add a knob of butter while they are cooking or toss them in melted butter when they are done.

If the beans are cooked without butter, they can be mixed with French dressing or mayonnaise for salads; or chopped and put into omelettes, quiches or other egg dishes.

Herring and French bean salad

4 herrings
4 oz (100 gr) lean bacon, finely
  chopped
4 flat anchovy fillets, finely
  chopped
for the dressing:
2 tablespoons olive oil
1 tablespoon wine vinegar
1 clove garlic, crushed with a pinch of salt
black pepper
8 green olives, stoned and quartered
tomato slices for garnish

3 tablespoons chopped lemon
  thyme or thyme
1 lb (450 gr) French beans

Preheat the oven to Reg 4/350°F, 180°C.
Slit the herrings down the belly, clean them and remove the

heads. Remove the back fins and the backbone but keep them joined down the back. Scatter the bacon and anchovies on one side of the fish. Sprinkle two tablespoons of the thyme over the top. Fold over the other side of the fish and reshape. Put the herrings into a greased ovenproof dish, cover them with foil, and bake in the oven for 30 minutes. Remove them from the oven and allow them to cool completely in the dish, still covered.

Meanwhile top and tail the beans and cook them without butter as described above, with the remaining thyme. Drain them and allow them to cool. Mix the oil, vinegar, garlic and pepper together and toss the beans and olives in this dressing, reserving one tablespoon. Keeping the herrings still folded, slice them in diagonal slices. Arrange the beans in a serving dish. Put the herring slices on the top and drip over the rest of the dressing. Garnish with tomato slices.

French bean supper

1 lb (450 gr) French beans   4 oz (100 gr) lean ham, diced
1 tablespoon chopped savory   6 eggs, beaten

Preheat the oven to Reg 4/350°F, 180°C and butter a round ovenproof dish.
Cook the beans with the savory according to the basic method (above), lay them in the dish, and scatter the diced ham over them. Beat the eggs together and pour them over the beans and ham. Season. Bake in the oven for 30 minutes, when it should be set and golden brown and able to be lifted easily from the dish.

♛   ♛   ♛

Coming along with French beans, and far more plentiful, are English runner beans. The shops are full of them all through the month and they always seem to be in just as good condition at the end as at the beginning.

Beans have a high moisture content, so if they are cooked for some time in rapidly boiling water they lose a good deal of their colour and flavour. Instead try the following basic recipe. Don't be put off by the lack of water – beans really will make their own.

Green beans with savory

1 lb (450 gr) runner beans, sliced	1 tablespoon chopped savory, or
1 oz (25 gr) butter	thyme or marjoram
1 medium onion, thinly sliced	4 tablespoons water

Melt the butter in a saucepan on a low heat and cook the onions in it until they are soft. Stir in the beans and the savory and seasonings and add the water. Cover tightly and simmer for 15 minutes.

My favourite way of cooking runner beans is to vary this recipe by the addition of two rashers of bacon. Finely chop the onion and bacon, and cook them in the butter until they are beginning to brown. Add the beans, herbs and water and carry on as above.

Spicy sausages can be used instead of bacon, and the next recipe makes a richer dish.

Green beans and sausage

1 lb (450 gr) runner beans, sliced	6 oz (150 gr) spicy sausage
½ oz (13 gr) butter	(Metwurst, Cabanos or Chorizo)
1 medium onion, sliced	cut into quarter-inch (6 mm)
1 dessertspoon paprika	slices
¼ pint (1·5 dl) stock	

Melt the butter in a saucepan on a low heat. Stir in the onion and paprika and cook gently until the onion is soft. Off the heat, blend in the stock and mix in the beans and sausage. Season, and set the pan back on the heat. Simmer very gently, covered, for 30 minutes.

Using oil instead of butter, the same method can be used to make a salad which can be eaten hot or cold.

Green bean salad

1 lb (450 gr) runner beans, sliced	1 large clove garlic, finely
4 tablespoons olive oil	chopped
1 large onion, thinly sliced	2 tablespoons wine vinegar

Heat the oil in a saucepan on a moderate heat. Stir in the beans, onion and garlic. Cover tightly and cook on a very low heat for 20 minutes, shaking the pan occasionally. Uncover and raise the heat. Stir in the vinegar, bring it to the boil and continue to boil until any liquid in the pan is reduced. Season, and serve hot immediately, or let it cool and serve it as a salad.

For a more substantial dish, beans can be mixed with potatoes.

Potatoes and beans boulangère

1½ lb (675 gr) new potatoes, scraped and cut into very thin rounds
salt, pepper
1½ lb (675 gr) runner beans, sliced

2 tablespoons chopped spring onions
1 tablespoon chopped savory
approx 1 pint (6 dl) stock
½ oz (13 gr) butter

Preheat the oven to Reg 4/350°F, 180°C and lightly butter an ovenproof dish.

Put a layer of potato into the bottom of the dish. Season them with pepper and a little salt, and strew some of the onion and savory over them. Cover this with a layer of beans. Repeat these layers, finishing with potatoes. Pour in enough stock to come three-quarters of the way up the vegetables and dot the top with butter. Bake for 1¼ hours and serve straight from the dish.

Chopped and cooked in stock, runner beans can make unusual soups. The next two recipes could also be made with any other variety of green bean.

Bean and bacon soup

¾ lb (325 gr) runner beans, chopped very small
6 oz (150 gr) lean bacon, diced
1 oz (25 gr) butter
1 medium onion, finely chopped

1 tablespoon flour
1½ pints (9 dl) stock
2 tablespoons chopped thyme and/or savory

Melt the butter in a saucepan on a low heat. Add the onion and bacon and cook them gently until they are beginning to brown.

Stir in the flour and blend in the stock. Bring to the boil, stirring and add the beans and herbs. Simmer, uncovered, for 20 minutes. Check the seasoning. If the bacon is chopped up very small the soup can be served as it is. Alternatively, work it in the blender and reheat to serve.

Runner bean soup

1 oz (25 gr) butter	1½ pints (9 dl) stock
1 large onion, finely chopped	1 heaped tablespoon flour
¾ lb (325 gr) runner beans, chopped very small	2 tablespoons chopped savory
	1 wineglass sherry

Melt the butter in a saucepan on a low heat and cook the onion in this until it is soft. Stir in the flour and blend in the stock. Bring it to the boil, stirring. Add the prepared beans and savory and simmer for 30 minutes, uncovered. Pour in the sherry, check the seasoning, and reheat to serve.

Here are two ways of using beans in the main dish, both using white wine.

Chicken with beans, celery and tomatoes

a 3-3½ lb (1·3-1·5 kg) roasting chicken, jointed	1 small onion, thinly sliced
1 oz (25 gr) butter	1 wineglass white wine
1 lb (450 gr) runner beans, cut into thin julienne sticks	1 teaspoon tomato purée
4 sticks celery, cut into julienne sticks	bouquet garni
	½ lb (225 gr) firm tomatoes, skinned and roughly chopped

Heat the butter in a large sauté pan or wide-bottomed casserole on a moderate heat. Brown the chicken joints in this, skin-side down first. Remove the chicken and lower the heat. Put in the beans, celery and onion, and stir them around to coat them with butter. Season, cover, and let them sweat for five minutes. Raise the heat again. Pour in the wine and stir in the tomato purée. Bring to the boil, replace the chicken and tuck in the bouquet garni. Cover and simmer gently for 45 minutes.

Remove the bouquet garni from the pan and put the tomatoes on top of the chicken. Cover again and simmer for a further five minutes. Serve the chicken on a bed of vegetables with any juice spooned over the top.

Veal and runner beans

2 lb (900 gr) pie veal, cut into half-inch (1·25 cm) dice
1½ lb (675 gr) runner beans, sliced
1 oz (25 gr) butter
1 large onion, sliced

2 wineglasses white wine
1 dessertspoon Dijon mustard
2 tablespoons mixed chopped thyme and marjoram

Melt the butter on a high heat in a wide-bottomed casserole. Brown the veal in this. Put in the beans and onion, lower the heat and continue cooking until the onion is soft. Add the wine and stir in the mustard, herbs and seasoning. Bring to the boil. Cover and cook on a very low heat for 30 minutes.

❀   ❀   ❀

Cucumbers are in the shops all the year round, but in August, like most salad vegetables, they drop considerably in price and are plentiful. You may also be able to buy the fatter, knobbly outdoor or ridge cucumbers, which have more flavour and substance and are very good served hot as well as in salads and pickles. The herb that goes best with them is dill, another difficult one to grow; but as with basil, if there is any at all in your herb garden it should be there in August. Failing this, tarragon, chervil or parsley can be used.

Ridge cucumber salad

1 ridge cucumber, diced but not peeled
2 hard-boiled eggs
4 tablespoons olive oil

1 dessertspoon Dijon mustard
1 tablespoon wine vinegar
1 tablespoon chopped dill

Rub the egg-yolks through a sieve into a bowl and cream them. Work in the olive oil, drop by drop. Beat in the mustard and add the vinegar, also drop by drop. Season. Chop the egg whites very finely, mix them with the dill and add them to the dressing. Stir the cucumber into the dressing.

Chill before serving either with cold meat, or as a first course with fresh granary bread.

Hot cucumber salad

½ large or 1 small ridge cucumber,
  thinly sliced, but not peeled
4 tablespoons olive oil
1 clove garlic, chopped

1 large Cos lettuce
  heart, shredded
1 tablespoon chopped dill
juice of 1 lemon

Heat the oil on a moderate heat and cook the cucumber and garlic in this until the cucumber is just beginning to soften. Quickly stir in the lettuce and dill and finally the lemon juice. Season, stir about to mix the ingredients and serve immediately with grilled steak or chops.

Lamb chops with cucumber and lettuce

4 lamb chops, boned
1 wineglass white wine
2 tablespoons chopped chervil
2 tablespoons chopped coriander
  leaves

1 teaspoon dill seeds
1 oz (25 gr) butter
1 ridge cucumber, sliced
1 Webb's lettuce heart, shredded
2 tablespoons double cream

Mix the chervil, coriander and dill with the wine and marinate the chops in this for four hours at room temperature. Dry them on kitchen paper when you are ready to cook them, reserving the marinade.

Melt the butter in a large sauté pan on a high heat. Brown the chops on both sides, lower the heat, cover, and continue to cook for ten minutes. Uncover the pan and raise the heat again to evaporate any excess moisture. Set the chops aside on a large serving dish to keep warm.

Keeping the heat high, quickly stir in the cucumber and lettuce. Make sure they are well coated with the pan juices and then stir in the marinade. Boil it to reduce it a little, stir in the cream, and let it bubble a moment. Season. Immediately arrange the vegetables round the chops, pour any excess sauce over them and serve.

Mackerel with cucumbers

4 medium mackerel
1 small ridge cucumber
4 tablespoons olive oil
1 clove garlic, finely chopped

½ lb (225 gr) tomatoes, skinned
    and roughly chopped
1 tablespoon chopped dill
1 tablespoon chopped basil

Fillet the mackerel and cut them into strips about half an inch (1·25 cm) wide. Slice the cucumber.

Heat the oil on a fairly high heat in a large frying pan, and when it is ready put in the mackerel strips. Fry them very quickly until they are only just done, remove them and lower the heat. Put in the cucumber and garlic and cook them until they are beginning to brown. Raise the heat again and add the tomatoes and herbs. Bring them to bubbling point, season, put in the mackerel and carefully mix it in to heat it through. Serve with buttered noodles.

Ridge cucumber with ham, eggs and cheese

1 ridge cucumber, cut into
    half-inch dice
1 oz (25 gr) butter
6 spring onions, chopped
4 hard-boiled eggs, chopped

4 oz (100 gr) lean ham, diced (or
    substitute salami or any kind of
    savoury sausage)
2 oz (50 gr) Cheddar cheese,
    sliced
1 dessertspoon Meaux mustard

Melt the butter in a frying pan on a moderate heat. Cook the cucumber and onions in this until they are just beginning to brown. Stir in the eggs, ham and cheese and heat through, not letting the cheese melt too much. Stir in the mustard and serve at once.

This makes a good lunch dish.

🙚   🙚   🙚

From March, right through the spring and summer, the only eating apples available are foreign ones which often seem rather flavourless, and by July there are only a few home-grown cooking apples available in certain areas and in others none at all. So what a joy it is when in August the first new English apples can be picked. The names are so attractive too – Beauty of Bath, Miller, George Cave, James Grieve, and Grenadier, the first of the cookers. An apple straight from the tree and some strong Cheddar cheese – what could be better? Dice them up with the first of the celery for a salad. Or try these other salad recipes.

Apple and radish salad

2 tart eating apples
20 large radishes
8 oz (225 gr) Derby Sage (or
  Cheddar) cheese

4 tablespoons olive oil
1 dessertspoon Meaux mustard

Chop the apples, radishes and cheese into even-sized pieces. Gradually blend the oil with the mustard, season, and mix the dressing into the salad.

Apple and kipper salad

4 kipper fillets
juice of 2 lemons
4 tart eating apples, finely diced
2 tablespoons horseradish sauce

Skin and dice the fish and soak it in the lemon juice for at least an hour. Mix the apples with the kippers and lemon juice and stir in the horseradish sauce. Serve with brown bread, garnished with cress.

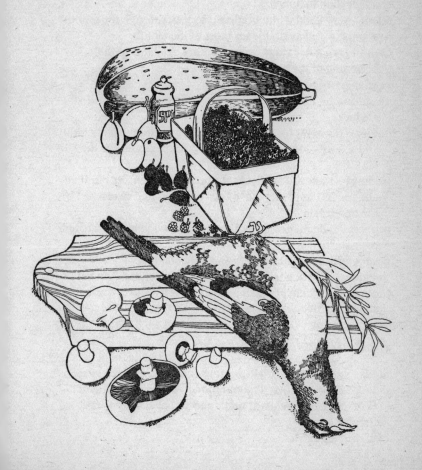

Vegetables available in September

beans, runner – all through the month

beans, French – they are still picked in September but in small quantities

beetroot – small ones in bunches are available

cabbage – primo cabbage finishes and is replaced by Christmas Drumhead. Savoys come in at the end of the month and occasionally red cabbages as well

carrots – these are now maincrop varieties and are sold loose rather than in bunches

celery – very good white English celery all through the month

courgettes – still available for most of the month

cucumbers – a few ridge cucumbers are available at the beginning of the month

vegetable marrow

mushrooms – field mushrooms can be found or bought if you are lucky

onions – the new crop are a good size now, and the baby onions and shallots come into the shops at the beginning of the month

parsnips – these are available all through September but they are best left until they have been softened and sweetened by the first frosts

peppers – red and green English ones are available all through the month

pumpkins – arrive at the very end of September

tomatoes – still in good supply and very sweet and firm

turnips – buy them by the bunch with the leaves on if you can, so you get two vegetables in one

Fruit available in September

apples – all kinds of English eating and cooking apples are in the shops in September. The commonest eating varieties are Worcester Pearmains at first, followed by Cox's Orange Pippins later

blackberries

citrus fruit – not really worth buying in September as it is very
  pithy
damsons
nuts – cob nuts
plums
pomegranates
strawberries – there may be a short-lived second appearance of
  strawberries and raspberries sometime during the month

Fresh herbs available in September

basil – finishes in September
bay
chervil – goes to seed in the beginning of the month, but a
  second crop springs up towards the end
chives – still going strong
coriander – this becomes scrappy towards the end of the month
dill – still producing good leaves
fennel – going to seed and the leaves become straggly
lovage – still rampant
marjoram – still plenty of soft leaves and stems
mint – grows well all through September
parsley – the new crop should come up towards the end of the
  month
rosemary – still has very soft leaves
sage – lots of soft leaves
savory – starts to get a little tougher towards the end of the
  month
tarragon – plenty of soft leaves but the plant becomes straggly
thyme – good soft leaves and tender stems

83   83   83

September is the harvest month, with misty mornings and
golden fields. We tend gradually to turn away from the more
frivolous foods of summer and think instead of the homely
English dishes that have been served at harvest suppers for
centuries.

  Field mushrooms grow up in fields and orchards in the heavy

September dews, with far more flavour than cultivated ones. If
you can only find or buy a few of these, cook them and enjoy
them in the traditional way – fried in bacon fat for breakfast.
But if you're lucky enough to find plenty, try some other ways
with them.

The larger and flatter, slightly concave field mushrooms are
ideal for stuffing, or at least for having slices of ham or cheese
laid on them. The following recipes can all be served as first
courses.

Stuffed mushrooms

8 medium mushrooms
2 oz (50 gr) melted butter
1 small onion
1 thick slice granary bread made
  into crumbs

10 sage leaves, finely chopped
8 thin pieces of Cheddar cheese
  the same size as the mushrooms

Remove the stalks from the mushrooms, and reserve them.
Brush the mushrooms with half the melted butter and grill them
under a high heat until they are almost done. Set them aside on
a heatproof plate.

Chop the onion and the mushroom stalks very finely. Cook
the onion on a low heat in the remaining melted butter until it is
soft. Add the chopped stalks, raise the heat and cook them for
two minutes. Remove the pan from the heat and work in the
crumbs, sage leaves and seasoning. Divide this mixture between
the mushrooms, top with the cheese, and grill them under a high
heat until the cheese has melted. Once the stuffed mushrooms
are done they are difficult to move because of the melted cheese,
so grill them on the serving plate.

You can vary this by using chopped mixed herbs instead of
sage and binding the stuffing with the juice of half a lemon.

Mushrooms with cheese and onion

8 large flat mushrooms
1 tablespoon melted butter
16 spring onions

8 thin slices Gruyère or strong
  Cheddar cheese
browned crumbs

Trim the stalks of the mushrooms to about half an inch (1·25 cm). Put the mushrooms on an ovenproof serving plate, brush them with melted butter, season with salt and pepper, and sprinkle over the chopped spring onions. Put them under a hot grill until they begin to bubble. Remove them from the heat and lay the cheese on top. Scatter over the browned crumbs and put them under the grill for a further half minute.

Mushrooms with cheese and bacon

12 medium mushrooms
12 chopped sage leaves
juice of 1 lemon
4 oz curd cheese
12 pieces of lean bacon, no larger than the mushrooms
1 tablespoon melted butter

Mix the sage leaves and lemon juice into the cheese and season. Brush the mushrooms with melted butter and put them on to a heatproof serving plate with a slice of bacon on each one. Grill them under a high heat until the bacon is crisp. Put a dollop of the cheese mixture on top of each mushroom and return them to the grill until they are just brown.

Because of their strong flavour, field mushrooms go well with spicy mustards.

Grilled mushrooms with tarragon mustard and tomatoes

12 large flat mushrooms, including the stalks
1 tablespoon melted butter
1 dessertspoon tarragon mustard
4 firm tomatoes, each cut into three slices
6 black olives, stoned and cut in half lengthways

Brush the mushrooms with melted butter and put them on to a heatproof serving plate. Chop the mushroom stalks and mix them with the mustard.

Grill the mushrooms under a high heat until they are heated through. Divide the stalk mixture between the mushrooms, spreading it over the surface. Season. Put them back under the grill until they begin to bubble. Put a slice of tomato and then one olive half on each mushroom. Put under the grill again until they are really hot and the olives are sizzling.

Field mushrooms are ideal for making a meatless pâté, but if you can't obtain them use open cultivated ones instead.

Mushroom pâté

4 oz (100 gr) mushrooms, finely chopped
1 oz (25 gr) butter
1 medium onion, finely chopped
4 oz (100 gr) curd cheese
4 tablespoons chopped mixed herbs

Melt the butter in a frying pan on a low heat and cook the onion in this until it is soft and just beginning to brown. Raise the heat a little, add the mushrooms, and cook them for four minutes.

Remove the pan from the heat and allow the mushrooms to cool a little. Put the cheese, mushrooms and herbs into the blender and work them until they are smooth. Season.

Divide the pâté into four individual soufflé dishes and chill it until it is firm. Serve it with brown toast.

ß   ß   ß

Another vegetable very often stuffed at harvest time is the marrow. Throughout September you can buy both long, cylindrical ones, and the less common dumpy, round ones. There is no difference at all in the flavour, but the round ones are easier to stuff and bake as they will remain steady while you put the stuffing in and will stand upright in the oven without having to be wedged.

Cooked on its own, marrow can be a tasteless, soppy vegetable, but spices or herbs can quite transform it, as in these two spicy soups.

Curried marrow soup

½ medium marrow, peeled, cored
 and sliced
1 oz (25 gr) butter
1 medium onion, sliced
1 dessertspoon curry powder

1 teaspoon turmeric
1 pint (6 dl) stock
1 bayleaf
4 slices lemon
2 tablespoons chopped mint

Melt the butter in a saucepan on a low heat. Add the marrow and onion and stir in the curry powder and turmeric. Cook gently until the onion is soft. Stir in the stock and add the bay-leaf. Bring to the boil and simmer for ten minutes. Allow the mixture to cool slightly before working it in the blender until it is smooth. Check the seasoning and return the soup to the saucepan to reheat.

Serve the soup with a slice of lemon and some chopped mint added to each serving dish.

Paprika marrow soup

½ medium marrow, peeled, cored
 and sliced
1 oz (25 gr) butter
1 medium onion, sliced
1 teaspoon caraway seeds

1 dessertspoon paprika
1¼ pints (1·5 dl) stock
2 pickled dill cucumbers, chopped
 very small

Melt the butter on a low heat in a saucepan. Stir in the onion, marrow, caraway seeds and paprika. Cover and cook gently for ten minutes. Stir in the stock, bring it to the boil, stirring, and simmer for a further ten minutes. Rub the soup through a sieve or work it in the blender until smooth. Return it to the rinsed-out pan. Check the seasoning, add the pickled cucumbers and reheat.

Curried marrow

1 small marrow, peeled, seeded
 and cut into one-inch (2·5 cm)
 chunks
1 oz (25 gr) butter

1 medium onion, sliced
1 dessertspoon curry powder
1 teaspoon caraway seeds
juice of 1 lemon

Melt the butter in a large frying pan on a low heat. Stir in the onion, curry powder and caraway seeds. Cook them very gently until the onion is soft. Stir the marrow into the curry mixture. Season. Cover, and continue to cook it gently, shaking occasionally, for ten minutes. Remove the lid and stir in the lemon juice. Serve immediately.

Red-hot marrow

1 small marrow, peeled and cut into one-inch (2·5 cm) pieces
1 oz (25 gr) butter
1 small onion, thinly sliced
1 clove garlic, finely chopped
1 heaped teaspoon paprika
¼ teaspoon cayenne pepper
½ lb (225 gr) firm tomatoes, skinned and sliced

Melt the butter in a saucepan on a low heat. Stir in the onion, garlic, paprika and cayenne, and simmer, covered, for ten minutes. Stir in the cubes of marrow. Season, cover again and continue to cook for a further ten minutes. Add the tomatoes, cover again, and cook for another five minutes.

Cold marrow salad

1 small marrow, peeled, seeded and cut into one-inch (2·5 cm) chunks
1 sprig mint
1 medium onion, finely sliced
2 tablespoons olive oil
1 teaspoon paprika
1 teaspoon ginger
1 tablespoon wine vinegar

Steam the marrow in a vegetable steamer with the sprig of mint for 20 minutes. (If you have no steamer, use a colander, covered with foil, on top of a saucepan of boiling water.) Cook the onion very gently in the oil with the paprika and ginger until it is soft. Off the heat, stir in the vinegar. Pour this mixture over the cooked marrow and stir them together well. Chill before serving.

This is very good with cold pork.

Marrow and cucumber salad

1 small marrow, peeled, cored and cut into one-inch (2·5 cm) dice
3 sprigs mint

½ cucumber, diced but not peeled
1 clove garlic, crushed with salt
5 fluid oz (1·5 dl) natural yoghurt
black pepper

Steam the marrow in a vegetable steamer with one sprig of mint for 20 minutes. (If you have no steamer, use a colander, covered with foil, on top of a saucepan of boiling water.) Cool the marrow and chill it slightly. Finely chop the remaining two sprigs of mint and mix them with the cucumber and garlic into the yoghurt. Season with black pepper. Mix the marrow into the cucumber and yoghurt and chill again before serving.

This method of steaming rather than boiling marrow is used again in the following salad in which the marrow is stuffed and served in two halves.

Stuffed marrow salad

1 small marrow
1 large bouquet garni
12 oz (325 gr) cottage cheese
6 oz (150 gr) cooked meat (ham, corned beef, salami, savoury sausage or a mixture)

6 small firm tomatoes, skinned, deseeded and roughly chopped
2 teaspoons made English mustard
2 tablespoons chopped chives

Cut the marrow in half lengthways and scoop out the pulp. Put the bouquet garni in one half and put the two halves back together. Steam them in a steamer or in a colander covered with foil over boiling water for 15 minutes, turning once to make sure the marrow cooks evenly. Drain the two halves well and allow them to cool completely.

Combine all the rest of the ingredients, apart from the chives. Set the two halves of the marrow side by side on a serving dish and pile the mixture into them. Strew the chopped chives over the top.

Here are two hot stuffed marrow recipes, one of them using the steaming method and the other starting with a raw marrow.

Ham-stuffed marrow

1 small to medium marrow, either round or long
1 sprig mint
6 oz (150 gr) lean ham, diced
2 oz (50 gr) Cheddar cheese, diced
2 firm tomatoes, skinned and chopped
6 spring onions, chopped
1 tablespoon chopped marjoram and savory
1 tablespoon chopped parsley
1 oz (25 gr) butter

Preheat the oven to Reg 4/350°F, 180°C and butter an ovenproof dish.

Cut the top off the marrow and scoop out the pips and pulp with a long spoon. Peel the marrow, including the cap that you cut off. Put the mint into the marrow and place it in a steamer or colander covered with foil. Steam it over a saucepan of boiling water, turning it once, for 15 minutes.

Mix the ham, cheese, tomatoes and onions together with the herbs and seasoning and pile them inside the marrow, pressing down well. Replace the cap and secure it with wooden cocktail sticks. If the marrow is a long one, prop it up in the dish with a triangular wedge of bread. If it is round, just stand it up. Rub softened butter all over the marrow and bake it in the oven for an hour.

Beef-stuffed marrow

1 medium marrow, round if possible
2 tablespoons beef dripping
1 lb (450 gr) lean stewing beef, shredded into small strips
¼ lb (100 gr) flat mushrooms, sliced
1 medium onion, thinly sliced
juice of ½ lemon
1 tablespoon chopped thyme
½ lb (225 gr) baby onions
½ lb (225 gr) small carrots
1 lb (450 gr) small new potatoes
(these last three are optional but they do make it a very attractive complete meal)

Preheat the oven to Reg 4/350°F, 180°C.

Take the top off the marrow and scoop out the seeds and pulp. Peel the marrow and the cap. Put 1½ tablespoons of the dripping into a baking tray and let it melt in the oven.

Melt the remaining dripping in a frying pan on a high heat. When it is smoking, put in the beef and brown it for several minutes. Quickly add the mushrooms and onion and stir them about in the pan, still on a high heat, until the onion is beginning to soften. Stir in the lemon juice, thyme and seasoning and remove the pan from the heat. Pile this mixture into the marrow, pressing it down well. Replace the cap and secure it with cocktail sticks. If the marrow is round, set it as it is in the melted dripping in the tin. If long, then prop up the top with a triangular wedge of bread. Brush the marrow with the melted dripping and put the tin back into the oven for thirty minutes.

While the marrow is cooking, scrape the potatoes and carrots and peel the onions. Blanch the carrots by putting them into salted water, bringing them to the boil, draining and refreshing them. After the first 30 minutes put the vegetables round the marrow in the tin and turn them over in the fat. Put them back into the oven for an hour, turning the vegetables and basting the marrow occasionally. Serve the marrow whole on a large dish surrounded by the vegetables.

The following recipe can be served either as a vegetable dish or as a first course. If the marrows are very small each person can have a complete half.

Marrow and tomato boats

2 very small round marrows, halved lengthways, and peeled, cored and seeded
1 lb (450 gr) tomatoes, skinned and sliced
2 tablespoons chopped lemon thyme or thyme
16 spring onions, chopped
8 tablespoons browned crumbs
4 tablespoons Parmesan cheese
1 oz (225 gr) melted butter

Preheat the oven to Reg 4/350°F, 180°C and grease an ovenproof dish.
Put a layer of tomato in the bottom of each half marrow. Scatter over some thyme and then some chopped onions; then tomatoes, thyme, onions and tomatoes, seasoning each layer. Mix the cheese and crumbs together and scatter them over the

top. Brush the outsides and cut edges of the marrows with melted butter and bake them in the greased dish for an hour.

Diced marrow can be given flavour by cooking it with the main dish.

Pork and marrow in mustard sauce

2 lb (900 gr) lean boneless pork, cut into smallish pieces
2 tablespoons pork dripping or lard
1 large onion, sliced
1 tablespoon flour
1 dessertspoon Dijon mustard

¾ pint (4.5 dl) stock
3 large pickled gherkins, finely chopped
bouquet garni of marjoram, savory and sage
1 small marrow, peeled, deseeded and chopped into small dice

Preheat the oven to Reg 4/350°F, 180°C.
Melt the fat in a casserole on a high heat. Brown the pork pieces all over in this, remove them and set them aside. Lower the heat, add the sliced onion and cook it until it is soft. Stir in the flour and mustard and blend in the stock. Stir it until it boils and add the pork, gherkins, bouquet garni and seasoning. Cover, and put the casserole in the oven for 30 minutes. Add the marrow to the dish and put it back into the oven for an hour.

Next a real harvest dish: pigeons used to be shot when they tried to steal the corn, so they always turned up on the supper table at this time of year.

Pigeons braised with marrow

4 pigeons
for the stuffing:
4 oz (100 gr) mushrooms
1 tablespoon dripping
4 oz (100 gr) brown breadcrumbs, preferably granary
4 tablespoons red wine
2 tablespoons mixed chopped marjoram, thyme and parsley

1 tablespoon dripping
3 rashers lean bacon, diced
1 large onion, sliced
1 tablespoon flour
1 wineglass red wine
1 wineglass stock
bouquet garni of marjoram, thyme and parsley
1 small marrow, peeled, cored and cubed

Preheat the oven to Reg 4/350°F, 180°C.

To make the stuffing, finely chop the mushrooms and cook them in the dripping on a high heat for about three minutes. Remove the pan from the heat and work in the breadcrumbs, wine, herbs and seasoning. Stuff the pigeons with this mixture and truss them.

Melt the dripping in a large flameproof casserole on a low heat and cook the bacon and onion in this until they are beginning to brown. Remove them and set them aside. Raise the heat to moderate and brown the pigeons all over. Set them aside with the bacon and onion. Stir in the flour and blend in the wine and stock. Bring to the boil, stirring. Replace the pigeons, bacon and onion and add the bouquet garni. Cover and put them in the oven for 30 minutes.

Add the marrow to the casserole and return it to the oven for an hour. Check the seasoning and serve the pigeons with the sauce poured over them, surrounded by the marrow.

      ❊   ❊   ❊

All through September you can buy bunches of baby beetroot. The beetroot recipes for April can be made with any size of beet, but the following dishes look really attractive if the smaller ones are used. The first two recipes contain allspice and juniper, both of which really enhance the delicate, slightly sweet, flavour of the vegetable, which is so often masked by sharp salad dressings.

Spiced lamb and beetroot

1 shoulder of lamb
8 baby beets
10 black peppercorns
6 allspice berries
6 juniper berries
1 tablespoon Dijon mustard
1 dessertspoon caraway seeds

1 oz (25 gr) butter or
  3 tablespoons melted lamb fat
8 small onions, peeled but not
  sliced
2 wineglasses red wine
1 tablespoon flour

Boil the beets in salted water for 30 minutes and peel them. Crush the spices together. Preheat the oven to Reg 4/350°F, 180°C.

Bone out the lamb and remove any excess fat. Spread the cut surface with the mustard and sprinkle over the caraway seeds. Roll it up and tie it with strong thread or fine cotton string. Heat the fat or butter on a low heat in a heavy flameproof casserole. Cook the onions very gently in this until they are just brown. Remove them and set them aside. Raise the heat to moderate and brown the lamb all over. Set it aside with the onions. Pour off all but a thin film of fat from the pan and set it back on the heat. Pour in the wine, stir in the spices and seasoning, and bring it to the boil. Replace the lamb and tuck the beets and onions round it. Cover the casserole and put it in the centre of the oven for 1½ hours.

Remove the lamb, carve it and arrange it on a dish with the vegetables. Put them to keep warm. Skim the juices in the casserole, putting about two tablespoons of the fat into a saucepan. Set this on a moderate heat and stir in the flour. Gradually blend in the juices from the casserole. Bring to the boil, stirring and let it simmer for a few minutes. Pour the sauce over the lamb before serving.

Boiled salt beef with mustard sauce

a 2-2½ lb (1-1·25 kg) piece salt beef (silverside or brisket), soaked overnight in cold water
10 cloves
10 allspice berries
10 black peppercorns
a few celery leaves or a stick of celery
1 lb (450 gr) baby beets, peeled and left whole
½ lb (225 gr) baby onions, peeled and left whole
1 bunch of baby carrots, scrubbed and cut into one-inch (2·5 cm) lengths if necessary

½ primo cabbage, cut into four wedges

for the dumplings:
4 oz (100 gr) self-raising flour, preferably 81 % wholemeal
2 oz (50 gr) beef suet
2 tablespoons mixed herbs
a little water

for the sauce:
1 tablespoon flour
1 dessertspoon dry mustard
juice of ½ lemon
2 tablespoons chopped parsley and/or chervil

Put the beef into a large saucepan with the spices, celery, beets and onions. Cover with water and bring gently to the boil, skim, and simmer for an hour. Add the carrots and continue cooking.

While the beef is cooking, make the dumplings. Mix the flour, suet and herbs together, add enough water to make a stiff dough, and form into balls about an inch (2·5 cm) in diameter.

Start to skim off any fat from the saucepan – you will need to reserve about two tablespoons for the sauce. When the carrots have been cooking for 25 minutes add the cabbage to the pan and put in the dumplings. Continue simmering for 20 minutes, when the beef will have cooked for 1½ hours. Arrange the carved beef, vegetables and dumplings on a serving dish and keep them warm.

Melt the skimmed-off fat in a saucepan on a moderate heat. Stir in the flour and mustard and let them cook for a few minutes. Blend in half a pint (3 dl) of the broth in which the beef cooked and bring it to the boil, stirring. Let it bubble for a moment. Stir in the lemon juice and the parsley and/or chervil. Serve the sauce separately.

Spiced beef and beetroot

2 lb (900 gr) lean stewing beef, cut into one-inch cubes	8 juniper berries, crushed
2 tablespoons beef dripping	8 allspice berries, crushed
1 large or 2 small onions, thinly sliced	1 dessertspoon soft brown sugar
2 wineglasses red wine	8 baby beets, peeled and halved
4 tablespoons red wine vinegar	2 tablespoons grated horseradish
	2 tablespoons sour cream
	1 dessertspoon dry mustard

Preheat the oven to Reg 3/325°F, 170°C.

Melt the dripping on a high heat in a heavy flameproof casserole. Brown the beef all over in this, remove it and set it aside. Lower the heat, stir in the onions and cook them until they are soft. Pour in the wine and the vinegar, raise the heat again, and bring them to the boil. Stir in the spices and sugar and add the meat and beetroot. Season. Cover the casserole and put it into the oven for 1½ hours.

Blend together the sour cream, mustard and horseradish and stir them into the casserole just before serving.

৪৩ ৪৩ ৪৩

Picking blackberries is a favourite occupation of the English in September. Unlike other Europeans, we tend to be slightly suspicious of many wild foods, but come blackberry time crowds of us flock out to the countryside with bowls and baskets. I haven't included recipes for blackberry pies and jams and jellies because there are so many for these. But how about a blackberry pickle?

Pickled beetroot and blackberries

12 oz (325 gr) cooked beetroot,
  sliced
8 oz (225 gr) ripe blackberries
½ pint (3 dl) wine vinegar
a small piece of cinnamon

10 allspice berries
10 cloves
a small piece of root ginger
1 tablespoon soft brown sugar

Simmer all the spices with the vinegar for 15 minutes. Strain the vinegar and return it to the saucepan. Add the sugar and stir the vinegar on a low heat until the sugar is dissolved. Add the beetroots to the pan with the blackberries. Bring them to the boil and immediately remove them from the heat. Cool the pickle and leave it for 24 hours before using it, then use it up within a week, keeping it in the refrigerator.

Soused mackerel and blackberries

4 small mackerel
1 small onion, sliced
8 oz (225 gr) blackberries
a small piece of cinnamon
1 bayleaf torn in half
2 tablespoons wine vinegar
shredded lettuce for serving

Preheat the oven to Reg 4/350°F, 180°C.
Clean the mackerel and remove the heads and fins. Lay them in a lightly oiled ovenproof dish, season and scatter the onion over the top. Put in the blackberries and tuck in the cinnamon and pieces of bay. Pour over the vinegar and cover with foil. Bake for 20 minutes.

Allow them to cool in the dish, still covered, and then chill them slightly. When you are ready to serve them, gently scrape the skin from the fish. Separate each half from the backbone and lay it on a bed of lettuce. Remove the onion, cinnamon and bayleaf from the dish and rub the liquid and the blackberries through a sieve. Spoon this sauce over the mackerel fillets to coat them, just before serving.

This makes a good light lunch or first course.

Hot blackberries and onion

8 oz (225 gr) blackberries
6 allspice berries
6 juniper berries
½ oz (13 gr) butter
1 medium onion, thinly sliced
juice of ½ lemon
brown bread and butter for serving

Crush the spices together. Melt the butter in a frying pan on a low heat. Add the onion and cook it gently until it is soft. Raise the heat, add the blackberries and spices and cook them briskly, stirring, for two minutes. Stir in the lemon juice and boil up for half a minute. Serve hot in small bowls with brown bread and butter as a first course.

❊   ❊   ❊

Think of blackberries, and you usually think of apples. Cooking apples are in season most of the year, from autumn to late June. Throughout this period, they gradually become softer and more pulpy, but this happens so gradually that we don't notice the change. Then suddenly, at the end of August, into the shops come crisp green ones again, and we realise how much better they are when they are fresh. Apples, like blackberries, are used mostly in sweet dishes – stewed or baked or put into pies or dumplings, but they are just as good in savoury dishes – usually with pork, but occasionally with other meats.

Pork chops for autumn

4 pork chops
1 dessertspoon chopped thyme
6 chopped sage leaves
1 large or 2 small cloves garlic,
   chopped
1 bay leaf, crumbled
2 medium onions, sliced

2 medium cooking apples, peeled,
   cored and sliced
2 green peppers, chopped
½ pint (3 dl) brown sauce (page 12)
1 oz (25 gr) butter or
   4 tablespoons pork fat
¼ teaspoon ground black pepper
¼ teaspoon fine sea salt

Crush together the thyme, sage, garlic, and bay. Rub them into the surface of the chops and leave them for four hours.

Melt the butter on a high heat in a heavy frying pan. Put in the chops, still covered with the herbs and garlic, and brown them on both sides. Lower the heat. Add the onion and the apple to the pan and continue cooking for 20 minutes, covered. Add the peppers, turn the chops, and cook for a further ten minutes, still covered. Remove the lid and stir in the brown sauce. Check the seasoning, raise the heat slightly, bring it to the boil, and serve immediately.

Grilled pork chops in cider sauce

4 pork chops
10 sage leaves, chopped
1 large clove garlic
¼ teaspoon salt
¼ teaspoon ground black pepper
2 large cooking apples
2 teaspoons ground cinnamon

for the sauce:
1 small onion, finely diced
1 small carrot, finely diced
½ stick celery, finely diced
2 tablespoons olive oil
1 level tablespoon flour
½ pint (3 dl) dry cider
2 cloves
a small piece of cinnamon

Crush together the sage, garlic, salt and pepper, rub them into the chops, and leave them to stand for four hours.

Meanwhile make the sauce. Cook the vegetables in the oil in a saucepan on a low heat until they are just beginning to brown. Stir in the flour and cook it until it browns. Off the heat, blend in the cider. Return the pan to the heat, bring the sauce gently to the boil and skim it if necessary. Add the cloves and cinnamon. Cover, and simmer on the lowest possible heat for 30 minutes. Strain it through a sieve, pressing down hard on the vegetables to extract all the juices. Return the sauce to the rinsed pan and simmer for a further five minutes.

When you are ready to cook the chops, preheat the grill to high. Scrape any pieces of the marinade off the chops. Lay them on the heated grill pan and cook them under a high heat until one side is completely done and golden brown. Turn them over and continue cooking under a high heat.

Have ready the apples, peeled, cored and sliced into rings. Just as the chops are done, lay the apple slices on top of them and sprinkle them with the cinnamon. Put them back under the grill (still high) and cook until the apples are done and are just beginning to melt into the pork. Arrange the chops on a serving dish and pour over the sauce.

Salt pork baked in cider

a 2½ lb (1·25 kg) piece of salt belly of pork (with bones)
1 carrot
1 onion
1 stick celery
bouquet garni of parsley, thyme and sage
a few black peppercorns
1 tablespoon made English mustard
about one tablespoon cloves
2 large cooking apples, peeled, cored and sliced
½ pint (3 dl) dry cider

Put the pork into a saucepan with the carrot, onion, celery stick, bouquet garni and peppercorns. Bring it slowly to the boil and simmer for an hour, skimming if necessary.

Preheat the oven to Reg 4/350°F, 180°C. Remove the pork from the saucepan, peel or cut off the rind and take out the bones. Spread the top thickly with the mustard and stick in the cloves about an inch apart all over the top. Put the pork into an ovenproof dish and lay the apple slices down either side of it. Pour round the cider.

Bake it in the centre of the oven for an hour. Serve it carved into slices with the apple rings arranged on top and any liquid from the dish spooned over it.

Pork and apple terrine

6 oz (150 gr) fairly lean pork, such
    as the lean end of a fresh belly,
    cut in quarter-inch (6 mm)
    cubes
4 oz (100 gr) lean bacon, cut into
    quarter-inch (6 mm) cubes

1 small cooking apple, diced into
    quarter-inch (6 mm) cubes
1 small onion, finely chopped
6 sage leaves, chopped

Preheat the oven to Reg 3/325°F, 170°C.

Mix the pork, bacon, apple, onion and sage together and press
them down into a 1 lb (450 gr) earthenware terrine. Cover and
put it into the oven for two hours. Remove from the oven and
set a weight on top until it is cool. Turn it out just before
serving.

Beef sausages with apple and tomato sauce

for the sausages:
1 lb (450 gr) coarsely minced good
    quality beef
1 oz (25 gr) butter
1 small onion, finely chopped
1 clove garlic, finely chopped
1 teaspoon turmeric
1 teaspoon ground cumin
½ teaspoon ground allspice

½ teaspoon cayenne pepper
1 tablespoon chopped mixed
    herbs
for the sauce:
1 lb (450 gr) cooking apples
2 strips lemon rind
3 ripe tomatoes, skinned and
    chopped
1 dessertspoon grated onion

To make the sausages, melt the butter on a low heat in a small
frying pan and cook the onion and garlic in this until the onion
is transparent. In a large mixing bowl beat the onion mixture,
spices, herbs and seasoning into the meat. Divide the mixture
into eight portions and form them into sausage shapes about
two inches long and one inch in diameter. When you are ready
to cook them, preheat the grill to high and grill them fairly close
to the heat until they are brown and crisp all round.

    Meanwhile make the sauce. Stew the apples with the lemon
rind until they are soft and then sieve them. You should have
about six fluid oz (1·8 dl) of purée. Put the purée with the
tomatoes and the onion into a saucepan and beat them together

over a moderate heat until the tomatoes begin to go pulpy. Sieve the mixture again to get rid of the tomato pips. Season, reheat, and serve either separately or poured over the sausages.

Herrings with bacon and apple sauce

4 herrings
oatmeal to coat them
for the sauce:

1 oz (25 gr) butter	2 teaspoons made English
4 rashers lean bacon, diced	mustard
1 large onion, sliced	juice of ½ lemon
1 large cooking apple, peeled,	1 tablespoon chopped thyme or
cored and finely chopped	lemon thyme

First make the sauce. Melt the butter in a saucepan on a low heat and cook the bacon, onion and apple together until the onion is soft and the apple pulpy. Blend the mustard with the lemon juice and stir these into the sauce with the thyme. Season and set aside.

Fillet the herrings and coat the fillets in oatmeal. Grill them under a preheated high grill until they are brown. They are such an oily fish that they will provide their own fat. Serve them with the sauce in blobs on the top.

       ❃   ❃   ❃

The other fruits of autumn are plums and damsons. The damson season usually lasts from late August until late September. They are a tart, hard little fruit, unsuitable for eating raw and needing a good deal of sugar when made into sweet dishes. However, as with redcurrants, you can take advantage of this sharpness and make them into a spicy sauce for serving with roast lamb.

Damson sauce for roast lamb

½ lb (225 gr) damsons, halved and	6 allspice berries
stoned if possible	6 cloves
1 small onion, sliced	1 wineglass red wine
a piece of cinnamon	

Put the damsons with the onion, spices and wine into a saucepan. Bring them gently to the boil and simmer for 15 minutes. Rub them through a sieve.

Serve the sauce separately with the lamb, hot if the meat is hot and cold if it is cold.

My favourite plums are Victorias, so sweet and juicy that raw they make a pudding in themselves. But if you can spare some from the pie or the fruit bowl they also go well with lamb, even though they are so much sweeter than damsons.

Spiced lamb with plums

1 best end of neck of lamb, boned   ½ oz (13 gr) butter or
¼ teaspoon ground cinnamon   2 tablespoons melted lamb fat
¼ teaspoon ground nutmeg   2 wineglasses white wine
1 medium onion, finely chopped   6 Victoria plums, stoned and
2 oz (50 gr) raisins, finely chopped   sliced

Preheat the oven to Reg 4/350°F, 180°C.

Sprinkle the cinnamon and nutmeg over the cut surface of the lamb and scatter the onion and raisins on top. Roll up the meat and tie it with strong thread or fine cotton string. Melt the butter or fat on a high heat in a heavy flameproof casserole. Brown the lamb all over in this. Pour in the wine, bring it to the boil and add the plums to the dish. Cover it and put it in the centre of the oven for 1¼ hours.

Remove the lamb, carve it and keep it warm. Rub the rest of the contents of the casserole through a sieve. Reheat the sauce, pour a little over the meat and serve the rest separately.

Vegetables available in October

beetroot – bunches at first, later slightly larger and sold loose

Brussels sprouts – all through the month they are small, firm, and tightly packed

Brussels tops – these come into the shops right at the end of October

cabbage – Savoy, Christmas Drumhead and January King are available all through the month

carrots – no bunches now, but they are medium-sized and very crisp and sweet

celery – excellent, sound and white

greens – these come into the shops right at the end of the month

marrow – these are only good in the first two weeks of October

onions – button onions are sold for pickling, and can be used in cooking

parsnips – I always wait for the frosts for parsnips, but they are widely available all through the month

peppers – there are a few English ones at the beginning of the month but they are rather bitter

pumpkin – this is the only month in which it is available

swede – this is really good in October

turnips – small ones are sometimes available, with a delicious flavour

watercress – crisp and large-leaved watercress comes back in October, not quite as hot as in the spring but very fresh

Fruit available in October

apples and pears – all types of English cookers and eaters are widely available all through the month

citrus fruit – less pithy and stringy than of late but still not a very good buy

nuts – new cob nuts and fresh 'wet' walnuts can be found

Fresh herbs available in October

bay

chervil – very short and difficult to pick now

chives – begin to die down later in the month

fennel – produces less and less leaves and longer stems

lovage – dies down completely by the end of October

marjoram – the stalks get shorter and tougher throughout the month

mint – begins to die down during the first two weeks

parsley – this should still be growing but the leaves get smaller

rosemary – still has fairly soft leaves

sage – its growth slows down considerably in October and by the end of the month there are no more new leaves

savory – begins to get tougher but there is still some new growth

sorrel – this will still produce a few leaves if the weather is warm

tarragon – this dies down in October

thyme – still produces new leaves, but they become tougher as the month goes on

🥬　　🥬　　🥬

I always associate October with a garden full of brown leaves, a pumpkin standing in the conservatory, and the smell of pickles wafting out of the kitchen door. All the summer vegetables have come to the end of their run and the shops begin to be filled with the first of the more substantial ones that will be with us all through the winter.

One vegetable, though, has a very short season and is available only in October. The beautiful creamy orange pumpkin is usually associated with the pies served at American Thanksgiving suppers, but it was in fact originally an English vegetable, eaten mainly by the poor, and taken to America by the Pilgrim Fathers. They used to hollow out the centre and fill it with apples and spices, and this was the original pumpkin pie.

There is very little flavour in the flesh of the pumpkin, so it can easily be turned into a sweet or a savoury dish, but it has one distinct quality which (together with the shortness of its season) makes it a very special vegetable – the texture of the pumpkin is as creamy as the colour of its skin.

To serve it as a vegetable, small cubes of pumpkin can be roasted round the joint, or slices of it can be fried in butter and sprinkled with plenty of black pepper. It can be cooked with spices, made into fritters, or served with butter and herbs.

Pumpkin paprika

1 slice of pumpkin about 6 inches (15 cm) thick diced into
   one-inch cubes
1 oz (25 gr) butter
1 medium onion, sliced
1 tablespoon paprika
4 tablespoons wine vinegar
1 teaspoon caraway seeds
1 dessertspoon kneaded butter

Melt the butter in a saucepan on a low heat. Put in the pumpkin, cover it, season, and cook for about ten minutes or until the cubes are just tender. Remove the pumpkin and keep it warm. Cook the onion in the pan, covered, for ten minutes. Stir in the paprika and cook, stirring, for five minutes. Replace the pumpkin and stir it around until it is covered with the paprika. Add the vinegar and caraway seeds and simmer, covered, for a further five minutes. Stir in a little kneaded butter to thicken the dish just before serving.

Pumpkin fritters

8 quarter-inch (6 mm) thick slices
   of pumpkin, with the pith and
   skin removed
for the fritter batter:
4 oz (100 gr) flour
1 teaspoon curry powder

1 teaspoon paprika
¼ pint (1·5 dl) milk
2 egg yolks
1 egg white, whipped

oil or fat for frying

To make the batter, add the curry powder, paprika and salt to the flour before working in the egg yolks and milk. Fold in the whipped egg white.

Dip the pumpkin slices in the batter and fry them in hot deep fat. Serve the fritters instead of potatoes as an accompaniment to cold meat.

Pumpkin beurre noir

4 one-inch (2·5 cm) thick slices of
  pumpkin, with the pith and skin
  removed
2 oz (50 gr) butter

juice of 1 lemon
1 tablespoon chopped capers
2 tablespoons chopped mixed
  herbs

Cook the pumpkin slices in a steamer or a colander covered with foil over boiling water for 20 minutes, turning the slices once.

While the pumpkin is steaming make the sauce to be ready at the same time. Heat the butter in a frying pan on a high heat until it browns. Stir in the lemon juice, capers and herbs. Season and remove from the heat immediately. Pour this over the pumpkin slices and serve as a first course.

The following recipe makes a good lunch or supper dish.

Pumpkin with bacon

1 six-inch (15 cm) thick slice of
  pumpkin, cut into small cubes
1 medium onion, chopped

2 tablespoons chopped parsley
8 bacon rashers

Preheat the oven to Reg 6/400°F, 200°C and lightly grease an ovenproof dish.
Lay the cubes of pumpkin in the dish and scatter over them the onion and parsley. Season, lay the bacon rashers over the top, and bake in the oven, uncovered, for 30 minutes.

Pumpkin can also be cooked to a purée for soups and other dishes. Dice it and cook it with about half an inch (1·25 cm) of water, covered, on a low heat for 15 minutes.

Golden pumpkin soup

6 fluid oz (1·8 dl) pumpkin purée
  (see above)
¾ pint (4·5 dl) stock
1 medium onion, roughly
  chopped

juice of ½ orange
1 dessertspoon tomato purée
¼ pint (1·5 dl) milk

Put the stock and onion into a saucepan, bring them to the boil and simmer, covered, for 20 minutes. Stir in the pumpkin, orange juice and tomato purée. Allow the mixture to cool slightly and work it in the blender until it is smooth. Return it to the saucepan, stir in the milk, season, and reheat without boiling.

Pumpkin soup

a piece of pumpkin about
  1½ inches (4 cm) thick, thinly
  sliced
1 oz (25 gr) butter

1 large onion, thinly sliced
1½ pints (9 dl) stock
1 clove garlic, finely sliced
grated nutmeg

Melt the butter in a saucepan on a very low heat and stir the pumpkin and onion into the pan. Cover them with a butter paper and a lid and let them sweat for five minutes. Stir in the stock and simmer, covered, for 15 minutes. Allow it to cool slightly.

Put the stock and vegetables into the blender with the garlic and work them until they are smooth. Return the soup to the saucepan, season, and grate in a little nutmeg. Reheat it and serve.

Pumpkin and turnip soup

6 oz (150 gr) pumpkin, thinly
  sliced
6 oz (150 gr) turnip, thinly sliced
¾ oz (19 gr) butter
1 medium onion, thinly sliced

1 pint (6 dl) stock
a bouquet garni which includes
  savory
2 tablespoons chopped savory

Melt the butter in a heavy saucepan on a low heat and stir in the vegetables. Cover them with a butter paper and a lid and allow them to sweat for five minutes. Stir in the stock and add the bouquet garni. Cover and simmer for 20 minutes. Remove the bouquet garni and allow the soup to cool slightly. Work it in the blender until it is smooth. Add the chopped savory and reheat.

The next recipe combines pumpkin purée with eggs to make a light meal.

Pumpkin bake

a slice of pumpkin, four inches
  (10 cm) thick, puréed as above
1 oz (25 gr) butter
4 oz (100 gr) lean bacon, diced

1 medium onion, sliced
4 eggs
2 oz (50 gr) grated Cheddar cheese
2 tablespoons chopped parsley

Preheat the oven to Reg 4/350°F, 180°C. Butter a shallow oven-proof dish, preferably a round one.
Melt the rest of the butter in a frying pan on a low heat and cook the bacon and onion in it until the onion is soft. Beat the eggs and stir the bacon, onion, cheese, parsley and finally the pumpkin into them. Season. Pour them into the prepared dish and bake them for 25 minutes.

The creamy texture of the pumpkin purée makes an ideal base for a very simple curry, which can be a good life-saver recipe if you want to produce a meal in a few minutes.

Simple pumpkin curry

1 lb (450 gr) any left-over meat or poultry
1 medium onion, sliced
1 dessertspoon curry powder
1 oz (25 gr) butter
1 4-inch (10 cm) slice pumpkin, puréed as above
1 tablespoon chopped herbs
lemon juice to taste

Gently cook the sliced onion in the butter with the curry powder until the onion is soft. Stir in the diced meat or poultry, the pumpkin purée and the herbs and lemon juice. Season and heat through.

Used in a more conventional curry recipe, pumpkin will cook down to make a thick sauce which is less stodgy than one made from lentils and less rich than one made from almonds.

Beef and pumpkin curry

2 lb (900 gr) stewing beef, cut into one-inch (2·5 cm) cubes
1½ oz (38 gr) butter
2 medium onions, sliced
1 dessertspoon turmeric
2 teaspoons ground ginger
¼ teaspoon cayenne pepper

¾ pint (4·5 dl) stock
1 large clove garlic, crushed with salt
4 tablespoons mango chutney
a slice of pumpkin about 6 inches (15 cm) thick, cut into one-inch (2·5 cm) cubes

Preheat the oven to Reg 4/350°F, 180°C.

Melt the butter on a high heat in a heavy, flameproof casserole and brown the cubes of beef all over. Remove the beef and lower the heat. Stir in the onion, turmeric, ginger and cayenne and cook them gently until the onion is soft. Blend in the stock and bring to the boil, stirring. Add the garlic, chutney, beef and pumpkin to the pan. Cover it and put it into the oven for 1½ hours.

The pumpkin will cook down to a pulp and provide the necessary thickening for the sauce.

The following recipes also make use of the pumpkin's creamy texture.

Pork with pumpkin and apple sauce

2 lb (900 gr) rolled shoulder of pork
½ oz (13 gr) butter
1 medium onion, sliced
6 oz (150 gr) raw pumpkin, chopped small

1 medium cooking apple, peeled, cored and sliced
a bouquet of sage leaves
6 cloves
¼ pint (1.5 dl) stock

Preheat the oven to Reg 4/350°F, 180°C.

Melt the butter in a heavy flameproof casserole on a high heat and brown the joint all over. Remove it and lower the heat. Stir in the onion and the pumpkin, cover them and let them sweat for five minutes. Add the apple to the pan with the sage and cloves. Pour in the stock, bring it to the boil and replace the pork. Cover the casserole and put in the oven for 1½ hours. Take out the pork, carve it and keep it warm. Rub all the contents of the casserole through a sieve. Reheat the sauce and serve it separately.

Meat balls in spiced pumpkin sauce

for the meat balls:
1 lb (450 gr) good quality beef, coarsely minced
8 allspice berries
8 black peppercorns
1 clove garlic, crushed with salt
6 sage leaves, chopped
1 egg, beaten
2 tablespoons seasoned flour
1 oz (25 gr) butter

for the sauce:
6 oz (150 gr) raw pumpkin, chopped small
1 teaspoon ground ginger
a little grated nutmeg
6 oz (150 gr) ripe tomatoes, skinned and roughly chopped

Crush the allspice berries and peppercorns together. Mix the spices, garlic and sage leaves thoroughly into the meat and beat in the egg. Form the mixture into twelve balls and coat them with the seasoned flour. Melt the butter in a saucepan or casserole on a moderate heat. Brown the meat balls all over and set them aside. Lower the heat. Add the pumpkin, ginger and nutmeg to the pan. Cover them and cook them gently for three minutes. Stir in the tomatoes and put the meatballs on top. Cover, and simmer very gently on top of the stove for 15 minutes, turning the meatballs once.

Remove the meatballs and place them on a warm serving dish. Rub the contents of the pan through a sieve. Reheat the sauce and pour it over the meatballs before serving.

☓ ☓ ☓

Sometimes at the beginning of October, you will be able to buy bunches of small, firm white turnips still with the tops on. If you are lucky enough to find these you will be buying two vegetables for the price of one.

Turnip tops are best cooked like spring greens (page 61), only for a longer time and with a little more water as they have quite a strong, irony flavour.

Turnips themselves were for a long time in this country looked upon only as cattle fodder, but they can in fact be quite delicious. They can be served as a single vegetable or incorporated into sauces, and small amounts added to the pot can give a distinctive and unusual flavour to dishes.

Turnips in lemon sauce

1 lb (450 gr) small white turnips, peeled and cut into quarter-inch (6 mm) slices
1 oz (25 gr) butter

1 dessertspoon Dijon mustard
juice of ½ lemon
1 tablespoon chopped parsley

Cook the turnips in boiling salted water for 15 minutes. Drain them and leave them to steam and dry. Melt the butter in a saucepan on a low heat and blend in the mustard and lemon juice. Put the turnips into the pan with the parsley and gently turn them over in the sauce until they are well coated.

Honeyed turnips

6 small turnips, peeled and cut in half and then into fairly thick slices
1 oz (25 gr) butter

1 medium onion, thinly sliced
1 dessertspoon clear honey
¼ pint (1·5 dl) stock
1 tablespoon chopped parsley

Preheat the oven to Reg 4/350°F, 180°C.
Melt the butter on a low heat in a flameproof casserole. Cook the onion in the butter until it is just beginning to turn golden. Stir in the turnips and coat them thoroughly with the butter. Add the honey and stir again. Cook gently for two minutes and then stir in the stock and parsley. Season. Cover with a butter paper and a lid and put them in the oven for an hour.

Turnips in orange sauce

1 lb (450 gr) white turnips, peeled and cut into half-inch (1·25 cm) dice
grated rind and juice of ½ medium orange

1 oz (25 gr) butter
¼ pint (1·5 dl) stock
1 tablespoon chopped parsley

Put the turnips into a saucepan with the grated orange rind and the butter and stock. Cover them and set on a moderate heat for 15 minutes when the turnips should be tender and the stock absorbed. Stir in the orange juice and the chopped parsley just before serving.

Turnips and orange are combined again in this recipe for lamb.

Lamb with turnip and orange

1½-2 lb (675-900 gr) lean boneless
  lamb, cut from the shoulder,
  cut in ¾-inch (2 cm) cubes
1½ oz (38 gr) butter
2 small turnips, finely diced
1 medium onion, chopped

grated rind and juice of 1 orange
enough stock to make up the
  orange juice to 7 fluid oz (2 dl)
3 teaspoons Dijon mustard
2 tablespoons chopped marjoram

Melt the butter on a high heat in a wide-bottomed casserole. Brown the pieces of lamb all over, in two batches if necessary. Remove them and set aside. Lower the heat right down and cook the onion and turnip in the pan until they are soft. Pour in the stock and orange juice and add the orange rind. Gently bring them to the boil and replace the lamb. Stir in the mustard and marjoram. Season, cover and cook on a very low heat for 30 minutes.

Turnip and horseradish salad makes a good accompaniment to cold beef. Here is a hot beef stew using both these ingredients.

Shin of beef with turnips and button onions

2 lb (900 gr) shin of beef, cut in
  ¾-inch (2 cm) dice
2 tablespoons beef dripping
4 medium turnips, cut in ¾-inch
  (2 cm) dice

24 button onions, peeled
1 dessertspoon dry English
  mustard powder
¾ pint (4·5 dl) stock
1 tablespoon grated horseradish

Preheat the oven to Reg 3/325°F, 170°C.
Melt the dripping on a high heat in a flameproof casserole and brown the beef well in this. Remove it and set it aside. Lower the heat and cook the turnips and onions in the dripping until

they start to brown. Stir in the mustard and blend in the stock.
Bring it to the boil and replace the beef. Cover the casserole and
cook it in the oven for 1½ hours. Stir in the horseradish and
check the seasoning just before serving.

Chicken with turmeric

a 3-3½ lb (1·3-1·5 kg) roasting chicken, jointed
½ lb (225 gr) Italian, Polish or Spanish spiced sausage, cut into
 1½-inch (4 cm) lengths
4 small turnips, peeled and quartered
6 sticks celery, cut into 1½-inch (4 cm) lengths
4 carrots, cut into 1½-inch (4 cm) lengths
2 medium onions, peeled and quartered
bouquet garni
up to 1½ pints (9 dl) stock
1 dessertspoon turmeric infused with 2 tablespoons boiling water

for the dumplings:
4 oz (100 gr) self-raising flour, preferably wholemeal
2 oz (50 gr) beef suet
1 tablespoon chopped parsley
1 tablespoon chopped thyme
enough water to bind to a stiff dough

Put the chicken, sausage, vegetables and bouquet garni into a
saucepan or casserole. Cover them with stock and pour in the
infused turmeric. Cover the pan, bring to the boil and simmer
very gently for 1½ hours.

To make the dumplings, mix together the flour, suet and herbs
and a pinch of salt and bind them to a stiff dough with the water.
Form into eight small balls and add them to the pan for the last
20 minutes of cooking. Check the seasoning and serve the
chicken, vegetables and dumplings arranged on a dish with a
little of the liquid spooned over them.

Turnips and onions can be made into a soubise-type sauce
which is best used in a dish which contains a sharper-flavoured
ingredient as well, to provide a contrast. In the first of these
recipes this is achieved by the use of raw vegetables and Dijon
mustard.

Roast lamb with turnip sauce

1 shoulder of lamb, boned
3 small turnips, grated
1 medium onion, finely chopped
3 teaspoons Dijon mustard

for the sauce:
1 oz (25 gr) butter   1 tablespoon flour
1 small turnip, grated   ½ pint (3 dl) milk
1 small onion, finely chopped

Preheat the oven to Reg 4/350°F, 180°C.
Mix together the turnips, onion and mustard. Spread them over
the cut surface of the lamb. Roll up the meat and tie it with
strong thread or fine cotton string. Roast the lamb to your
liking.

To make the sauce, melt the butter in a saucepan on a low
heat. Stir in the turnip and onion and cook gently until the onion
is soft. Blend in the flour and milk. Bring them to the boil and
cook, stirring, until thick. Cool slightly and put them through
the blender until smooth. Season. Reheat and serve the carved
lamb and the sauce separately.

In the next recipe, lemon and English mustard provide the
sharpness.

Cod in turnip sauce

2 lb (900 gr) cod fillets, skinned and cut into serving pieces
1 dessertspoon dry mustard
juice of 2 lemons

for the sauce:
1 medium turnip, grated   1½ oz (38 gr) flour
1½ oz (38 gr) butter   ¾ pint (4·5 dl) milk
1 large onion, finely chopped
4 medium potatoes, peeled
4 medium turnips
2 tablespoons grated Cheddar cheese

Mix the mustard with the lemon juice, brush this over the cod
and let it stand for 30 minutes.

To make the sauce, cook the onion and grated turnip slowly in the butter until the onion is soft and just beginning to turn brown. Blend in the flour and stir in the milk. Bring it to the boil and stir until it is thick. Season, and leave it aside until required.

Boil the potatoes and the whole turnips in salted water together until they are tender. Slice them and arrange them in rows on an ovenproof serving dish. Keep warm.

Grill the fish under a high heat until it is golden and cooked through (about six minutes). Place the fish on the sliced turnip and potato. Reheat the sauce, and pour it over the top. Strew over the grated cheese. Put the dish back under the high grill until the cheese is brown and bubbly.

The same basic sauce can also be made into a soufflé.

Turnip soufflé

6 oz (150 gr) grated turnip	1 heaped teaspoon grated
1 oz (25 gr) butter	horseradish
1 medium onion, finely chopped	½ pint (3 dl) milk
1 tablespoon flour	4 eggs, separated
1 heaped teaspoon dry mustard	1 egg white (optional)
	1 tablespoon browned crumbs

Preheat the oven to Reg 5/375°F, 190°C and prepare a soufflé dish (p 15).

Melt the butter in a saucepan on a low heat. Stir in the turnip and onion and cook them gently until they are just beginning to brown, stirring occasionally. Stir in the flour, mustard and horseradish, and blend in the milk off the heat. Bring to the boil, stirring, and cook until thick. Allow to cool, and put into a mixing bowl. Beat in the egg yolks, stiffly whip the whites and fold them into the mixture. Season. Quickly pile the mixture into the soufflé dish and dust the top with browned crumbs. Put it into the centre of the oven for 35 minutes.

❃   ❃   ❃

All through October you can buy button onions, fiddly to peel, but really worth the trouble as they are so much sweeter than their larger relatives. They are mostly sold for pickling, but replacing sliced onions in stews and casseroles, incorporated into sauces, cooked with other vegetables or simply on their own, they make an attractive as well as a tasty little vegetable.

In the following recipe they make a piquant sauce for lamb chops.

Lamb chops with button onion sauce

4 good-sized lamb chops	½ pint (3 dl) stock
2 tablespoons chopped marjoram	1 tablespoon chopped parsley
1 oz (25 gr) butter	1 tablespoon chopped capers
24 button onions, peeled	1 dessertspoon vinegar from the
1 tablespoon flour	capers or white wine vinegar

Scatter the marjoram over the chops, season them and grill them under a high heat to your liking.

Melt the butter in a saucepan on a low heat and cook the onions, covered, until they are golden brown and tender, shaking occasionally. Stir in the flour and off the heat blend in the stock. Return to the heat, bring to the boil and stir in the parsley, capers and vinegar. Simmer for ten minutes and serve the chops with the sauce poured over them.

In the next two recipes button onions both give flavour in the cooking and make the dish look attractive.

Best end of lamb goulash

1 large or 2 small pieces best end neck of lamb, chined and with any excess fat removed	16 button onions, peeled
	a bouquet garni which includes a few celery leaves
8 medium carrots, cut in ¾-inch (2 cm) dice	1½ pints (9 dl) stock
	1 oz (25 gr) butter
4 sticks celery, cut in ¾-inch (2 cm) dice	1 dessertspoon paprika
	1 dessertspoon caraway seeds
4 small turnips, cut in ¾-inch (2 cm) dice	2 tablespoons chopped capers
	1 tablespoon flour

Put the meat and vegetables into a large saucepan. Tuck in the bouquet garni and season well with black pepper. Pour in the stock. Bring slowly to the boil, and simmer gently for 1¼ hours uncovered. Allow it to cool. Take the meat from the stock and discard the bones and any more fat. Dice the lean meat and set it aside. Reserve the vegetables and stock separately.

In the rinsed-out pan, melt the butter on a low heat. Stir in the paprika and the caraway seeds and cook very gently for five minutes. Stir in the flour and blend in the stock (¾ pint (4·5 dl) or just over). Bring it gently to the boil and stir in the capers. Add the vegetables and meat, and let them stand for at least an hour for the flavours to blend. Check the seasoning and reheat gently before serving.

Chicken and button onions in lemon sauce

a 3-3½ lb (1·3-1·5 kg) roasting chicken
4 sprigs lemon thyme, or thyme
4 sprigs parsley
1 tablespoon turmeric
for the sauce:
1 oz (25 gr) butter
1 tablespoon flour
juice of ½ lemon
1 tablespoon chopped parsley

25-30 button onions, peeled
1 carrot
1 stick celery
10 peppercorns

Put two sprigs each of lemon thyme and parsley inside the chicken. Truss it and rub the turmeric into the skin. Put the chicken and onions into a large saucepan or casserole with the carrot, celery, and peppercorns and the other sprigs of lemon thyme and parsley. Pour in water to the top of the thighs. Bring it slowly to the boil and poach gently for an hour, covered. Remove the chicken and the onions. Strain and reserve the stock. Allow the chicken to cool, take it off the bones, and cut it into chunks.

Melt the butter on a moderate heat in a large pan. Blend in the flour and half a pint (3 dl) of the reserved stock. Bring to the boil and stir until it is thick. Stir in the lemon juice and season.

Gently fold in the chicken pieces, the onions and the chopped parsley. Serve with buttered rice.

And finally, two vegetable dishes with button onions.

Beetroot and onion casserole

8 small beetroots
16 button onions, peeled
1 oz (25 gr) beef dripping
1 teaspoon soft brown sugar
juice of ½ lemon

Parboil the beetroots in salted water for 30 minutes. Drain and peel them. Preheat the oven to Reg 4/350°F, 180°C.

Melt the dripping on a low heat in a flameproof casserole. Cook the onions gently in this until they are beginning to brown. Add the beetroots to the casserole with the onions and continue cooking for five minutes. Sprinkle over the sugar. Cover and put into the oven for 45 minutes. Take the casserole from the oven and put it on a high heat on top of the stove. Add the lemon juice, season, bring it to the boil, give the vegetables a stir and serve immediately.

Brussels sprouts and button onions

1 lb (450 gr) small Brussels
  sprouts, cleaned and trimmed
16 button onions, peeled
1 oz (25 gr) butter

¼ pint (1·5 dl) stock
1 tablespoon mixed chopped
  thyme and marjoram

Put all the ingredients together in a saucepan, season and set it on a moderate heat for 25 minutes, covered. By this time all the stock should be absorbed and the vegetables tender and shiny.

☙ ☙ ☙

As well as pickling a few onions, I use the last of the summer vegetables to make chutneys.

Piccalilli

1 large cucumber
1 small marrow
1 large cauliflower
for the pickle:
1½ pints (9 dl) white wine vinegar,
  or white malt vinegar
1 oz (25 gr) pickling spice
4 oz (100 gr) demerara sugar
1 rounded dessertspoon ground
  ginger

1 lb (450 gr) onions
2 tablespoons salt

1 tablespoon turmeric
1 tablespoon dry mustard
1 dessertspoon flour

Cut the vegetables into small pieces and put them into a large bowl, with salt between the layers. Leave them for twelve hours. Drain them and rinse in a colander. Boil one pint (6 dl) of the vinegar with the pickling spice for five minutes. Strain it and put it in a large saucepan. Blend the spices and flour with the remaining half pint (3 dl) of vinegar and put these into the pan with the rest. Bring the pickle to the boil and stir in the vegetables. Simmer for ten minutes. Allow it to cool before putting it into screw-topped jars. It will keep for up to six months.

This is the time of year when tomato growers clear out their greenhouses and get rid of all the green tomatoes which are obviously not going to ripen. Here is a good long-lasting chutney to make from them.

Green tomato chutney

5 lb (2·25 kg) green tomatoes
5 medium onions, peeled and
  chopped
3 green peppers, deseeded and
  chopped
5 medium cooking apples, peeled,
  cored and chopped
¾ pint (4·5 dl) white malt vinegar

½ lb (225 gr) soft brown sugar
grated rind of 2 oranges
grated rind of 1 lemon and juice of
  1½ lemons
2 oz (50 gr) sea salt
1 teaspoon ground black pepper
1 teaspoon ground mace
1 teaspoon ground ginger

Simmer the tomatoes in water for 15 minutes and skin them, keeping them immersed until you are ready to skin each one.

Cut them in half and scoop out the seeds. Put the seeds into a sieve over a preserving pan or large saucepan and rub them with a wooden spoon to extract all the juice. Put the tomato halves into the pan. Add the juice and all the other ingredients to the pan. Bring the mixture slowly to the boil and simmer for two hours, when it should be rich and pulpy. Put the chutney into screw-topped jars and put the lids on when it is cool. It will keep for six months or more.

೫೫   ೫೫   ೫೫

In October Conference pears are really hard and crunchy. They are best eaten raw, with a good ripe Brie, Demi Sel or other soft but not too strong cheese.

Here are two first-course salads using pears with curd cheese which has a lighter flavour more suitable for the beginning of the meal.

Pear and curd cheese salad

4 firm Conference pears
4 oz (100 gr) curd cheese
juice of 1 lemon
2 tablespoons chopped fresh cob nuts

Peel the pears and cut them in half lengthways. Discard the cores and then scoop out enough flesh from the pears to leave quarter-inch (6 mm) thick cups. Chop the scooped-out flesh. Brush the shells with lemon juice. Blend the remaining lemon juice with the cheese and mix this with the chopped pear flesh. Pile this back into the pear cups and scatter the chopped nuts over the top.

Pear salad with ham

4 small, firm Conference pears, peeled and cut into slices two inches (5 cm) by half an inch (1·25 cm)
3 oz (75 gr) lean ham, finely diced
the bulbs of 4 spring onions (or 1 small onion), chopped
4 oz (100 gr) curd cheese
2 tablespoons sour cream
juice of 1 lemon

Mix the ham and onions with the cheese and cream. Turn the pear slices in the lemon juice. Pile the cheese on to four small plates or one large one (on lettuce or cress if you like). Garnish with the pieces of pear. Top with a sprig of parsley.

The next pear salad uses tarragon for flavour.

Pears in tarragon dressing

4 firm Conference pears, peeled and chopped
4 tablespoons double cream
1 dessertspoon tarragon mustard
1 dessertspoon wine vinegar

or instead of the last two use tarragon vinegar and Dijon mustard
8 large lettuce leaves
4 tablespoons chopped walnuts

Blend the mustard and cream together and beat in the vinegar. Coat the pears in the dressing. Pile them onto lettuce leaves and scatter the chopped walnuts over the top.

Vegetables available in November

beetroot
Brussels sprouts – in excellent condition, firm and tightly packed
Brussels tops – tender and tasty
cabbage – Christmas Drumhead, January King, Savoys and red
   and white varieties available all through the month
carrots – in perfect condition
cauliflowers – these are variable but it is not a very good month
   for them
celery – in peak condition
greens – these become tougher towards the end of the month
leeks – these are good if you can get them, but in some years
   there aren't many in November
onions – there are still some button onions available, and the
   English crop are large and sound
parsnips – very sound and a good size all through the month
potatoes – excellent
swedes – excellent
turnips – excellent
watercress – this depends on the weather; too many frosts will
   make the leaves turn yellow very quickly

Fruit available in November

apples and pears – at the beginning of the month there are
   plenty of dessert apples and pears, but the supplies dwindle
   during the last week, as one supply from the cold store is used
   up and we have to wait for the Christmas stocks to be released
   at the beginning of December. Cooking apples are plentiful
   throughout the month
citrus fruit – some lovely green satsumas start arriving in the
   shops at the end of the month; oranges and grapefruit are
   still South African but are slightly sweeter and juicier than
   they have been
nuts – chestnuts and English cobs and walnuts are in the shops
   all through the month; all the other varieties from abroad
   come in for the Christmas season.

Fresh herbs in November

bay
chervil – only if the weather is very mild and even then it is scrappy
marjoram – this has woody, shorter stems and small leaves
parsley – growth is very slow in November
rosemary – the leaves gradually become tougher as the month goes on
sage – very tough leaves now and no new growth at all
savory – woody stems and tougher leaves, but there are plenty of them
sorrel – there are one or two leaves if the weather is mild
thyme – this has very woody stems and rather tough leaves

Although weatherwise it is often the 'dull November' of the old rhyme, this is by no means a dull month for food. The shops are really well stocked with all kinds of winter vegetables which are freshly harvested and firm, and not too huge. Towards the end of the month window displays look brighter and more tantalising as the countdown to Christmas begins.

And at the beginning of the month we have Guy Fawkes Night, which to me always means baked potatoes. Nothing can match the flavour of one that has been buried in the ashes of the bonfire, eaten with loads of butter (and probably a good deal of ash as well!), but even baking in the oven brings out the best in a potato. Like all the other roots, potatoes are particularly good in November. You can safely serve baked ones to your guests without worrying that they are going to cut one open in anticipation, butter at the ready, only to find that it is full of black lumps.

A baked potato must have a crispy skin; you can achieve this by scrubbing it, pricking it twice on both sides with a fork and then putting it into the centre of a hot oven Reg 4/350°F, 180°C for 1½ hours. If there is nothing else in the oven that will spoil, you can make it even better by raising the heat to Reg 5 or 6/ 400°F, 200°C or for the final 15 minutes.

Here are some ways of adding flavour and variety to baked potatoes.

Baked potatoes with sage

4 baked potatoes
2 oz (50 gr) butter
1 tablespoon chopped sage

Melt the butter and cook the sage in it for half a minute. Split the potatoes in half and pour over the butter and sage mixture. Season.

Tomato and Worcestershire potatoes

4 baked potatoes
1 oz (25 gr) butter
1 tablespoon tomato purée
1 tablespoon Worcestershire sauce
4 medium tomatoes, each cut into four slices
1 tablespoon grated Parmesan cheese

Cut the potatoes in half and scoop out the middles. Mash them with the butter, tomato purée and Worcestershire sauce. Pile the mixture back into the shells. Put two tomato slices on each, sprinkle with the Parmesan, and put them back into the oven until the Parmesan has melted.

Sage and apple potatoes

4 baked potatoes
2 oz (50 gr) butter
12 sage leaves, chopped
1 lb (450 gr) cooking apples, peeled and thinly sliced

Cut the potatoes in half and scoop out the middles. Mash them with half the butter and the sage. Put the mixture back into the shells and pile the apple slices on them. Dot the remaining butter on top, and put them back in the hot oven for 20 minutes.

These go well with roast pork.

Baked potatoes with anchovy sauce

4 baked potatoes
2 oz (50 gr) butter
4 anchovy fillets, chopped
1 tablespoon capers, chopped

Heat the butter on a high heat until it is brown. Stir in the anchovies and capers and pour it immediately over the halved potatoes.

Baked potatoes with cheese and parsley

4 baked potatoes
10 tablespoons grated Cheddar cheese
4 tablespoons chopped parsley

Cut the potatoes in half and scoop out the middles. Mash them with all but two tablespoons of the cheese, and the parsley and seasoning. Pile the mixture back into the shells and sprinkle the remaining cheese over them. Put them back into the oven until the cheese is melted and bubbly.

Baked potatoes with capers and onions

4 baked potatoes
2 oz (50 gr) butter
1 tablepsoon chopped capers
1 dessertspoon anchovy essence
2 large onions, sliced into rings

Cut the potatoes in half and scoop out the middles. Mash them with half the butter, the capers and the anchovy essence. Put the mixture back in the shells and lay the onion rings on top. Dot them with the remaining butter and put them back in the oven for 30 minutes so the onions can brown.

Mashed potatoes are the best kind to serve with spicy casseroles. Peel them first and cook a small sliced onion with them. Then mash them all together to a smooth creamy texture with butter and a little milk. It is a good idea to cook more than you need so that you can have potato cakes the next day.

Potato cakes

Mash the potatoes as described above and leave them until they are quite cold and firm enough to handle, preferably overnight.

Preheat the oven to Reg 6/400°F, 200°C and thickly butter a baking tray. Form the potatoes into small balls with your hands, put them on the baking tray, and press them down to make thin cakes about two inches (5 cm) in diameter and half an inch (1·25 cm) thick. Brush them with beaten egg and put them into the oven until they are golden brown (about 45 minutes).

Potatoes can also be boiled with an equal quantity of either turnip or parsnip, and then puréed all together.

As November is such a good month for potatoes, here are some more recipes for them.

Potato cubes with parsley

4 medium potatoes, peeled and
   cut in quarter-inch cubes
4 tablespoons olive oil

1 large onion, finely chopped
4 tablespoons chopped parsley
½ pint (3 dl) boiling water

Heat the oil on a moderate heat in a large frying pan. Add the potatoes and onions and fry them until they are golden, stirring them around frequently. Stir in the boiling water and the parsley, season and continue to cook until all the water has evaporated.

Glazed potato wedges

4 large even-sized potatoes,
   scrubbed but not peeled
1½ oz (38 gr) butter
½ pint (3 dl) stock

4 tablespoons chopped parsley
2 bayleaves
2 tablespoons grated cheese

Cut each potato in half lengthways and cut each half into four long wedges shaped like melon slices. Melt the butter on a high heat in a large frying pan or sauté pan and brown the potatoes on both the flat sides of the wedge. (Do them in batches if the pan is too small to take all the potatoes at once). Return all the potatoes to the pan. Pour in the stock and bring it to the boil. Add the parsley and bay leaves. Cover tightly and simmer gently for 30 minutes by which time the stock should have reduced to a sticky glaze. Check it occasionally and add more stock if necessary towards the end. Season if necessary and scatter in the grated cheese two minutes before the end so it just has time to melt.

Julienne potatoes and herbs

Cut the potatoes into very thin julienne sticks and sauté them in a large frying pan or paëlla pan in a mixture of oil and butter on a moderate heat. When they are a golden brown, toss in any mixture of chopped mixed herbs that you like.

Casserole of bacon and potatoes

6 even-sized potatoes, about
    4 inches (10 cm) long and
    2 inches (5 cm) wide, peeled and
    quartered

1 oz (25 gr) butter
2 rashers lean bacon, diced
1 small onion, sliced
¼ pint (1·5 dl) stock

Preheat the oven to Reg 4/350°F, 180°C.
Melt the butter in a flameproof casserole on a low heat and cook the bacon and onion in this until they are golden. Meanwhile, round off the edges of the potatoes with a peeler so they look like new potatoes. Stir them into the bacon and onion and pour in the stock. Put them into the oven for an hour and check the seasoning before serving.

Here are two recipes for large potato cakes, both of which look attractive and unusual on the dinner table.

Savoury potato cake

4 medium potatoes
4 oz (100 gr) butter
2 eggs, beaten
2 tablespoons chopped parsley

4 oz (100 gr) self-raising flour,
    preferably 81 % wholemeal
2 tablespoons milk

Preheat the oven to Reg 3/325°F, 170°C, and line a 1 lb (450 gr) loaf tin with a butter paper.

Boil the potatoes in their skins, peel them and mash them without milk or butter. Rub them through a sieve. Cream the butter in a mixing bowl and beat in the potato. Beat in the eggs, a little at a time, and then mix in the parsley. Add the flour bit by bit, and finally beat in the milk. Season, put the mixture into the loaf tin and bake it in the centre of the oven for 1½ hours.

If you have any of this left over, it is good fried in dripping or bacon fat and served with a fried egg on the top.

Mashed potato and onion cake

4 medium potatoes
1 medium onion
2 oz (50 gr) butter
2 oz (50 gr) grated Cheddar cheese (optional)

Boil the potatoes in their skins, peel them while they are still hot and mash them. Preheat the oven to Reg 5/375°F, 190°C.

Finely chop the onion. Melt the butter in an eight-inch (20 cm) skillet or deep sandwich tin on a moderate heat on top of the stove. Add the onion and cook it until it is brown. Keeping the pan on the heat, mix the potatoes into the butter and onion. Season. When they are well mixed, press the mixture down and cover it. Leave it on the heat for three minutes to let the under-side brown. Remove the lid, and put the pan or tin into the oven for 20 minutes. Turn out the cake, and the outside should be golden brown.

If you are using the cheese, sprinkle this over the top for the last ten minutes of cooking, so that when you turn out the cake the cheesey taste will be underneath as a surprise.

ɮ   ɮ   ɮ

The darker and longer nights always remind me of Sunday teas round the fire with boiled eggs, toast, crumpets, cheese and crunchy white celery.

In November English celery is in really peak condition as

there have been no severe frosts yet to make the sticks soft in the middle or brown-speckled. Although buying it still with the root on and covered in rich black earth makes a little more work than buying the ready-washed variety, it's so worth it for the flavour and texture. A stick of celery just plain and alone is treat enough, especially if it includes the inner part of the root, but it can be chopped up and mixed with so many different things for winter salads as well. Celery and apple is a good combination, especially if you use the sweeter types of cooking apple. Mix in some fresh chopped walnuts and coat it with mayonnaise or Fresh dressing. For a first course, celery can accompany all types of spicy sausages like cabanos or Chorizos; surprisingly, as the textures are so different, it goes well with grapefruit.

The wide ends of celery sticks can be filled with the other salad ingredients.

Celery and apple boats

the wide bottom halves of 8 sticks celery
2 large cooking apples, peeled and cut into quarter-inch (6 mm) dice
4 oz (100 gr) curd cheese
2 tablespoons chopped walnuts

Mix the apples with the cheese. Pile the mixture into the celery sticks and scatter the chopped walnuts over the top.

Stuffed celery and tomatoes

the wide ends of 8 sticks celery
4 large firm tomatoes, skinned and halved
4 oz (100 gr) curd cheese
1 tablespoon tomato purée

1 teaspoon paprika
a few drops Tabasco sauce (or a tiny pinch of Cayenne pepper)
4 pickled gherkins, chopped very small

Soften the cheese in a bowl and work in the tomato purée, paprika and Tabasco sauce. Scoop out the seeds from the tomatoes and rub them in a sieve over the bowl of cheese to extract all the juice. Blend this well into the cheese. Stuff the pieces of celery and the tomato halves with the cheese mixture. Scatter the gherkins over the top.

Celery is just as delicious cooked as it is raw, either on its own, or with another vegetable, in a casserole, or incorporated into a main dish. Strong-flavoured English celery also makes a simple soup, but the recipe is not really suitable for the green varieties.

Celery soup

8 sticks celery
1½ oz (38 gr) butter
1½ tablespoons flour
1½ pints (9 dl) stock

4 fluid oz (1·5 dl) double cream
2 tablespoons grated Cheddar
  cheese

Melt the butter in a saucepan on a low heat and stir in the celery. Cover the pan and let it sweat for five minutes. Stir in the flour and blend in the stock. Bring it gently to the boil, stirring, and simmer for 20 minutes, uncovered. Stir in the cream, check the seasoning, and reheat the soup.

Serve the soup in individual bowls with the cheese floated on the top at the last minute.

Lamb chops with celery and mushrooms

8 small lamb chops
½ oz (13 gr) butter or
  2 tablespoons lamb fat
4 oz (100 gr) mushrooms, sliced

1 large onion, sliced
6 large sticks celery, sliced
1 wineglass dry white wine
1 dessertspoon tomato purée

Heat the fat in a heavy sauté pan or large frying pan on a high heat and brown the chops in this on both sides. Lower the heat to moderate and continue cooking for seven minutes, turning the chops from time to time. Add the mushrooms, onion, celery and seasoning to the pan with the chops and continue cooking until the onion is beginning to brown. By this time the chops should be done, so remove them from the pan and keep them warm. Raise the heat, pour in the wine and stir in the tomato purée. Boil until the liquid is reduced by half. Pile the vegetables on to a warm serving dish and set the chops on top.

Leeks and celery cooked with tomatoes

4 small thin leeks, cut into
  half-inch (1·25 cm) slices
6 sticks celery, thinly sliced
1½ oz (38 gr) butter

4 tomatoes, skinned, deseeded and
  roughly chopped
2 tablespoons chopped parsley
approx ½ pint (3 dl) stock

Melt the butter on a low heat in a heavy saucepan. Stir in the
leeks and celery. Cover them and let them sweat for five minutes.
Add the tomatoes and parsley and enough stock to come half-
way up the vegetables. Cover, check the seasoning, and cook on
a moderate heat for 25 minutes.

Red celery

8 large sticks celery, cut into
  julienne sticks
1 medium onion, thinly sliced
¼ pint (1·5 dl) stock

1 teaspoon tomato purée
1 teaspoon paprika
1 oz (25 gr) butter

Put the celery and onion into a saucepan with the stock, tomato
purée, paprika and butter and set them on a moderate heat for
20 minutes, covered.

If you can get one, use a wild rabbit for the next recipe – they
are so much more tasty than tame ones.

Rabbit and celery in cider

1 wild rabbit
2 tablespoons seasoned flour
1 oz (25 gr) bacon fat or pork
  dripping
4 oz (100 gr) lean bacon, diced

3 sticks celery, diced
1 medium onion, sliced
¼ pint (1·5 dl) dry cider
1 tablespoon chopped mixed
  parsley and sage

Joint the rabbit. Remove all the meat from the bones and dice
it fairly small. Toss the meat in the seasoned flour. Melt the fat
on a low heat in a heavy sauté pan or large frying pan. Put in
the bacon, celery and onion and cook them until the onion is
soft. Remove them and set them aside. Raise the heat and add

a little more fat if necessary. Put in the pieces of rabbit and fry them until they are brown, moving them around all the time so they don't stick together. Pour in the cider and bring it to the boil. Stir in the herbs, season, and replace the vegetables and bacon. Cover the pan and cook on the lowest heat possible for an hour.

Chicken, celery and leeks in cheese sauce

a 3-3½ lb (1·3-1·5 kg) roasting
   chicken
1 teaspoon ground nutmeg
1 teaspoon ground cinnamon
2 sprigs parsley
for the sauce:
1 oz (25 gr) butter
1 tablespoon flour
2 oz (50 gr) grated Cheddar cheese
2 tablespoons chopped parsley

6 sticks celery, cut in one-inch
   (2·5 cm) squares
6 small leeks, cut in one-inch
   (2·5 cm) squares

Mix the spices together and rub them into the skin of the chicken. If you have any left over, rub the inside as well. Put one sprig of parsley inside the chicken and truss it. Put the chicken into a large saucepan or casserole. Surround it with the vegetables, tuck in the other parsley sprig and season. Put in enough cold water to just cover the thighs. Cover the pan, bring the water to the boil and simmer very gently for an hour.

Allow the chicken to cool in the stock before removing it. Take the meat off the bones and cut it into cubes. Remove the leeks and celery from the stock and strain off ½ pint (3 dl) stock for the sauce.

Melt the butter in a saucepan on a moderate heat. Stir in the flour and blend in the stock. Stir until it boils. Beat in the grated cheese and parsley. Mix in the celery, leeks and diced chicken and serve garnished with watercress to give a contrasting taste and colour.

ॐ   ॐ   ॐ

Carrots are in perfect condition in November, crisp and crunchy for salads and a good size for cooking. For salads they can be cut into thin sticks or grated and mixed with yoghurt, sour cream dressing or a simple French dressing. Grated carrot is delicious mixed with grapefruit in a salad especially if you use lots of garlic and pepper. Here is a carrot and curd cheese salad which makes a refreshing first course.

Carrot and curd cheese salad

4 medium carrots, grated
4 oz (100 gr) curd cheese
juice of 1 lemon

1 clove garlic, crushed with salt
2 tablespoons chopped raisins
watercress for serving

Combine the cheese, lemon juice, garlic and a little pepper. Mix the carrots and raisins into the cheese mixture. Pile it onto the centre of a large serving plate or four small ones and surround it with sprigs of watercress.

Carrots always make good thick soups, either on their own or mixed with other vegetables.

Carrot and orange soup

12 oz (325 gr) carrots, sliced
2 medium onions, sliced
1½ oz (38 gr) butter
1½ pints (9 dl) stock

juice of 2 large oranges and pared
  rind of one
4 tablespoons double cream

Melt the butter on a low heat in a saucepan and stir in the carrots and onions. Cover them and let them sweat for five minutes. Pour in the stock, bring to the boil and simmer, covered, for 15 minutes. Allow to cool slightly and work the vegetables and stock in the blender until smooth. Pour in the orange juice and blend for a few seconds more. Put the soup back into the saucepan and stir in the cream. Season, and reheat gently without boiling.

  Cut the pared rind of one of the oranges into thin slivers. Simmer them in water for five minutes and drain them well. Float them on top of the soup just before serving for a garnish.

Carrot and leek soup

3 large carrots	1½ pints (9 dl) stock
3 small leeks, sliced	2 tablespoons chopped parsley
1 oz (25 gr) butter	

Grate half a carrot and set it aside. Slice the rest. Melt the butter on a low heat in a saucepan. Stir in the sliced carrot and leeks, cover them and let them sweat for ten minutes. Stir in the stock, bring it to the boil and simmer gently for 20 minutes uncovered. Allow the soup to cool before working it in the blender until smooth. Return it to the pan, check the seasoning and reheat it.

Pour the soup into bowls and float the grated raw carrot and the chopped parsley on the top.

Carrot and turnip soup

8 oz (225 gr) carrots, thinly sliced	1½ pints (9 dl) stock
8 oz (225 gr) turnips, thinly sliced	2 teaspoons made English
4 oz (100 gr) onion, finely chopped	mustard
1½ oz (38 gr) butter	1 dessertspoon grated horseradish

Melt the butter on a low heat in a saucepan. Stir in the vegetables, cover them and let them sweat for seven minutes. Pour in the stock, bring it to the boil and simmer for 15 minutes, uncovered. Allow the soup to cool slightly and work it in the blender until smooth. Return it to the saucepan and stir in the mustard and horseradish. Reheat.

Carrots, like many vegetables, are best cooked so that they can absorb any liquid which is added to them.

Glazed carrots in stock

1 lb (450 gr) carrots, sliced
1½ oz (38 gr) butter
½ pint (3 dl) stock
2 tablespoons chopped parsley

Put the carrots into a heavy saucepan with the butter, stock and seasoning. Cover them and set them on a moderate heat for 20 minutes. Take off the lid and continue to cook until all the moisture has evaporated and the carrots are glazed. Toss in the parsley.

Carrots with capers and lemon

1 lb (450 gr) carrots, sliced into thin rounds
1½ oz (38 gr) butter
½ pint (3 dl) stock
grated rind and juice of 1 lemon
1 dessertspoon chopped capers

Melt the butter in a saucepan on a low heat and stir in the carrot slices. Cover them and cook them gently for seven minutes. Pour in the stock and lemon juice and add the lemon rind and seasoning. Raise the heat and boil fairly rapidly until all the stock is absorbed and the carrots are slightly glazed. Toss in the chopped capers just before serving.

Carrots and sprouts with tomato purée

½ lb (225 gr) carrots, thinly sliced
½ lb (225 gr) Brussels sprouts, trimmed
1 dessertspoon tomato purée
1 oz (25 gr) butter
¼ pint (1·5 dl) stock

Put all the ingredients in a saucepan. Cover and set on a moderate heat for 20 minutes. Check the seasoning before serving.

Diced braised carrots and celery

¾ lb (325 gr) carrots, diced very small
4 sticks celery, diced very small
1 oz (25 gr) butter
1 tablespoon tomato purée
½ pint (3 dl) stock
bouquet garni
1 bayleaf

Preheat the oven to Reg 4/350°F, 180°C.
Melt the butter in a small casserole on a low heat. Stir in the vegetables. Cover them with a butter paper and a lid and let them sweat for five minutes. Stir in the tomato purée and stock and put in the bouquet garni and the bayleaf. Season. Put the casserole into the oven for an hour.

Put into the pot, carrots are one of the essential ingredients of familiar dishes like Lancashire hot-pot and Irish stew. Here are some more meat dishes which use them.

Braised beef and carrots

2 lb (900 gr) stewing beef, cut into one-inch (2·5 cm) cubes
2 tablespoons beef dripping
1 lb (450 gr) carrots, thinly sliced
2 medium onions, thinly sliced
1 wineglass white wine
½ pint (3 dl) stock
1 large clove garlic, chopped
1 lb (450 gr) tomatoes, skinned and chopped
2 tablespoons tomato purée
bouquet garni

Preheat the oven to Reg 3/325°F, 170°C.
Melt the dripping on a high heat in a heavy flameproof casserole. Brown the cubes of beef all over and remove them. Lower the heat and stir in the carrots and onions. Cover them with a butter paper and a lid and let them sweat for seven minutes. Pour in the wine and stock, and add the garlic, tomatoes, tomato purée, bouquet garni and seasoning. Bring them to the boil and replace the meat. Cover the casserole and put it in the oven for 1½ hours.

Stuffed chicken with carrots and tomatoes

a 3-3½ lb (1·3-1·5 kg) chicken
for the stuffing:
½ oz (13 gr) butter
1 small onion, finely chopped
6 oz (150 gr) grated carrots
2 tomatoes, skinned and chopped
grated rind and juice of ½ orange
1 oz (25 gr) butter
10 oz (250 gr) carrots, cut into julienne sticks
¼ pint (1·5 dl) stock, made from the giblets
4 tomatoes, skinned, deseeded and chopped
juice of ½ orange
bouquet garni
½ oz (13 gr) kneaded butter

Preheat the oven to Reg 4/350°F, 180°C.
To make the stuffing, melt the butter in a small frying pan on a low heat and cook the onion in this until it is soft. Mix in the carrots, tomatoes and orange rind and juice. Continue cooking

until the tomatoes are mushy and mixed well into the carrots. Stuff the chicken with this mixture, and truss it.

Melt the butter on a moderate heat in a large flameproof casserole. Brown the trussed chicken all over in this, taking care not to damage the skin as you turn it over. Take out the chicken and lower the heat. Stir in the carrots, cover them, and let them sweat for five minutes. Set the chicken back in the casserole, pour in the stock and bring it to the boil. Put in the tomatoes and tuck in the bouquet garni. Season, cover the casserole and put it into the oven for 1¼ hours.

Remove the chicken and keep it warm. Strain the juices from the casserole and put the carrots on to a warm serving dish. Put the sauce back into the casserole and stir in the orange juice. Thicken as necessary with kneaded butter. Carve the chicken and arrange it on the carrots with spoonfuls of the carrot stuffing. Pour the sauce over the top before serving.

Veal in Marsala with carrots and celery

2 lb (900 gr) pie veal, cut into
  ¾-inch (2 cm) cubes
1 oz (25 gr) butter
12 oz (325 gr) crisp thin carrots,
  thinly sliced

4 sticks celery, thinly sliced
1 medium onion, thinly sliced
2 wineglasses Marsala or sherry
2 tablespoons chopped parsley

Melt the butter on a high heat in a wide-bottomed casserole. Brown the pieces of veal all over in this. Remove them, lower the heat, add the vegetables and cook them gently for three minutes, stirring. Pour in the Marsala and bring it to the boil. Put the veal back in the casserole, with the chopped parsley. Season, cover the casserole and set it on a very low heat for 45 minutes, by which time most of the liquid will be absorbed and the vegetables soft.

ॐ   ॐ   ॐ

Different types of green cabbage are available during most of the year, but it is only in the winter months that you can buy the crinkly Savoy. Its texture is less good than that of the firmer white or green cabbages for eating raw, but it has a more savoury flavour and never goes too limp when cooked. The really dark outer leaves of the Savoy are extremely tough and are one of the few parts of any vegetable that I throw away, but the next layer of large leaves are good for stuffing as the crinkled texture prevents them from tearing.

Stuffed cabbage leaves

12 large Savoy cabbage leaves
1 lb (450 gr) good quality sausage meat, or ½ lb (225 gr) good quality minced beef and ½ lb (225 gr) sausage meat mixed
2 tablespoons chopped mixed herbs
1 small onion, finely chopped

a little flour
½ pint (3 dl) stock
½ oz (13 gr) kneaded butter
1 dessertspoon tomato purée
1 dessertspoon Worcestershire sauce
2 tomatoes, skinned, deseeded and cut into strips

Preheat the oven to Reg 4/350°F, 180°C.
Blanch the cabbage leaves for three minutes in rapidly boiling water. Drain them and let them steam dry. Thoroughly mix the meat with the herbs and onion. Divide the mixture into twelve and put a portion on each leaf. Roll up the leaves, the stem-end first and then the sides, and fold them over. Lightly dust them with flour. Put them into a deep dish or casserole and pour over the stock. Cover them and cook them in the oven for 45 minutes. Take them out and put them on a serving dish to keep warm.

Pour the stock in which they cooked into a saucepan, bring it to the boil and stir in the kneaded butter, tomato purée and Worcestershire sauce. Add the tomatoes to the pan and heat them through. Check the seasoning and pour the sauce over the stuffed cabbage leaves before serving.

The stuffing in this recipe can be varied; you can use minced beef only, instead of half sausage meat, or perhaps minced pork with sage. Minced cooked meats bound with potatoes or beaten egg can also be used, or for a complete change, flaked smoked haddock and rice.

Because of its strong flavour the Savoy cabbage can be spiced, or cooked with wine or cider.

Braised Savoy cabbage in cider

1 Savoy cabbage (inner leaves
  only), shredded
1 oz (25 gr) butter
1 large cooking apple, thinly
  sliced

1 large onion, thinly sliced
4 tablespoons dry cider
1 tablespoon wine vinegar

Preheat the oven to Reg 4/350°F, 180°C.
Blanch the cabbage in boiling salted water for two minutes.
Drain it well. Melt the butter in a casserole on a low heat and
cook the apple and onion gently in this until they are soft.
Remove them and set them aside. Take the casserole off the heat.
Put in a layer of one third of the cabbage, then half the apple
and onion, then cabbage, the remaining apple and onion, and
finally a layer of cabbage. Season. Mix the cider and vinegar
together and pour them into the casserole. Cover, and put them
into the oven for an hour.

Here is a simpler recipe, cooked on top of the stove.

Savoy cabbage with apple and onion

1 Savoy cabbage (inner leaves
  only), shredded
1 large cooking apple, thinly
  sliced

1 large onion, thinly sliced
1 oz (25 gr) butter
¼ pint (1·5 dl) stock

Put all the ingredients into a heavy saucepan. Season, cover
them and set them on a moderate heat for 20 minutes, stirring
occasionally.

Savoy cabbage, celery and savory in white wine

1 Savoy cabbage (inner leaves
  only), shredded
2 oz (50 gr) butter
6 large sticks celery, sliced

1 large onion, sliced
2 tablespoons chopped savory
1 wineglass white wine
1 wineglass stock

Put the butter in the bottom of a large saucepan. Add the vegetables and the savory on top of the butter and pour in the wine

and stock. Season, and set the saucepan on a moderate heat for 30 minutes, stirring occasionally.

Spiced tomato cabbage

1 small Savoy cabbage (inner leaves only), finely shredded
1 tablespoon Worcestershire sauce
1 tablespoon tomato purée
¼ pint (1·5 dl) stock
1 tablespoon olive oil

4 allspice berries and 2 cloves, crushed together
1 clove garlic, crushed with a pinch of sea salt
2 firm tomatoes, peeled, deseeded and chopped

Blend together the Worcestershire sauce, tomato purée, stock, oil, spices and garlic. Put the cabbage into a heavy saucepan and pour in the mixture. Set the pan on a moderate heat for 20 minutes. Toss in the tomatoes and check the seasoning just before serving.

Although Savoy cabbage is no good for cold salads, it can be made into hot ones. Here is one with pork, to be served as a main dish.

Hot pork and Savoy cabbage salad

1 lb (450 gr) belly of pork, diced
2 sprigs rosemary, finely chopped
2 cloves garlic, finely chopped
½ large or 1 very small Savoy cabbage (inner leaves only), shredded

1 large eating apple, peeled and diced
2 tablespoons wine vinegar
2 tablespoons mayonnaise

Heat a large frying pan or paëlla pan on a high heat with no fat. Add the pork, the rosemary and the garlic. Fry, stirring all the time, until the pork is brown and crisp and the fat is beginning to run (about ten minutes). Stir in the cabbage and apple, and continue to cook, still stirring, for two minutes. Mix in the vinegar and quickly bring it to the boil. Remove the pan from the heat and stir in the mayonnaise. Serve immediately, hot.

Vegetables available in December

beetroot
Brussels sprouts – still small, crisp and tasty
Brussels tops – very good and tender all through the month
cabbage – Christmas Drumhead, January King, Savoys, red
    and white cabbages are all still available
carrots – these are excellent all through the month
celery – if there are very severe frosts this will have brown soft
    patches; otherwise it is in excellent condition
chicory – not a very abundant vegetable but it first comes into
    the shops in December
greens – these usually alternate with Brussels tops at this time
    of the year, but they are not as tender
leeks – these are excellent and in good supply
onions – good quality large ones and button onions can
    still be bought
parsnips – excellent, firm and large
swede – very good all through the month
turnips – also very good
watercress – this is only good if there are no frosts

Fruit available in December

apples and pears – all kinds of English apples and pears are
    available all through the month, but just after Christmas the
    supplies may drop slightly as we wait for the next batch to
    come out of the cold store
cooking apples – in good supply all through the month and still
    crisp
citrus fruit – really good oranges and satsumas, and grapefruit
    are juicy again by now
grapes – these, particularly the sweet white Spanish ones, are
    cheap
nuts – all kinds of nuts are in the shops for Christmas
rhubarb – the first forced rhubarb arrives late in the month

Fresh herbs available in December

marjoram – tiny leaves and tough stems but still usable
parsley – very tiny leaves in December and not very productive
rosemary – slightly tough leaves but plenty of them
sage – very tough, almost dry leaves, but still usable
savory – still has lots of leaves but the steams are short and very
  woody
thyme – a lot of leaves but woody stems

℞   ℞   ℞

If you love cooking, what better time of the year is there than
Christmas? All through the month preparations are made and
meals planned, and never are the food shops better stocked. As
well as buying special ingredients for all the Christmas fare you
can take advantage of the shops' willingness to sell more unusual things at this time of the year (such as jars of olives or
whole pieces of candied peel) and stock up your store cupboard
for the next few months.

Although I seem to be stirring and mixing something on every
day in December, I tend to disregard vegetables, while I turn my
thoughts to puddings, pies, meats and terrines. There are plenty
of really good vegetables about, though – all kinds of roots and
cabbages; and all the apples and pears are taken fresh and crisp
from the cold store.

There is plenty of English fruit, and also cheap grapes, satsumas, and the first of the juicy sharp oranges from Spain. After
several months of pithy, dry oranges these are a real treat –
lovely, if a little messy, to eat on their own as a sweet, a fresh
ingredient in green salads, and good for cooking as well.

These recipes use satsumas or oranges, or sometimes both.

Tomato and orange salad

Mix equal amounts of chopped orange segments with chopped
tomatoes. Toss them in French dressing and serve them on a
bed of lettuce.

Carrot, turnip and satsuma salad

2 medium carrots, grated
2 medium turnips, grated
2 satsumas

1 clove garlic, crushed with salt
juice of 1 lemon
10 fluid oz (3 dl) plain yoghurt

Separate the segments of the satsumas and cut each one in half.
Blend the lemon and garlic into the yoghurt. Mix the dressing
into the vegetables and satsumas.

Curried Savoy cabbage with satsumas

1 small Savoy cabbage (inner
  leaves only), shredded
1 small onion, finely sliced
½ oz (13 gr) butter

¼ pint (1·5 dl) stock
1 heaped teaspoon curry powder
2 satsumas

Put the cabbage and onion into a saucepan with the butter,
stock and curry powder and set them on a moderate heat for
20 minutes. Pull the satsumas into segments and cut each segment in half. Toss the segments into the cabbage for the final
minute of cooking so they just heat through.

Beef with lemon and orange

2 lb (900 gr) shin of beef, cut into
  one-inch (2·5 cm) cubes
2 tablespoons seasoned flour
2 oz (50 gr) beef dripping
2 medium onions, finely chopped
6 sticks celery, cut in half-inch
  (1·25 cm) dice
1 pint (6 dl) stock

10 allspice berries and 10 black
  peppercorns, crushed together
2 tablespoons chopped marjoram
  and savory
2 small oranges
grated rind and juice of 1 lemon
4 tablespoons sour cream

Preheat the oven to Reg 3/325°F, 170°C.
Coat the beef with seasoned flour. Melt half the dripping in a
heavy flameproof casserole on a high heat and brown the beef
cubes all over in this. Remove the beef and lower the heat. Add
the remaining dripping to the casserole and gently cook the
onions and celery in this until the onions are soft. Raise the heat

again and pour in the stock. Add the crushed spices. Stir until
it boils, scraping in any brown pieces from the bottom of the
pan. Replace the beef and add the herbs. Put into the oven for
1½ hours.

Meanwhile, pare the rind thinly from the oranges and cut it
into thin slivers. Blanch them by putting them into cold water
and bringing them to the boil. Drain them. Peel the oranges and
cut each segment into three. When the beef is cooked, stir in the
lemon juice and rind and the sour cream and put the casserole
back into the oven for a few minutes to heat through again. Stir
in the orange pieces just before serving in a warm serving dish
with the slivers of orange rind over the top.

Whiting with orange and satsumas

8 whiting fillets, skinned
for the marinade:

grated rind and juice of 1 large orange	1 tablespoon olive oil
1 small onion, finely chopped	1 dessertspoon chopped thyme or lemon thyme
1 teaspoon dry mustard	

1 small green cabbage, shredded	4 tablespoons water
1 medium onion, sliced	1 dessertspoon chopped thyme or lemon thyme
½ oz (13 gr) butter	
2 tablespoons white wine	2 satsumas

Mix all the ingredients for the marinade together. Spoon half of
them into a large flat dish. Lay the whiting on top and spoon
over the rest. Leave them for at least four hours.

Put the cabbage and onion into a saucepan with the butter,
wine, water and thyme. Season and set them on a fairly low heat
for 25 minutes, shaking occasionally. Skin the satsumas and
divide each one in half vertically. Slice each half and toss them
into the cabbage. Put the cabbage mixture into a flat, ovenproof
dish and preheat the grill to high. Remove the whiting from the
marinade, brushing off all the pieces of onion. Lay it on top of

the cabbage and put the dish under the grill until the whiting are golden and cooked through.

White wine and olives give a completely different flavour to this next beef dish.

Beef with celery, orange and olives

2 lb (900 gr) shin of beef, cut into
  ¾-inch (2 cm) cubes
3 tablespoons beef dripping
2 medium onions, thinly sliced
8 sticks celery, sliced
1½ tablespoons flour
½ pint (3 dl) stock
½ pint (3 dl) white wine

grated rind and juice of 1 large
  orange
2 tablespoons mixed chopped
  thyme or lemon thyme and
  parsley
12 green olives, stoned and
  quartered

Preheat the oven to Reg 3/325°F, 170°C.
Melt the dripping on a high heat in a heavy flameproof casserole. Brown the pieces of meat all over in this. Remove them and set aside. Lower the heat and stir in the onion and celery, and cook them until they are beginning to soften. Stir in the flour and keep stirring until it browns. Blend in the stock and wine and bring them gently to the boil, stirring. Replace the meat and stir in the orange rind and juice, herbs and olives. Cover the casserole and put it into the oven for 1½ hours.

Check the seasoning and serve with a green salad of lettuce and cress, to which you have added another chopped orange.

Stuffed herrings with oranges

4 herrings with soft roes
1 oz (25 gr) butter
1 small onion, finely chopped
1 oz (25 gr) granary breadcrumbs

2 Spanish oranges
4 tablespoons chopped watercress
4 tablespoons oatmeal

Remove the heads from the herrings, slit them down the belly and clean them, reserving the roes. Remove the fins and backbone, but keep them joined down the back. Finely chop the roes.

Melt the butter in a frying pan on a low heat and gently cook the onion in this until it is soft. Raise the heat, add the roes to the pan, and cook them briskly for three minutes, stirring all the time. Remove them from the heat and work in the crumbs, the grated rind of one of the oranges, the watercress and seasoning. Stuff the herrings with this mixture, reshape them and coat with oatmeal. Preheat the grill to high. Remove the remaining rind and pith from the oranges with a sharp knife and cut each one across into eight slices.

Grill the herrings until one side is golden brown. Turn them over carefully and brown the other side. Put four orange slices on each herring, tapering them down according to size towards the tail. Put them back under the grill until the oranges are sizzling.

♧   ♧   ♧

There are all kinds of nuts in the shops in the weeks leading up to Christmas. They can be chopped up and sprinkled over creamy soups or over the top of meat dishes in the same way as parsley. Walnuts are good in salads, especially with crunchy cabbage or celery, and almonds are delicious salted. Instead of buying almonds in their shells for salting, save yourself a little trouble by buying them shelled in a packet. Don't buy ready-blanched ones for salting or they will be too dry.

Salted almonds

8 oz (225 gr) almonds
3 tablespoons olive or peanut oil
1 tablespoon fine sea salt

Put the almonds in a little cold water in a shallow pan and bring them quickly to the boil. Drain them. Squeeze them out of their shells – gently, or they will ping across the room! Heat the oil in a heavy frying pan on a moderate heat. Put in the blanched almonds and fry them until they are golden brown, stirring them around for most of the time to make sure they colour evenly. Have ready a piece of kitchen paper, folded double and sprinkled with the salt. Put the hot almonds straight onto this from the pan and move them around until they are coated with the salt. When they are cool, put them into an airtight jar and keep them to serve with drinks before Christmas lunch.

Chestnuts can be used quite a lot in cooking, but these are really difficult and fiddly to peel. The best way is to nick off the tops with a sharp knife and simmer them for ten minutes in lightly salted water. Take them off the heat, but keep them immersed until you peel them, otherwise they will dry up and you will have to start all over again. The following recipes for chestnuts only use a few, so the preparation time isn't too lengthy.

Chestnut soup

¾ lb (325 gr) chestnuts, peeled and skinned
1 large onion, sliced
1½ pints (9 dl) stock
2 tablespoons double cream
a little grated nutmeg

Put the chestnuts into a pan with the onion and barely cover them with some of the stock. Season with black pepper. Simmer gently for 20 minutes or until the chestnuts are tender. Put the chestnuts and onion into the blender with all the stock (in two batches if necessary) and work it until the soup is smooth.

Return the soup to the pan and reheat it. Check the seasoning, and pour it into small soup bowls. Dribble the cream in circles over each dish and grate over a little nutmeg.

Chestnut and watercress soup

8 oz (225 gr) chestnuts, peeled and finely chopped
1 large onion, finely chopped
1 oz (25 gr) butter
1½ pints (9 dl) stock
2 bayleaves
1 bunch watercress, finely chopped

Melt the butter on a low heat in a saucepan. Stir in the chestnuts and onion and cook them slowly until the onion is golden. Stir in the stock, add the bayleaves, bring it gently to the boil, stirring, and simmer for 15 minutes. Check the seasoning. Remove the bayleaves and add the watercress to the pan just before serving.

Brussels sprouts and chestnut soup

8 oz (225 gr) Brussels sprouts, finely chopped
8 oz (225 gr) chestnuts, peeled and finely chopped
1 oz (25 gr) butter

1 large onion, finely chopped
a little grated nutmeg
1½ pints (9 dl) stock
bouquet garni

Melt the butter in a saucepan on a low heat and stir in the Brussels sprouts, chestnuts, onion and nutmeg. Cover and cook them gently for ten minutes. Stir in the stock and add the bouquet garni. Bring to the boil and simmer for 15 minutes. Allow to cool slightly. Remove the bouquet garni, work in the soup in the blender until smooth, and reheat.

The next recipe again uses the delicious combination of Brussels sprouts and chestnuts, this time in a stuffing for chicken.

Chicken with Brussels sprouts and chestnuts

a 3-3½ lb (1·3-1·5 kg) roasting chicken
1¼ lb (600 gr) Brussels sprouts
¼ lb (100 gr) chestnuts, peeled and finely chopped
1 medium onion, finely chopped
1 oz (25 gr) butter
2 tablespoons chopped parsley

juice of ½ lemon
a little grated nutmeg
1 small carrot, finely chopped
½ stick celery, finely chopped
¼ pint (1·5 dl) stock, made from the giblets
bouquet garni

Preheat the oven to Reg 3/325°F, 170°C.
To make the stuffing melt half the butter in a frying pan on a low heat and sauté half the onion in this until it is golden. Add the chestnuts to the pan and mash them with the onion over the heat until they are well blended together. Remove them from the heat. Boil ¼ lb (100 gr) of the sprouts in salted water until they are tender, and mash them with the chestnuts and onion. Mix in one tablespoon of the parsley, the lemon juice and nutmeg. Stuff the chicken with this mixture and truss it.

Melt the remaining butter on a moderate heat in a large flameproof casserole. Brown the chicken all over in this, turning it carefully so as not to break the skin. Remove the chicken, lower the heat and stir in the carrot, celery and the rest of the onion. Cover them with a butter paper and a lid and let them sweat for five minutes. Set the chicken on the top of the vegetables, pour over the stock and surround the chicken with the rest of the sprouts. Tuck in the bouquet garni and grate over a little more nutmeg. Put it into the oven for 1¼ hours.

Take out the chicken and carve it. Arrange it on a warm serving dish with the Brussels sprouts. Strain the juices from the casserole and return them to the heat. Boil to reduce a little and stir in the remaining chopped parsley. Check the seasoning and serve the chicken with the sauce poured over it, with spoonfuls of the stuffing on top.

If you like, you can add some more peeled chestnuts to the Brussels sprouts that are cooked round the chicken, but this isn't essential.

Here is another recipe for a chestnut stuffing, this time for lamb.

Lamb with chestnut stuffing

2½ lb (1·125 kg) best end or loin of lamb, boned
for the stuffing:
¼ lb (100 gr) chestnuts, peeled and   1 small stick celery, finely chopped
    finely chopped   ¼ pint (1·5 dl) stock
½ oz (13 gr) butter   1 teaspoon chopped rosemary
1 small onion, finely chopped   grated rind and juice of ½ lemon

1 large onion, thinly sliced
4 tablespoons stock
½ pint (3 dl) brown sauce (page 12)

Preheat the oven to Reg 4/350°F, 180°C.
To make the stuffing, melt the butter on a low heat in a small frying pan and cook the onion and celery in this until they are beginning to soften. Stir in the chestnuts and the stock. Cover and simmer gently until all the stock is absorbed and the chestnuts are soft. Mash them to a purée with the back of a spoon. Mix in the rosemary and the lemon rind and juice.

Bone the lamb. Spread the stuffing over the cut surface of the lamb. Roll up the joint and tie it with strong thread or fine cotton string. Put it in a roasting tin and roast it for $1\frac{1}{2}$ hours. After the first 15 minutes, scatter the sliced onion round the lamb, and stir it several times during cooking. When the lamb is cooked, remove it, carve it and keep it warm. Remove the onion and set it aside. Pour off any excess fat from the pan and deglaze it with the stock. Pour in the brown sauce and put back the onion rings. Bring it to the boil, stirring, and simmer for one minute. Pour the sauce over the lamb to serve.

☣   ☣   ☣

Brussels sprouts are the vegetable most often served with the Christmas turkey. When they are small and tightly packed they are a very tasty little vegetable and can be quite simply boiled until they are just tender and tossed in butter and a little chopped parsley to go with the rich stuffings and sauces of the Christmas meal. But during the rest of the month, try these recipes to go with plainer meals and make the sprouts more interesting.

Purée of Brussels sprouts

Boil them until they are tender and mash them with butter, double cream and nutmeg.

Brussels sprouts braised with onions

1 lb (450 gr) Brussels sprouts, trimmed and cut across in quarter-inch (6 mm) slices	1 oz (25 gr) butter a little grated nutmeg $\frac{1}{4}$ pint (1·5 dl) stock
1 large onion, sliced	

Preheat the oven to Reg 4/350°F, 180°C.
Melt the butter in a flameproof casserole on a low heat. Stir in the onion and Brussels sprouts and grate in the nutmeg. Cover with a butter paper and a lid and let them sweat for five minutes. Pour in the stock and cover them again. Cook them in the oven for 45 minutes, check the seasoning and serve.

Brussels sprouts dijonnaise

1 lb (450 gr) Brussels sprouts 1 teaspoon Dijon mustard
¼ pint (1·5 dl) stock ½ oz (13 gr) butter
2 tablespoons chopped parsley

Put all the ingredients into a saucepan and set them on a moderate heat for 20 minutes. Check the seasoning before serving.

Paprika Brussels sprouts

1 lb (450 gr) Brussels sprouts 1 teaspoon tomato purée
¼ pint (1·5 dl) stock ½ oz (13 gr) butter
1 teaspoon paprika

Put all the ingredients into a saucepan and set them on a moderate heat for 20 minutes. Check the seasoning before serving.

Brussels sprouts with tomatoes and garlic

1 lb (450 gr) Brussels sprouts 1 clove garlic, finely chopped
4 large tomatoes, skinned, seeded ½ oz (13 gr) butter
  and roughly chopped ¼ pint (1·5 dl) stock

Put all the ingredients into a saucepan and set them on a moderate heat for 20 minutes. Check the seasoning before serving.

Brussels sprouts and leeks

1 lb (450 gr) Brussels sprouts
4 small leeks, cut into ¾-inch (2 cm) lengths
¼ pint (1·5 dl) stock
1 teaspoon tarragon mustard, or lots of black pepper

Put all the ingredients into a saucepan, cover, and set on a moderate heat for 20 minutes. Check the seasoning before serving.

Brussels sprouts niçoise

1 lb (450 gr) Brussels sprouts,
 trimmed and cut across in
 quarter-inch (6 mm) slices
2 flat anchovy fillets
½ oz (13 gr) butter

¼ pint (1·5 dl) stock
1 dessertspoon tomato purée
1 clove garlic, finely chopped
6 stoned black olives, cut into thin
 slivers

Preheat the oven to Reg 4/350°F, 180°C.
Pound the anchovies to a paste. In a casserole gently warm the
butter and stock together until the butter has melted. Stir in the
anchovies and the tomato purée. When they are all blended
together, stir in the sprouts, garlic and olives. Bring them to the
boil and put them into the oven for 45 minutes.

Chopped up small with either mayonnaise or French dressing,
Brussels sprouts make crunchy side-salads. Here's a recipe for a
hot Brussels sprouts salad.

Hot Brussels sprouts salad

1 lb (450 gr) Brussels sprouts, cut
 into quarter-inch (6 mm) slices
2 tablespoons olive oil
a 3-inch (7·5 cm) piece of savoury
 garlic sausage, diced very small

1 clove garlic, finely chopped
1 tablespoon wine vinegar
1 teaspoon Dijon mustard

Heat the oil on a high heat in a large frying pan and fry the
diced sausage and garlic until they are brown. Add the sprouts
and stir them about for three minutes. Blend together the vinegar and mustard and quickly stir them into the salad. Bring to
the boil and serve immediately.

Next, a simple Brussels sprouts soup.

Brussels sprouts soup

1 lb (450 gr) Brussels sprouts, sliced
1½ pints (9 dl) stock
4 fluid oz (1·5 dl) double cream
grated nutmeg

Put the sprouts into a pan with the stock and simmer them for 20 minutes. Allow them to cool and work in the blender until smooth. Return to the pan, stir in the cream and nutmeg, check the seasoning and reheat.

Brussels sprouts go well with pork and can be cooked with it to blend the flavours.

Marinated pork with Brussels sprouts

1½ lb (675 gr) lean, boneless pork	½ pint (3 dl) dry white wine
1 dessertspoon chopped sage	1 lb (450 gr) Brussels sprouts, cut
2 small cloves garlic	into quarter-inch (6 mm) slices
sea salt, black pepper	1 oz (25 gr) butter or pork
6 oz (150 gr) lean bacon	dripping

Crush the sage and garlic with a pinch of sea salt and ground black pepper. Rub them into the surface of the pork. Cut both the pork and the bacon into strips 1½ inches long (3·75 cm) and a quarter of an inch (6 mm) wide and thick. Put them into a bowl, turn them in the wine and leave them for about four hours. Drain the meat from the marinade and reserve both.

Melt the dripping on a high heat in a wide-bottomed casserole or large sauté pan. Brown the strips of pork and bacon in this, keeping the heat high to drive away any moisture. When the meat is brown and slightly sticky pour in the marinade. Bring it to the boil, stirring, and immediately lower the heat right down. Stir in the sprouts. Cover, and cook on the lowest heat possible for 25 minutes. Check the seasoning and serve with buttered noodles.

Stuffed pork chops with Brussels sprouts and orange

4 pork chops, with no long loin bone, but not trimmed short	1 oz (25 gr) granary breadcrumbs
1 lb (450 gr) Brussels sprouts	grated rind and juice of 1 orange
2 tablespoons pork dripping	1 dessertspoon chopped rosemary
1 small onion, finely chopped	1 clove garlic, chopped

Boil ¼ lb (100 gr) of the sprouts until they are tender and mash them. Trim and slice the remaining ones ¼ inch (6 mm) thick. Melt half the fat in a small frying pan and cook the onion gently in this until it is soft. Remove the pan from the heat and work in the mashed sprouts, the breadcrumbs, orange rind and rosemary. Season.

Place the chops on a flat surface, put the stuffing under the long part of the chops and shape them into ovals with the tail of the chops round the stuffing. Tie them round with fine string or strong thread. Melt the remaining fat in a large frying pan on a moderate heat. Fry the chops in this for about ten minutes on each side. Carefully remove them with a large slice, keeping the stuffing in place, and keep them warm. Lower the heat and stir in the remaining sprouts and the garlic. Cook gently, stirring, until they are just beginning to soften. Raise the heat slightly. Stir in the orange juice, season, and bring to the boil. Place the sprouts on a warm serving dish with the chops on top, removing the string from the chops at the last minute.

ଷ   ଷ   ଷ

If goose is on the menu for Christmas dinner, red cabbage is a good accompaniment, especially if it is cooked with apples whose sharpness will counteract the fattiness of the bird. The following recipe includes chestnuts, but they can be omitted.

Braised red cabbage and chestnuts

1 small red cabbage, shredded
1 oz (25 gr) butter
1 large onion, sliced
1 large cooking apple, peeled and
  sliced
2 tablespoons wine vinegar

1 tablespoon soft brown sugar
2 tablespoons water
¼ lb (100 gr) chestnuts, peeled (see
  page 256)
a little kneaded butter

Preheat the oven to Reg 4/350°F, 180°C and lightly butter a small ovenproof casserole.

Blanch the cabbage in boiling salted water for two minutes and drain it well. Melt the butter in a frying pan on a low heat and cook the onion and apple in this until they are soft. Mix the vinegar, sugar and water together.

Put a layer of cabbage in the bottom of the casserole, season, and sprinkle over it a little of the sugar and vinegar mixture. Cover it with a layer of apple and onion, and again season and sprinkle with the sugar and vinegar. Then add a few chestnuts. Continue these layers, finishing with one of cabbage. Cover with a butter paper and a lid and put into the centre of the oven for an hour. Mix in the kneaded butter and put back for a further five minutes.

The next recipe keeps the crunchiness of the red cabbage.

Red cabbage on top of the stove

1 small red cabbage, shredded	4 tablespoons olive oil
1 large cooking apple, sliced	1 tablespoon redcurrant jelly
1 medium onion, sliced	2 tablespoons red wine vinegar

Heat the oil on a low heat in a large frying pan or paëlla pan. Gently cook the cabbage, onion and apple in the oil until they are just beginning to go limp. Stir in the redcurrant jelly, and when it has dissolved raise the heat to moderate and quickly stir in the vinegar. Season. Bring to the boil and serve immediately.

Red cabbage and beef make a hearty meal for winter days.

Braised beef and red cabbage

2 lb (900 gr) shin of beef, diced	$\frac{1}{2}$ pint (3 dl) stock
2 tablespoons seasoned flour	4 tablespoons wine vinegar
2 oz (50 gr) butter	1 tablespoon redcurrant jelly
24 button onions, peeled	12 allspice berries, crushed
1 small red cabbage, shredded	

Preheat the oven to Reg 4/350°F, 180°C.
Coat the beef in seasoned flour. Melt 1$\frac{1}{2}$ oz (38 gr) butter on a high heat. Brown the beef all over in this and set it aside. Turn the heat right down, add the remaining butter to the casserole and cook the onions in it until they are becoming transparent.

Stir in the cabbage. Pour in the stock and vinegar and add the redcurrant jelly. Bring them slowly to the boil, and when the jelly has melted stir in the allspice and replace the beef. Cover the casserole and put it in the centre of the oven for 1½ hours. Serve with a green salad.

Index

Theodora FitzGibbon
A Taste of Ireland £1.25

There is a flourishing Irish cookery tradition : Irish recipes are to be
found tucked away in odd corners of magazines and in cookery books,
but many of these recipes come from private family papers which
have never before been published. They are accompanied by a
remarkable series of historic photographs.

A Taste of London £1.50

The food of London is as varied as its inhabitants and its history, and
Theodora FitzGibbon has mingled London's history with many
excellent recipes. The superb historic photographs give a unique and
touching insight into the bygone days of London.

A Taste of Scotland £1.25

The range of Scots cooking is wide, which is not surprising when
one considers the influence of Scandinavia and the 'well keipt
ancient alliance, maid betwix Scotland and the realme of France',
which inspires stovies, Lorraine soup, even haggis, not to mention
Mary Stuart's favourite biscuits. The photographs – from between
1845 and 1900 – cast their own poignant spell.

A Taste of Wales £1.25

Here are many dishes whose Welsh names are themselves poetry :
Cawl Cymreig, Brithyll â Chig Moch, Pwdin Efa, Teisen Nionod.
'Once more Theodora FitzGibbon explores the food of another
country of Britain ... authenic, historical recipes are interleaved
with superb touching photographs dating from the later years of the
nineteenth century' THE TIMES

A Taste of the West Country £1.25

'What a tasty dish ! Dozens of them and all with regional
connections ... Somerset braised lamb, clotted cream and
syllabub ... the recipes for these and many more are presented each
facing a period photograph' EXETER EXPRESS AND ECHO

The Times Cookery Book 95p
Katie Stewart

Carefully chosen from the recipes published in *The Times* over the
last few years, and including many new ones, this collection of
recipes by Katie Stewart is practical, varied and imaginative.
Selected to suit both everyday needs and special occasions, these
recipes provide a rich source of new ideas for anyone who enjoys
cooking.

New Casserole Treasury 60p
Lousene Rousseau Brunner

This collection of over four hundred delicious casserole recipes
comes from many countries, from great chefs and country kitchens.
And the ingredients range from truffles and pâté to cabbage and
beer.
Her clear, detailed and precise instructions make these dishes a joy
for even the most inexperienced cook to create.

You can buy these and other Pan books from booksellers and
newsagents , or direct from the following address :
Pan Books, Cavaye Place, London SW10 9PG
Send purchase price plus 15p for the first book and 5p for
each additional book, to allow for postage and packing
Prices quoted are applicable in UK

While every effort is made to keep prices low, it is sometimes
necessary to increase prices at short notice. Pan Books reserve the
right to show on covers new retail prices which may differ
from those advertised in the text or elsewhere